HOW TO DO YOUR

CASE

STUDY

SAGE | 50 YEARS

SAGE was founded in 1965 by Sara Miller McCune to support the dissemination of usable knowledge by publishing innovative and high-quality research and teaching content. Today, we publish more than 850 journals, including those of more than 300 learned societies, more than 800 new books per year, and a growing range of library products including archives, data, case studies, reports, and video. SAGE remains majority-owned by our founder, and after Sara's lifetime will become owned by a charitable trust that secures our continued independence.

Los Angeles | London | New Delhi | Singapore | Washington DC

HOW TO DO YOUR

CASE

STUDY

2ND EDITION

GARY

THOMAS

$SAGE

Los Angeles | London | New Delhi
Singapore | Washington DC

Los Angeles | London | New Delhi
Singapore | Washington DC

SAGE Publications Ltd
1 Oliver's Yard
55 City Road
London EC1Y 1SP

SAGE Publications Inc.
2455 Teller Road
Thousand Oaks, California 91320

SAGE Publications India Pvt Ltd
B 1/I 1 Mohan Cooperative Industrial Area
Mathura Road
New Delhi 110 044

SAGE Publications Asia-Pacific Pte Ltd
3 Church Street
#10-04 Samsung Hub
Singapore 049483

Editor: Jai Seaman
Assistant editor: James Piper
Production editor: Katherine Haw
Copyeditor: Richard Leigh
Proofreader: Neil Dowden
Marketing manager: Ben Sherwood
Cover design: Shaun Mercier
Typeset by: C&M Digitals (P) Ltd, Chennai, India
Printed and bound in Great Britain by
CPI Group (UK) Ltd, Croydon, CR0 4YY

© Gary Thomas 2016

This edition published 2016

First edition published 2011

Library of Congress Control Number: 2015936406

British Library Cataloguing in Publication data

A catalogue record for this book is available from
the British Library

ISBN 978-1-4462-8264-9
ISBN 978-1-4462-8265-6 (pbk)

CONTENTS

About the author		ix
Preface		x
About the companion website		xiii

PART 1 GETTING YOUR BEARINGS — 1

1 What is a case study? — 3

Is the case study scientific? — 7
Some definitions — 9
What is a case? — 11
What *is* and *is not* a case? — 14
What is the case study good and not good for? — 17
If you take only one thing from this chapter, take this … — 23
Further reading — 24

2 The case study and research design — 25

Doing the right kind of research — 25
What is design? — 26
First things first: your purpose — 27
Next, your question — 28
Literature review — 30
How to go from idea to question to case study — 31
Questions and different approaches to research — 35
Design frames and methods — 37
Using storyboards to help you design your case study — 38
If you take only one thing from this chapter, take this … — 44
Further reading — 45

3 The whole is more than the sum of the parts: seeing a complete picture — 46

Break things down or see them as wholes? — 46
Gestalt psychology — 50
Dramas, theatres and stages — 51

Ecological psychology   53
Systems thinking   56
If you take only one thing from this chapter, take this ...   59
Further reading   61

4 Rigour and quality in your case study: what's important?   62

Is the 'sample' important in case study?   62
Do I have to worry about reliability and validity in a case study? 64
Triangulation   67
Positionality   68
Generalisation   68
Finding or regularising   73
Quality   74
If you take only one thing from this chapter, take this ...   76
Further reading   76

5 Ethics   78

Your participants   78
Vulnerable groups   79
Participants' activity   80
Deception or concealment   81
Confidentiality and anonymity   81
Data security and stewardship   82
Consent   83
Contacting participants   89
Care for your participants – and yourself   89
Where do I put discussion about ethics in my case study write-up? 90
Getting clearance – ethical review   90
If you take only one thing from this chapter, take this ...   93
Further reading   93

PART 2   SELECTING A CASE AND CONDUCTING THE STUDY   95

**6 Different kinds of case studies: selecting a subject
  for your case study   97**

How do you select your case study subject?   98
Same starting points, different paths – there's no right way   111
Kinds of case studies   112
If you take only one thing from this chapter, take this ...   117
Further reading   118

7   Your purpose: thinking about the object of your study   **119**

Intrinsic   120
Instrumental   120
Evaluative   121
Explanatory   123
Exploratory   126
If you take only one thing from this chapter, take this …   132
Further reading   132

**8   Your approach: theory testing or theory building;
      interpretation or illustration**   **134**

Theory testing or theory building   135
Drawing a picture – illustrative–demonstrative   141
Interpretative   147
Experimental   153
If you take only one thing from this chapter, take this …   158
Further reading   159

9   Your process: the shape, style and manner of your case study **161**

The single case   162
Time as a dimension of the case study   165
The multiple or collective or comparative case (or cross-case analysis) 172
Nested case studies   177
Parallel and sequential studies   180
If you take only one thing from this chapter, take this …   182
Further reading   183

PART 3   COLLECTING EVIDENCE, ANALYSING AND
          WRITING UP   185

10 Out in the field: some ways to collect data and evidence   **187**

Interviews   189
Accounts   190
Diaries   191
Group interviews and focus groups   191
Interrogating documents   193
Questionnaires   193
Observation   196
Image-based methods   198
Measurements and tests   199

	Official statistics and other numerical data	200
	If you take only one thing from this chapter, take this …	201
	Further reading	202
11	**Analysis: a toolkit for analysing and thinking in case study**	**203**
	Interpretative inquiry: eliciting themes	204
	Constant comparative method	204
	Theme mapping	206
	NVivo	207
	Grounded theory	210
	Thick description	211
	Word clouds	212
	Sociograms	212
	Systems thinking	214
	Drawing storyboards – the nuts and bolts	217
	Developing your theory	219
	Using narrative	225
	Think drama	229
	Being intuitive and imaginative	232
	If you take only one thing from this chapter, take this …	234
	Further reading	235
12	**Writing your study**	**236**
	Structure	236
	Writing up your case study	238
	Two examples of good analysis, argument and writing	244
	Some rules for writers	247
	If you take only one thing from this chapter, take this …	249
	… and this – a final thought	250
	Further reading	251
	Other reading	252
	References	253
	Index	261

ABOUT THE AUTHOR

Being of a nervous disposition as a child, Gary Thomas failed to write anything on his 11-plus examination paper, which inaction took him to secondary modern school. His subsequent zigzag through the education system gave him broad experience of its good and bad sides.

 He eventually became a teacher, then an educational psychologist, then a professor of education at the University of Birmingham, where his teaching, research and writing now focus on inclusive education and the methods used in social science research.

He has led a wide range of research projects and has received awards from the AHRC, the ESRC, the Nuffield Foundation, the Leverhulme Trust, the Department for Education, charities such as Barnardos and the Cadmean Trust, local authorities and a range of other organisations. He has written or edited 20 books and lots of boring academic articles.

He has two grown-up daughters, one baby daughter and – at current reckoning – two grandchildren. He likes, in alphabetical order, cats, chess, cycling, gardening, dogs and writing. He dislikes Chelsea tractors, pomposity and people who try to make things sound more complicated than they are (in that order).

Despite supporting Aston Villa football club, he maintains an optimistic outlook on life.

PREFACE

At its best, the case study provides the most vivid, the most inspirational analysis that an inquiry can offer. Einstein did it; Newton did it. Sociologists do it; psychologists do it. Doctors do it; teachers do it; lawyers do it; nurses do it. It is done across the disciplinary and methodological spectrum, and even though this book is, first and foremost, for those in the applied social sciences and humanities, I hope it will also be useful to students and researchers in other fields. I've been delighted with the reception of the first edition, which seems to be used by researchers in a variety of disciplines. The new edition contains much more material on ethics and data collection, and has new sections on analysis, including material on grounded theory, sociometry and NVivo.

The case study provides a form of inquiry that elevates a view of life in its complexity. The contrasting view, of course, is that an inquiry is best conducted by breaking life up into digestible, study-sized chunks. We all like easily digestible food, but it's not often the most nutritious.

It's the realisation that complexity in social affairs is frequently indivisible which has led to the case study having the status of one of the most popular and most fertile design frames for researchers' work. It's a design frame with huge potential, but it also has its restrictions. Sometimes I feel that students stumble into a case study without really being sure of its benefits or its limits. So, in this book, I look at not just how to do a case study but also at what case studies are good for and what they are not good for.

The case study has branched out and blossomed from its origins, which were, according to White (1992), in the professional training of lawyers at the Harvard Law School in the nineteenth century. It was the appropriately named Christopher Columbus Langdell, the first dean of that law school, who set the ball rolling in 1870. Actually, I've taken White's word for it that it was Christopher Columbus Langdell who named the case study method, but, of course, the 'method' is so obvious it is difficult to make an argument for it needing to be 'pioneered' or invented at all. Rather in the way that America was bound to have been discovered with or without the voyage of the first, and rather more famous, Christopher Columbus, the case study method would have been stumbled on even without the insights of his nineteenth-century namesake.

Others could quite legitimately claim to have been the first to develop a systematic method for looking at single cases, even if they didn't think to call their method the 'case method' or 'case study'. Jean Marc Gaspard Itard and his study of Victor, the 'wild boy of Aveyron', at the beginning of the nineteenth century could equally take the accolade, as could Frédéric Le Play in his celebrated studies of French working people in the middle of that same century. (Le Play used a case method wherein he would invite himself to reside with ordinary families for extended periods until he got to know them intimately. Whether or not his uninvited sojourns in the cottages of poor coalminers of the Jura were exuberantly welcomed by his hosts is unrecorded – one can imagine some Pythonesque tableaux – but his rich analyses were lauded in both political and literary circles.)

All of this pioneering work originated in the social sciences and the humanities, but one of the points I try to make throughout the book is that researchers use case studies far less self-consciously and less apologetically in fields separate from these. In these other fields, inquirers seem to be more inclined to do what comes naturally – to adopt methods that are right for the questions in hand without undue hand-wringing about the correctness of this or that method. Given that there has indeed been hand-wringing and uncertainty about how best to use case studies, particularly in the applied social sciences, I hope this book will offer some clear advice to students on how best to do such an inquiry, with lots of examples of how it can be used most fruitfully.

In my examples I have drawn on instances of real or possible case studies that could be done by real students doing real inquiries. I have done this rather than use high-profile, well-known case studies carried out by teams of sociologists, each taking several years to complete. These iconic examples can provide pointers and flashes of insight that can inspire and give ideas, but, if I read too many of these, I find I can become daunted rather than inspired, thinking, 'How on earth could I ever do anything like this?' So, the examples I have given are, in the main, real, adapted (and many thanks to the students from whom I have stolen them) or sometimes imagined.

I've assumed people will be reading this book because they want to do a case study, not because they want to find out about the case study method per se. There must, I suppose, be a very limited number of research methodologists who are interested in the case study in and of itself, but my assumption is that these are not the principal audience for this book. Looking at the books available on the topic, though, it is almost as if it were the other way round. It is almost as though authors are writing books on case studies as if most people want to pursue an academic interest in the case study method rather than want to find out about it so that they can do one better.

I've also wanted in this book to provide not just a primer on the case study but also something rather more eclectic than is to be found in most of the books available on the topic. In my experience, nearly all of the academic writing on the case study has been done by sociologists seeing it as a form of inquiry for sociology alone. While the case study has a long and fascinating tradition in sociology, it's not owned by sociology. Indeed, as I've noted, the method can be used almost anywhere, and I try to make this point in the book by taking examples from different areas of inquiry.

I also try to show how different insights about holistic inquiry from different academic domains can have wider application and how ideas from across a spectrum of disciplines have commonality.

I should note that parts of Chapter 4 in this book have been published in the journals *Qualitative Inquiry* and the *Oxford Review of Education* (Thomas, 2011a, 2011b).

There are too many colleagues, friends and students to thank by name, but I do really want to thank them all for their ideas and time. Thanks especially to Jai Seaman at SAGE, who commissioned this second edition and coordinated readers' comments to provide such an enormously helpful plan of action for the new volume. Many thanks to all of Jai's colleagues at SAGE for their help in putting the new book together, especially Katherine Haw, Richard Leigh and their colleagues in the production department at SAGE.

ABOUT THE COMPANION WEBSITE

Visit **https://study.sagepub.com/thomascasestudy2e** to find a range of additional resources to aid your study, including:

- **Checklists** to help you track your progress at each stage in the research process
- **Template consent forms** to be distributed to research participants
- **Links to ethics guidelines** by professional organisations
- **Selected journal articles** giving you free access to scholarly journal articles chosen for each chapter to expand your knowledge and reinforce your learning of key topics

PART 1

GETTING YOUR BEARINGS

In this first part of the book, I look at:

- what the case study is, and the kinds of inquiries for which it may be useful

- some ground rules for the conduct and design of a case study

- what we are trying to do with the case study as a form of inquiry – namely, look at a situation in its completeness and all its complexity

- why, throughout the history of inquiry, people have felt that it is a good idea to examine something in its completeness

- some of the ways in which the success of a case study may be measured

- the ethical dimensions of case study.

1

WHAT IS A CASE STUDY?

If you use case study as the design frame for your research you will be concentrating on one thing, looking at it in detail. When you do a case study, you are interested in that thing in itself, as a whole.

I'm using the word 'thing' advisedly since the thing may be a person, a group, an institution, a country, an event, a period in time or whatever. You may be looking at the process of a medical diagnosis with one patient or you may be looking at relationships among a gang of teenagers or you may be looking at one student's learning in class. You may be looking at a family or at IKEA's development as a business or at the USA's political stance at the time of the Cuban missile crisis. Any of these 'things', these phenomena, could form the subject of a case study. What is of interest is the uniqueness of the thing and the thing in its completeness.

Being about one thing, it is about the particular, rather than the general. You can't generalise from one thing, so there is no point in trying to do so – no point, in other words, in trying to say, 'This is the case here, so it is also the case there, there and there.' You cannot, for example, say, 'The treatment of this patient with influenza with our new drug Flugone has worked. Hooray! Let's give it to everyone with influenza.'

Because you are not able to generalise from this one case, there is no point in thinking about all of the sampling techniques that are used with other kinds of research. The only sense in which 'sampling' is relevant in a case study is the sense in which you go out and find the subject of your case study.

The main feature of your choice of case will be the interest that you have in the subject of the study. Why are you interested in it? It could be interesting because …

> A case study is about the particular rather than the general. You cannot generalise from a case study.

- you are intimately connected with it – perhaps it is a child in your class, a patient in your hospital or a project in your company

- it is a conspicuously good example of something in which you are interested – for example, IKEA as an example of a successful business

- it is different from what is typical – it is an 'outlier' that shows something remarkable by virtue of its difference from what seems to be the norm, such as, perhaps, Kerala as a state in India where, despite widespread poverty, people have a far longer life expectancy than they do elsewhere in India.

Singleness is the watchword with a case study.

Should you worry about this singleness? You may, after all, have heard people being snooty about 'anecdotal evidence' – in other words, evidence that comes from just one situation or one event. Such anecdotal evidence is uncorroborated by evidence from different experiences. Social science is about getting beyond what is merely anecdotal, some would say.

Certainly, when we want to generalise – to say that this phenomenon has occurred in this sample of people and we can generalise this finding to the wider population – clearly we cannot use just one person's experience or a single set of uncorroborated observations as the basis for this. That is why such trouble has to be taken in many kinds of research to establish the sample as being *representative* of the wider population. If we want to generalise we need to make the basis of our generalisation clear. What gives us grounds to make the claim that we *can* generalise?

What we are talking about with a case study, though, is a different kind of inquiry from those where generalisation is expected to follow. Here we are talking about understanding *how* and *why* something might have happened or why it might be the case. The assumption in a case study is that, with a great deal of intricate study of one case, looking at your subject from many and varied angles, you can get closer to the 'why' and the 'how'. As Becker (2014: 3) puts it: 'Everything present in or connected to a situation I want to understand should be taken account of and made use of. If it's there, it's doing something, however unimportant that thing seems, no matter how unobtrusive it is.'

You'll notice that although the assumptions about valid processes of inquiry and analysis differ from those in many kinds of social research (for we are not working from samples that enable us to generalise), assumptions about the use of evidence do not change. With a case study there is still the assumption that we must collect good evidence and lots of it. In the modern phrase, we must 'drill down' as deep as we possibly can to get evidence, penetrating into every nook and cranny, and squeezing out every little bit that can be found.

To mix our metaphors even more, we must look at our subject from many and varied angles, to develop what the great historian–philosopher Michel Foucault (1981) called 'a polyhedron of intelligibility'. By this he meant that inquiries in the humanities and social sciences are too often one-dimensional, as if

> **Two important things about a case study:**
>
> 1 you drill down further
> 2 you create a three-dimensional picture – or what Foucault called a 'polyhedron of intelligibility'.

we are looking at our subject just from one direction. In looking from *several* directions, a more rounded, richer, more balanced picture of our subject is developed – we get a three-dimensional view.

It is not just in the social sciences and the humanities that this multifaceted view is valuable. In what are taken to be 'harder' sciences, such as biology, astronomy and geology, and in many applied sciences, such as palaeoanthropology (the study of humanoid fossils), the case study is one of the principal methods used.

Let's look at astronomers. They can't experiment with the stars and, although there are a lot of stars (around 10^{22} – that's 1 with 22 noughts after it), when something unusual happens in the sky, astronomers have to make inferences from a very small number of cases – often, only one case. Their work is carried out by means of case study. As evidence accumulates bits of it are patched together. Astronomers try things out with the data they amass, trialling various models and explanations.

For example, in 1967, an astronomical phenomenon (to which the name 'pulsar' was later given) was discovered by the astronomer Jocelyn Bell Burnell and her colleagues with the then new radio telescope at Jodrell Bank. As she was drinking her tea one morning and eating her Penguin biscuit for elevenses, gazing into the green cathode-ray tube, Jocelyn noticed something unusual. Something in a distant galaxy was giving off massive pulses of radio energy at fantastically regular intervals. The rhythm was as regular as an atomic clock.

How could this amazingly regular pulse be accounted for? At first, it was thought by these hard-nosed scientists that this was a message from intelligent life and the pulsar was given the name LGM-1 (Little Green Men 1). There was no better explanation for this regular-as-clockwork beep-beep-beeping; nothing else in the known universe did anything like this. The astronomers had to make judgements based on their existing knowledge of phenomena such as this, and the best they could come up with at the time was little green men trying to communicate with us.

This pulsing phenomenon was *a case* – *The Case of the Beeping Astronomical Phenomenon*, Sherlock Holmes might have called it – and astronomers had to go about studying it idiographically (see box for definition). In fact, the case study is sometimes called idiographic study since the ideas are all based on and rooted in a single picture – the picture drawn by the inquirer. Given that there was only this case to study and little green men provided a possible, yet unlikely, source of explanation, the scientists let this explanation suffice for the time being.

> *Idiograph* – a symbol, a drawing or figure that stands for an idea (from the Greek *idea* meaning ... er ... 'idea', and *graphein* meaning 'to write').

To go beyond this simplistic (that is to say, too simple) explanation, Jocelyn and her astronomer colleagues had to come up with different kinds of observations and work on different explanations. They had to look in different ways

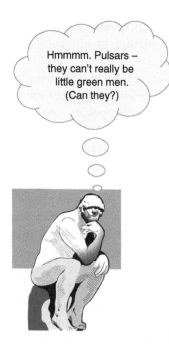

Hmmmm. Pulsars – they can't really be little green men. (Can they?)

Figure 1.1 Problems are solved by *thinking*, not by a special method

at the pulse to work out what it might be. By using their existing knowledge and theoretical speculation – putting forward and rejecting or accepting plausible hypotheses – they eventually worked out these regular pulses were the flashes of radiation from a collapsed neutron star that was spinning very fast to give out a directed and extraordinarily condensed beam of light, like a lighthouse.

The important point about this story is that this conclusion was arrived at not by studying thousands or hundreds or even tens of these pulsars, but by studying just one or two pulsars in a great deal of detail and employing a great deal of thinking (see Figure 1.1). Hugely significant scientific conclusions were drawn from this case. Much of the most important natural scientific endeavour and discovery has been achieved in similar ways. Indeed, it is worth noting that Einstein's *annus mirabilis* papers (including his conclusions on special relativity and mass–energy equivalence) were produced with little more than 'thought experiments' and a pencil, while Darwin's theory of evolution could be said to have been based on the insights he gained from a series of meticulously conducted case studies. From Einstein's 'thought experiments' to Darwin's finches to Jocelyn Bell Burnell's pulsar, the study was of *cases*.

The key, I think – and I am now moving back more single-mindedly to social research – is in what Flyvbjerg (2001: 132) calls 'getting close to reality'. By this he means keeping in contact with the subject of study and thinking with your own experience and your own intelligence. It is this 'staying real' that the case study is particularly good at encouraging, for it eschews methodological formulae and endorses and stimulates a critical, creative approach to problem-solving.

Flyvbjerg puts the emphasis in this 'getting close to reality' on 'little questions' and 'thick description' (of which more in Chapter 11). We sometimes ignore these little questions in the 'Big Science' view of what research should be like. Flyvbjerg (2001: 133) quotes Nietzsche as saying that 'all the problems of politics, of social organization, and of education have been falsified through and through ... because one learned to despise "little" things, which means the basic concerns of life itself'. As Flyvbjerg points out, small questions often lead to big answers.

For me, the truth of Flyvbjerg's point is exemplified in one of the best case studies I have ever read: *A Glasgow Gang Observed* (Patrick, 1973). It was written by a young sociologist named James Patrick (a pseudonym, for reasons that will become obvious), who had infiltrated a gang in the Maryhill district of Glasgow. By hood-winking members of the gang into believing that he was like them, then joining the gang and becoming a participant in its activities, Patrick was able to paint a detailed picture of the way that it operated. Although it is a case study – there is only a single gang, not 50, from which to generalise – it gives, through sparkling analysis, an understanding of gangs. Even though there is no pretence that this is a representative picture or that all gangs are like this, we can nevertheless get a rich understanding of the dynamics, tensions and motivation of gangs in general.

I'll let Flyvbjerg (2001: 135–6) have the last word on this since he puts it so nicely:

> practical rationality and judgment evolve and operate primarily by virtue of deep-going case experiences. Practical rationality, therefore, is best understood through cases – experienced or narrated – just as judgment is best cultivated and communicated via the exposition of cases … which is why … Ricahrd Rorty [says]: 'the way to re-enchant the world … is to stick to the concrete.'

A lot can be achieved by recourse to the concrete. We escape from a tendency too often found in academic writing to obfuscate with abstractions rather than clarify with specificity; to bring a fog over the topic in hand with abstract words and the seeking of generalisation where none is possible and none is helpful.

The great writer Harold Evans (2000: 32) said that the abstract should be 'chased out' in favour of the specific. He was talking of journalism rather than academic inquiry and writing, but I think his point is just as relevant in the academy, if not more so. It is a point that is especially germane to the use of the case study, where the reason-for-being concerns the validity of the concrete and the specific. Evans (2000: 33) quotes from C.E. Montague: 'The great escape should be from "mere intellectualism, with its universals and essences, to concrete particulars, the smell of human breath, the sound of voices, the stir of living".

You should, in a case study, be able to smell human breath and hear the sound of voices. Nothing is lost in their refraction through our own understanding as interpreting inquirers. In fact, much is gained as we add a separate viewpoint – one that moulds and melds the experiences of others through our own understandings.

Is the case study scientific?

If people are ever sniffy about the case study with you – or, indeed, if ever you have doubts yourself about the validity of this method – then you should remind yourself of the pedigree of the case study in the natural sciences. It has a lineage of highly significant advances coming out of case studies – idiographic analysis.

The interesting thing about scientists' own reflections on their work and the methodological traditions in which it grew is that it is generally accepted there is no particular, correct or proper way of generating or marshalling evidence and undertaking inquiries. As Einstein put it, the creative scientist must be an 'unscrupulous opportunist'. The essence of science, he said, is the seeking 'in whatever manner is suitable, a simplified and lucid image of the world ... There is no logical path, but only intuition' (cited in Holton, 1995: 168).

> There are many ways of being scientific. The case study is one of them.

Some students in the social sciences seem unaware of this methodological eclecticism. In fact, they may assume that 'serious' scientific inquiry is of a different character from that of the case study and necessarily involves quantification, isolation and manipulation of variables and carefully controlled experiments. This, however, is a product only of a particular kind of mid-twentieth-century thinking on research and method.

In a classic article reviewing this mindset, two social scientists, Parlett and Hamilton (1987), suggested that social science – particularly education and psychology – had assumed the methods of social science should, at their best, properly involve work with large datasets from which generalisations could be made.

Parlett and Hamilton saw this attitude as wrong-headed. They saw the mistake as having emerged from an expropriation by the social sciences of the outlook and methods of certain branches of the biological sciences. In particular, they said, the methods of agricultural scientists and medics had been seen by large sections of the social science establishment as the template within which to fit. They described this outlook, this way of doing social science, as conforming to what they called the *agricultural–botany paradigm*. Plant scientists do most of their work comparing the growth of fields of wheat or potatoes or soya beans that have been subjected to different treatments, but you can't, they suggested, treat social analysis in the same way that you treat plant analysis.

Their point was that the evaluative methods of agricultural scientists are fine and dandy for studying agriculture, but the trouble is that people are not ears of wheat, nor are they potatoes or even soya beans. We cannot, when we set up social scientific experiments, make assumptions about 'before' and 'after' conditions in the same way that agricultural scientists do, because there aren't befores, middles and afters as there are in fields of crops being given extra doses of fertiliser or different insecticides.

People do odd things, in a way that potatoes don't. People are, in the jargon, *agents* in their own destiny (in the way that potatoes aren't) and in the habit of making subtle or even drastic changes to the conditions for a trial. The measures used to assess change can't be taken with a tape-measure or a pair of callipers; they have to be undertaken with test scores, attitude ratings and so on. The trouble is that the latter are assumed to be of the same order of robustness as the assessments – simple measures of length and weight – that are made of plant growth. They're not. These social and psychological measures are not the same as centimetres and grams (which get gold star status in the measuring stakes because a centimetre is always a centimetre); they are far less trustworthy – in fact, they can be downright deceitful. In short, Parlett and Hamilton argued, studies undertaken in education and social sciences in this tradition fall short of their own claims that they are controlled, exact and unambiguous. (See also my own musings on this subject: Thomas, 2009.)

The long and the short of this is that there is no one way to be scientific and the case study is just as scientific as the next way to carry out an inquiry. As Einstein said (see above), science is not about a method, but about intuition or thinking – it's about supplying answers to questions with good evidence and good reasoning, which can be done in a variety of ways, with the principal feature of importance being the thought and analysis that go into providing those answers.

We sometimes get too hung up, I think, on the shibboleths of science – that is, the things taken to be core to the enterprise of science, such as causation and generalisation. Einstein's point is that it is *not* these that are at the core of good scientific thinking. Rather, it's about making connections and having insights and testing these out, in whatever way. The great sociologist Howard Becker (1998: 41) put it this way when he wrote about how the connections we seek are multistranded and multidirectional, such that causality is a less than helpful concept in social science:

> there are many modes of connection, for which we use words like 'influence' or 'causality' or 'dependence'. All these words point to variation. Something will vary and something else, dependent on what happens to the first thing, will undergo some change as well. The things that so vary will often influence each other in complicated ways, so that 'causality' is not really an appropriate way to talk about what we want to emphasize.

Some definitions

The case study is not a method in itself. Rather, it is a focus and the focus is on one thing, looked at in depth and from many angles. Bob Stake (2005: 443) puts it this way:

> Case study is not a methodological choice but a choice of what is to be studied … By whatever methods, we choose to study *the case*. We could study it analytically or holistically, entirely by repeated measures or hermeneutically, organically or culturally, and by mixed methods – but we concentrate, at least for the time being, on the case.

So, you have the focus for the case and you choose methods to help you inquire into the subject. I'll discuss some of those methods in Chapters 10 and 11.

Stake goes on to emphasise the importance of the singular in the case. So, a doctor may be a case to be studied, but it is difficult to see how methods of 'doctoring' could be a case. Nor could the reasons for child neglect be considered a case, says Stake (2005: 444), since 'We think of those topics as generalities rather than specificities. The case is a specific One' – note the upper-case 'O'.

Helen Simons (2009: 21) sums this up well in her definition of the case study:

> Case study is an in-depth exploration from multiple perspectives of the complexity and uniqueness of a particular project, policy, institution, programme or system in a 'real life' context. It is research-based, inclusive of different methods and is evidence-led. The primary purpose is to generate in-depth understanding of a specific topic (as in a thesis), programme, policy, institution or system to generate knowledge and/or inform policy development, professional practice and civil or community action.

Stake (1995: xi) makes a similar point: 'Case study is the study of the particularity and complexity of a single case, coming to understand its activity within important circumstances.'

Both of these experts stress particularity and complexity and the real-life circumstances within which the research occurs. Looking at a number of definitions of the case study, Helen Simons says that what unites them is a commitment to studying the complexity that is involved in real situations and defining the case study other than by methods.

Still on the question of definition, Hammersley and Gomm (2000: 2) make the point that all research is, in a sense, case study because 'there is always some unit, or set of units, in relation to which data are collected and/or analysed'. They suggest that the important distinction between the case study and other kinds of research is the number of cases investigated and the amount of detailed information which can therefore be collected about each one. Whereas with social surveys, for example, you find a little bit – perhaps just one set of questionnaire responses – from each of the many people participating, with a case study you are finding much, much more, but about a very limited number.

A summary of Hammersley and Gomm's table outlining the differences between the case study and two other forms of research (experiment and survey) is given in Table 1.1.

The choice of one case (or a small number) is made with a trade-off in mind, they say. You choose your very restricted sample so that you can gain greater detail, but this is at the expense of being able to make generalisations about your findings.

Table 1.1 A comparison of the case study with other forms of inquiry (liberally adapted from Hammersley and Gomm, 2000)

	Case study	Experiment	Survey
Investigates ...	one case or a small number of cases	a relatively large number of cases	a relatively large number of cases
Data collected and analysed about ...	a large number of features of each case	a small number of features of each case	a small number of features of each case
Study of ...	naturally occurring cases where the aim is not to control variables	cases where the aim is to control the important variables	naturally occurring cases selected to maximise the sample's representativeness of a wider population
Quantification of data ...	is not a priority	is a priority	is a priority

To Hammersley and Gomm's table I would add ...

	Case study	Experiment	Survey
Using ...	many methods and sources of data	one method	one method
Aiming to ...	look at relationships and processes	look at causation	look for generalisation

Like Hammersley and Gomm, Ragin (1992: 5) also offers a definition by presenting a contrast with what we might call 'variable-led research':

> The ... case-oriented approach places cases, not variables, center stage. But what is a case? Comparative social science has a ready-made, conventionalized answer to this question: Boundaries around places and time periods define cases (for example, Italy after World War II).

Ragin's definition does two things. It contrasts the emphasis on cases with an emphasis on variables in other kinds of research, but it also introduces the important idea of the *boundary*.

What is a case?

When I was writing this book, a moment of delightful serendipity occurred when, by mistake, I pressed the thesaurus button on my word processor while the cursor was stationed over 'case'. I give a summary of the meanings it came up with in Table 1.2.

I had thought that I knew what 'case' meant, but this serendipitous opening led me to some personal research into the meanings of 'case'. It turns out

Table 1.2   Meanings given for 'case'

Container	Situation	Argument
box	instance	reason
casing	event	defence
crate	occurrence	justification
suitcase	state of affairs	rationale
folder	circumstances	basis

(if my less-than-scrupulously-thorough research is correct) that the rather different meanings of 'case' arise because the word is taken from two similar-sounding Latin roots that have arrived, after corruption, at the same word, 'case', in English. The two roots are:

• *capsa*, meaning 'box', 'container' and, thus, 'case'

• *casus*, meaning 'event', 'fall', 'accident' and, thus, 'case'.

Kelly (1993: 35) notes that the *Oxford Latin Dictionary* lists 11 different meanings for the word 'case', suggesting that 'the term was just as confusing in Latin as in English'.

Anyway, this personal etymological quest led me to realise that the use of 'case' in 'case study' ticked two important boxes – by good luck, probably, rather than good planning – about the essence of this kind of inquiry. Quite fortuitously, therefore, it is an entirely appropriate term for what is done in a case inquiry. Let's look at these two meanings, plus the other one identified by my computer's thesaurus.

The case as container

The first column in Table 1.2, headed 'Container', is about the physical, concrete meaning of 'case'. While I hadn't at first considered that this was relevant to the case study, interestingly it emphasises the *containment* of a case study. A case, in the example of a crate or suitcase (see Figure 1.2) or even a pencil case, is 'bounded': you close it and clip the latches and that's it. The case – think 'suitcase' – is everything that is in it: T-shirts, jeans, socks, underwear, washbag, flip-flops, sunglasses, and so on.

At the risk of going from the ridiculous to the sublime, this is, in fact, similar to something the great philosopher Ludwig Wittgenstein said in the opening line of his famous *Tractatus*: 'The world is everything that is the case' (see Kenny, 1993: 3). Wittgenstein's language is sometimes thought to be a little mysterious, enigmatic or even poetic – as if he were teasing his merely mortal readers with riddles, saying,

'I'm not giving you answers, peasants: go away and think about it.'

Wittgenstein's enigmatic statement is relevant to the case study. Wittgenstein scholars (see Biletzki, 2009) have understood the great philosopher's 'The world is everything that is the case' to mean that the world in which we are interested, as inquirers, is composed of facts and states of affairs and objects, all of which are in a constant interrelationship with one another. Like the zillions of atoms in a box, they bounce into one another, they fit or don't fit with each other and intermesh in myriad ways, and the result is inherently highly complex and could

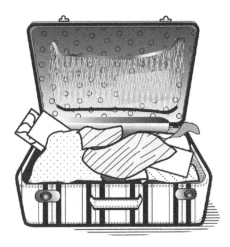

Figure 1.2   The case as a container

have taken any one of a number of other forms in our box. This is, in a sense, what the case study is about: the focus is on the complexity. That is, we have a state of affairs bounded by the case (think 'suitcase' again) and we study the complexity of what is in there.

So, there we are: the case is like a suitcase or possibly a wrapper.

The case as situation, event

Here, 'case' means a particular instance, an event, a happening, and the set of circumstances that surround this. So, this is different from the bounded (suit)case since it is less about the parameters that define the extent of the subject and more about a set of conditions or a state of affairs.

This, too, very nicely defines what happens when a case study is undertaken. A case study is about a set of circumstances in its completeness and the case is described – marked out – by those circumstances. It is the circumstances of the instance that are being studied. Where did it happen? When? What had happened before? Who was around? What was in the news? How did all of this affect what was going on and how events turned out?

An important feature of the case here is that, as Mitchell (2006: 31) puts it, there is, in ordinary use of English, 'a strong connotation that the word "case" implies a chance or haphazard occurrence' and this haphazardness entails specificity or particularity. This is an important point to make, for, as I discuss in Chapter 4 regarding 'samples', there can be no assumption that the case is in any way representative of a wider whole – it is a one-off, defined by the peculiar circumstances that you, the researcher, describe.

The case as argument

Figure 1.3   Your arguments are the fibres that hold your study together

The clue to the meaning of 'case' here is in statements such as 'The case for … is as follows' or 'Here is the case for the prosecution'. 'Case' is thus now being taken to mean a rationale, an argument.

This is not, if I am honest, likely to be relevant to the origins of the term 'case study'; nor is it likely to have been influential in the term's take-up as describing a form of inquiry. It *is* interestingly relevant, however, since a case study involves the rationale of one thing relating to another or possibly causing another. It involves your train of reasoning about the interrelationships between the elements of your study. It involves you justifying your reasoning and the conclusions with which you emerge, using evidence drawn from your empirical work. It is essentially about the arguments that you make to connect the elements of your observations. The arguments that you pose are like the fibres and ropes that hold all of the disparate elements together (see Figure 1.3).

What *is* and *is not* a case?

I noted earlier Stake's distinction between a study of *a doctor*, who could form the subject of a case study, and *doctoring*, which could not. On his or her own, though, even the doctor would not be a case – at least, not a very interesting or informative one. To be a case – an interesting one – we would have to be able to say that the doctor was a case *of* something (you should have an idea of what he or she is a case *of* at the outset). It will then be this analytical focus that crystallises, thickens or develops as the study proceeds. Indeed, it's the way this emerges, grows and develops that is at the heart of the study.

So, the Korean War would not be a case unless it was a case *of* something. Is it a case of a war? If so, can you say that it is a case of an especially remarkable or unusual *kind* of war? Perhaps it may be, by contrast, essentially a case of a border dispute, but one that has blown up out of proportion. Is it a case of US resistance to what was assumed to be communist expansion? Just chronicling the story of the Korean War would not be a case study. An exploration of any one of these 'ofs' – any of these analytical backdrops – however, *would* make a fascinating case study.

The importance of the analytical frame

Wieviorka (1992: 159) explains the distinctions I have drawn in my Korean War example by noting that when we talk about a case we, in fact, are talking about two elements:

1 what he calls a 'practical, historical unity' (the Korean War in my example) – this is, in essence, the *subject*

2 what he calls the 'theoretical, scientific basis' of the case (such as US resistance to communist expansion, in my example) – this is the *analytical frame* or what we could call the *object*.

So, just extending the war theme for a moment, we could not have a case study entitled 'World War II: a case study'. It is not a case study *of* anything. 'World War II: a case study of a "just war"', however, would contain both of the elements outlined by Wieviorka. It would make an interesting piece of work since it could examine in detail the notion of a just war, played out and exemplified through the case of World War II.

> **Case study research comprises two parts:**
>
> 1 **a subject**
> 2 **an analytical frame or object.**

Alternatively, take the example of a hospital ward. Would a description of this ward constitute a case study? In my opinion, it would not – it's not a case *of* anything. It becomes a case *of* something, as I explain in more detail in Chapter 6, when you can explain the analytical frame through which you might be viewing it. It might:

- be a good example of that analytical frame

- demonstrate something interesting in terms of your analysis because of its peculiarity

- be an example of an analytical focus that arises by virtue of your personal experience.

As I indicate in Table 1.3, the analytical focus must extend beyond mere description.

Table 1.3 What is and is *not* a case?

Subject (the 'practical unity')	What would not (on its own) constitute a case study?	What would be a case study?
Jesson Ward at Parktown Children's Hospital	a simple description of the ward	an analysis of why it is thought to be an outstanding children's ward
Editorials in the *Daily Globe* for the six days in week beginning 5 March	a content analysis of each editorial	a case study analysis of a newspaper proprietor's influence over the content of editorials
Aleksandr the meerkat	the rise of this advertising phenomenon	a case study analysis of the exemplary use of personality and a storyline in advertising

So, a case study is like one of those capsules with two halves: each half, each ingredient, is necessary in order for the other half to work, as shown in Figure 1.4. It has to contain the 'practical, historical unity', as Wieviorka (1992: 159) puts it (or 'the subject' in plain English), *and* it has to contain the analytical frame (or 'object'). It is not complete without both parts in place: one will not work without the other.

Wieviorka (1992: 160) continues:

> For a 'case' to exist, we must be able to identify a characteristic unit … This unit must be observed, but it has no meaning in itself. It is significant only if an observer … can refer it to an analytical category or theory. It does not suffice to observe a social phenomenon, historical event, or set of behaviors in order to declare them to be 'cases'. If you want to talk about a 'case', you also need the means of interpreting it or placing it in a context.

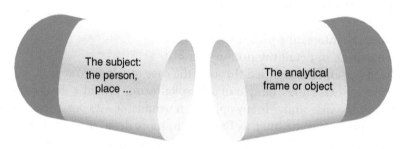

Figure 1.4   The two parts of a case study, each part needing the other

Let's take one more example and put it in the two-part capsule. Let's take as our subject the 1923 hung parliament in the UK. A narrative of this on its own is not a case study. How can we put it in the context of an analytical frame?

We first of all have to remember that we are looking at this *one* hung parliament – the *1923* one. We are looking at it as one of a set of hung parliaments. *Why* are we looking at this particular one? Perhaps it is an especially interesting one or an unusual one concerning the negotiations and the 'horse-trading' that occur among party leaders at the beginning of a hung parliament, just after the election result has been finalised and announced. This, then, would be our analytical frame. Clearly, a range of analytical frames *could* potentially accompany the subject, but we would need to choose one (or more) of these (see Figure 1.5).

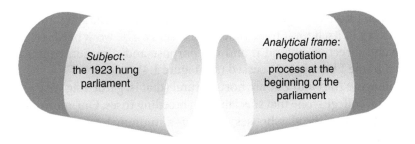

Figure 1.5   Putting the two parts together

What is the case study good and not good for?

Let's start with what the case study is *not* good for. It's not good for generalising from …

It's not good for generalising from (yes, I said 'not')

In the history of social inquiry there have been two broad lines of thought about the way that inquiries can and should be done. One suggests that we should collect lots of data about an issue and then generalise from it. The other suggests that, with certain questions, we are better learning from a specific example. As I shall discuss in Chapter 3, the ancestry for those lines of thought is as old as the Athenian hills. As far as I am concerned, both of these forms of inquiry are perfectly legitimate for their own purposes, but it is important not to get them mixed up. We cannot, for example, come up with potential reasons for Billy hitting Ryan repeatedly by doing an experiment – at least not in the formal sense of the word 'experiment'. Nor can we generalise about the success of a drug after observing its success in the case of one patient.

Throughout this book I shall be making a bit of a meal of the difference between generalisation and particularisation. I do so because a misunderstanding of the purposes of research and what we can get from inquiries is at the root of many a wild goose chase by students and other first-time researchers.

The assumption made by some is that *all* research has to be governed by identical ground rules – ones that stress sampling, generalisation and induction. Induction is the process of deriving a general principle on the basis of many observations gathered from experience.

I feel that I need to make this point so emphatically and repeatedly because students often misunderstand the purpose of the case study. The case study is about one thing, as I keep saying, but the unitary nature of the thing we are studying is unsatisfactory in itself for it to be called a case study. The work needs to have some purpose and direction behind it and the purpose and direction comes from the analytical frame I have just discussed (see Figure 1.4).

Let's imagine Alex and Zac are horticultural (that is, gardening) researchers at a horticultural college – one that specialises in breeding roses. One morning, on their routine daily tour of the glasshouses, Zac finds a stunning new white rose, the buds having just burst into flower. The flowers are fabulous; they're almost luminous. He bends to sniff one and immediately swoons as its perfume is hypnotic. Zac cuts the stem from the plant (don't worry, there are plenty more buds) and runs to Alex, calling: 'Hey, Alex, come and see this!' As he reaches her, he holds out the rose for her to smell. She nearly faints as she takes in the perfume – Zac has to hold out a hand to support her. Here, Zac is offering Alex the rose as an example of a new and particularly beautiful rose. (It will certainly become a garden classic.)

Now, if you will, replace Alex and Zac in your mind with Paula, who is a lecturer in plant science in the botany department of Gotham University. Quentin is among a group of students listening to Paula give a lecture. Paula holds up a white rose to the class. The point she wants to make is that roses are not alone in the family *Rosaceae* – they are but one particular genus, *Rosa*, of the family *Rosaceae*, which also contains blackberries, apples and strawberries (yes, extraordinary, but true).

In both of these cases, the roses are offered for a purpose, but *not* as examples from which we can generalise. Because on each occasion it is *one* rose, we can make no generalisations about it. We cannot look at each rose and say, 'All roses are white'. Nor can we look at it and say, 'All roses are perfumed' or 'All roses have thorns'. It would be wrong, in other words, to generalise from this one rose. In each case, the rose is serving a particular exemplary function of an analytical category.

I'll come back to this in a moment (under the next heading, 'It's good for uniqueness'), but before I do so I'd just like to spend a moment looking at a real-life example that I think shows why we should restrict the conclusions we draw from case studies. The case study has a fine history in medical education, particularly in psychiatry, where Sigmund Freud unpacked many of his new ideas through descriptions of cases. Freud, however, does something inappropriate, in my opinion, in one of his more famous cases and this serves as a good example of what should *not* be done with a case study.

The case was of a young woman to whom he gave the pseudonym Anna O. She had developed a set of neurotic behaviours, including a repeated paralysis, an inability to speak and a fear of drinking water. Of this latter characteristic, Freud (1957/2009) writes:

> It was in the summer during a period of extreme heat, and the patient was suffering very badly from thirst; for, without being able to account for it in any way, she suddenly found it impossible to

drink. She would take up the glass of water that she longed for, but as soon as it touched her lips she would push it away like someone suffering from hydrophobia. As she did this, she was obviously in an absence for a couple of seconds. She lived only on fruit, such as melons, etc., so as to lessen her tormenting thirst. This had lasted for some six weeks, when one day during hypnosis she grumbled about her English 'lady-companion', whom she did not care for, and went on to describe, with every sign of disgust, how she had once gone into this lady's room and how her little dog – horrid creature! – had drunk out of a glass there. The patient had said nothing, as she had wanted to be polite. After giving further energetic expression to the anger she had held back, she asked for something to drink, drank a large quantity of water without any difficulty, and awoke from her hypnosis with the glass at her lips; and thereupon the disturbance vanished, never to return.

The idea in the popular mind that personal acknowledgement and acceptance assist in the process of 'healing' is linked to many and varied contributory ideas stemming from psychoanalysis. Freud concludes:

> Ladies and Gentlemen, if I may be allowed to generalize – which is unavoidable in so condensed an account as this – I should like to formulate what we have learned so far as follows: *our hysterical patients suffer from reminiscences*. Their symptoms are residues and mnemic symbols of particular (traumatic) experiences.

Freud asks here if he 'may be allowed to generalize'. Well, no, sorry Sigmund, you can't generalise. You can't generalise – at least not in a useful way – from this case study. We can certainly take inferences and interpret these in the context of our personal knowledge and that which comes by virtue of our reading. It is wrong, however, to generalise and conclude, as Freud is encouraging us to do here, that reminiscence is the basis of a hysterical reaction. How could this be a useful generalisation? You or I would not develop a fear of drinking water if, like Anna O., we had witnessed a friend's dog drinking from a glass (well, I wouldn't – I would think it was rather sweet, though you may be a more sensitive soul).

No, Anna O.'s reaction was in the context of the era in which the episode happened and Anna's own history, which, of course, Freud went on to analyse in some detail. His analysis in these terms is as particular and as positioned as it is fascinating. However fascinating, though, Freud was not right to generalise from this one case to others and we can now appreciate, as twenty-first-century readers, why this is so, why it was incorrect to generalise.

We can appreciate that such a reaction was not a function simply of the individual psychological history of this patient, but also of the social, moral and political context of the age. It was a time, in our terms now, of heightened sensitivity to what would have been considered vulgarity. If Anna O. could be taken in a time machine to watch one of today's stand-up comedians, she would not just go off her water, she would have a fit of the vapours and probably never recover.

It's good for uniqueness

Going back to the rose, what would have been the purpose of offering the rose as a single case? For Zac, the horticulturalist, its uniqueness would be defined by its beauty and fragrance, placing it in a special position in relation to other roses. For Paula, the botanist, its uniqueness is defined by its exemplification of the unique genus, *Rosa*, of the family *Rosaceae*. The list of potential uniquenesses could go on, as shown in Table 1.4.

Table 1.4   One thing, one unique story

	Unique relative to what?	How might a case study, in showing the rose in its completeness, be interesting or instructive?
As a rose	All other garden plants	Showing how the rose is different from other garden plants, such as in repeat flowering. Showing how it is particularly susceptible to disease, compared with others
As a white rose	All other roses when used as emblems	A study of the significance of the white rose and its symbolic place in the history of different nations – in the Wars of the Roses, for example. Its cultivation and its popularity following this emblematic use
As a fragrant rose	All other roses	A case study of this rose and its selective breeding vis-à-vis fragrance. Its particular features that mark it out as an example of genetic mutation, including a discussion of the special difficulties in getting this variety to graft to the usual rootstocks

The point I am trying to make is that, if we are using the rose as an object for an inquiry, we are looking at its particular features in their variety and their completeness. We are, in other words, seeing the rose in terms of broader analytical categories, for, to quote from Wieviorka (1992: 160) again, the 'case' in itself (the rose) has no meaning in itself: 'It is significant only if an observer ... can refer it to an analytical category'. Wieviorka continues:

> If you want to talk about a 'case', you also need the means of interpreting it or placing it in a context ... Regardless of the practical approach for studying it, a case is an opportunity of relating facts

and concepts, reality and hypotheses. But do not make the mistake of thinking that it is, in itself, a concept. A case draws its unity not from the theoretical tools used to analyse it, but from the way it takes shape. (1992: 160)

Ragin (1992) makes an interesting point here, drawing from a seminar that he organised with Howard Becker – co-author of the celebrated case study *Boys in White* (Becker et al., 1961/1980). He says that Becker would continually pull the rug from under people's feet at the seminar by saying that cases should not be defined at the outset but, rather, *emerge* as the inquiry progresses. We should always be asking, Becker is suggesting, 'What is this a case *of*?' We should ask this question again and again, Becker advises, as our evidence accumulates around potential explanations (or 'theories'). The 'object' is then the explanation.

It's interesting to look at Becker's insight in the case of the three approaches to the rose set out in Table 1.4 because it puts the emphasis on the analytical part of the study – the explanation. It is the explanation and the theorising that are key in foci (roses in this case) that are quite similar.

A rich picture – with boundaries

A case study will not tell you the kinds of things that an experiment will tell you about causation (although you may choose to use an experiment as part of a case study, and this is covered in Chapter 8). What it does offer you is a rich picture with many kinds of insights coming from different angles, from different kinds of information. So, you may go into your case study and do interviews, make observations, keep a diary, look at statistics. Nothing is ruled out. The case study is a frame that offers a boundary to your research. Equally, you could think of the case study as representing the end of a searchlight beam. Everything at the end of the beam is seen in bright light and thrown into sharp relief, shadows and all. You study what is in the beam of light and your subject of interest in it is, 'What happened here? How did it happen? What was connected to what? Why did it happen?'

The end of a beam of light has a boundary, an edge, just as a case study has a boundary. Your case study is defined not so much by the methods that you are using to do the study, but the edges you put around your case – the direction in which you want your research to go and how far. You will define these at the outset. Perhaps you will say, 'I want to look at how IKEA grew to be the biggest furniture retailer in the world'. In making this examination you will be defining the subject of your case study by its growth, and growth implies development over time. Time implies history, with a beginning, middle and end.

Let's look at this particular example, defined by these parameters.

In this case study your principal theme of interest, we have just decided, will be growth. This case study will be focusing on change over time, beginning perhaps with a reconnoitre of the available statistics, to establish the grounds for your case. You will want to establish that IKEA really *is* the biggest furniture retailer in the world by comparing it with other retailers. You will want to show how it has grown over time, examining its turnover and profit figures since its creation by Ingvar Kamprad in Sweden in 1943. What does the graph of turnover figures look like over the years? Alternatively, you could show, on a series of maps, each representing a ten-year period, the countries in which IKEA stores have existed. You may be able to find out the figures you need quite easily or you may need to go to some quite obscure sources.

This gathering and plotting of basic data on turnover and profit over the years since 1943 provides the *boundary* for your case study. It says, 'This has happened: IKEA really is the biggest and it has become the biggest in a period of less than 50 years'.

This, though, is not enough for a case study. Simply to show the growth over time is not sufficient. You have the boundaries defined by the growth, but now you want to know how and why the growth has happened and, while you will not be able to provide a definitive answer, the case study should provide you with enough evidence to make a convincing argument. You will need to click together bits of information like pieces in a jigsaw, bits of evidence that you collect in support of any one of a number of tentative ideas – sometimes called hypotheses or theories – about the growth of the company.

If you are thinking about the growth of the company, what might be plausible ideas to explain its growth? Let's have a look at a few.

The company may have grown because its founder had one big idea or a series of good ideas, such as realising the:

- potential of sawdust and chipboard for making cheap furniture

- willingness of consumers to build their own furniture from a kit if the price and design are right

- ability and willingness of consumers to carry away their own flat-packed furniture with the advent of mass car ownership.

If any of these were important, where did Kamprad's ideas come from? Did he work in a sawmill and notice the abundance of sawdust? Did he work in retailing and realise the wastage involved in 'transporting air' in assembled furniture? Was it, instead, down to the retailing technique employed in IKEA stores, wherein consumers are encouraged to walk along a certain route through the store, being encouraged to buy as they make their extended and unexpected walk? (How many times have I come away from IKEA with something like a never-to-be-used Benthölme drawer-tidy precisely because I was steered along such a route?)

How could you go about finding out which of these potential ideas was important? Clearly the ideal would be an interview with Ingvar Kamprad, to ask him about your tentative theories, but I doubt if he gives many interviews. You will almost certainly have to rely on printed biographies of him. The Wikipedia entry for him, for example, tells us that in 1976 he wrote a manifesto detailing the IKEA concept of frugality and enthusiasm. We learn that he also worked with Swedish journalist Bertil Torekull on the book *Leading by Design: The IKEA Story* (Kamprad, 2000). In the autobiographical account, he further describes his philosophies and the trials and triumphs of the founding of IKEA. Also, that he began to make a lot of money when he was a child by buying matches cheaply in bulk and then reselling them at a profit. He expanded to fish, ballpoint pens and pencils.

Already we can see that he seems to be one of those people who almost can't help but make money. It's not as if he had an especially good idea about furniture or an especially wonderful insight into how it could be mass-produced. Rather, the seed seems to have come from his dynamism in finding ways to sell. Alongside this, he apparently drives a 15-year-old Volvo, flies only economy class and encourages IKEA employees to always write on both sides of a piece of paper. So, an obsession with economy, paring expenses down to the very last little bit, also comes through.

This is the kind of emerging information on which the narrative in a case study is built. The analysis begins to 'thicken' in this way around one theme.

If you take only one thing from this chapter, take this …

- A case study is about seeing something in its completeness, looking at it from many angles. This is good science. In fact it is the *essence* of good science.

- Although we cannot generalise from a case study, generalisation is not always what is wanted from the inquiry process. We don't always want or need to generalise and some of the most inspired and insightful research, of any kind, has come about as the result of case studies.

- What the case study is especially good for is getting a rich picture and gaining analytical insights from it. The 'analytical' bit is important: each study has a subject of interest (a person, place, event or phenomenon) and an analytical frame within which it is studied.

- Definitions of case study stress singularity and in-depth inquiry. The definition that I shall adopt for case study is as follows:

  > Case studies are analyses of persons, events, decisions, periods, projects, policies, institutions or other systems which are studied holistically by one or more methods. The case that is the subject of the inquiry will illuminate and explicate some analytical theme, or object.

FURTHER READING 📖

Bailey, M.T. (1992) 'Do physicists use case studies? Thoughts on public administration research', *Public Administration Review*, 52 (1): 47–55.
A widely cited article that provides an interesting contrast to the stance I have taken in this chapter, in that it defends case study research as meeting scientific criteria of generalisability, transferability and replicability.

Campbell, D. (1975) '"Degrees of freedom" and the case study', *Comparative Political Studies*, 8 (2): 178–93.
A classic paper in which Donald Campbell – one of the most respected proponents of experimental method – comes round to seeing the value of the case study.

Cohen, M.F. (2007) *An Introduction to Logic and Scientific Method*. New York: Harcourt, Brace.
Originally published (with Ernest Nagel) in 1934, this is a magnificent, if slightly dated, outline of what constitutes science. It is good on the duty of doubt in science. See especially Chapters 2 and 12.

Gomm, R., Hammersley, M. and Foster, P. (eds) (2000) *Case Study Method*. London: Sage.
This book offers, as the editors put it, the most influential and important articles on the case study. See especially the introduction by Hammersley and Gomm for an excellent overview.

Hammersley, M. (1992) *What's Wrong with Ethnography?* London: Routledge.
See Chapter 11, 'So, what are case studies?' By comparing the case study with surveys and experiments, Hammersley aims to show that these methods are not as different from each other as we sometimes assume and the differences that do exist between these ways of structuring research hinge on *case selection*.

Patrick, J. (1973) *A Glasgow Gang Observed*. London: Methuen.
This is a book I never tire of recommending. Like Becker et al.'s *Boys in White* (1961/1980), it is as good as a novel, describing the author's infiltration of a gang of young men in Glasgow.

Ragin, C.C. and Becker, H.S. (eds) (1992) *What is a Case?* Cambridge: Cambridge University Press.
Many excellent articles are included here. See especially Ragin's introduction.

Simons, H. (2009) *Case Study Research in Practice*. London: Sage.
An excellent, practical book on conducting a sociologically framed case study. Taken from the point of view of a student making her way through the process.

Stake, R.E. (1995) *The Art of Case Study Research*. Thousand Oaks, CA: Sage.
Stake, R.E. (2005) 'Qualitative case studies', in N.K. Denzin and Y.S. Lincoln (eds) *The Sage Handbook of Qualitative Research* (3rd edn). Thousand Oaks, CA: Sage.
Stake is one of the doyens of the case study method and his work is well worth reading.

Thomas, G. (ed.) (2014) *Case Study Methods in Education. Volume 1: Methodological Issues around the Use of Case Studies in Social Science*. London: Sage.
In this volume I have collected some iconic references for case study, including some of the key ones drawn upon in this chapter.

2

THE CASE STUDY AND RESEARCH DESIGN

Doing the right kind of research

Research can take many shapes and forms, and this is true in any field of endeavour. Imagine you are a research biologist interested in the anatomy of ants (or beetles or some other creepy-crawly). If this were the focus of your interest you would surely choose to explore this interest in a laboratory, using scalpels and pipettes and magnifying glasses and microscopes, taking notes and recordings as you needed them. You would not choose to go on a field trip with a tent and heavy boots and a pair of binoculars. What would be the point if you were interested in these little insects' anatomy? The sensible thing would be to do your work where you had the opportunity to do it in comfort and with access to all of the instruments and facilities (including a kettle) that you needed.

This seems obvious – and it *is* obvious to biologists. You don't often find them doing daft things, using an inappropriate research design. It's also interesting that they often do case studies, but they don't bother to call them case studies. Perhaps this is because, for them, the issues are clear and there is little uncertainty or handwringing about design and methodology. I wish the same were true for the social sciences. Unfortunately it is not. This is because it is sometimes very unclear where our focus should be. It's not obvious sometimes whether a research question should lead us to look in great detail at particular interactions between people or the same question ought to lead to straightforward counting or perhaps some kind of small experiment or some other research design. Because of these uncertainties, we often spend a great deal of time excitedly discussing methodology in the social sciences – angst with which natural scientists are not in general troubled. As psychologist Philip Levy (1981) put it, you don't find astronomers agonising over method or writing articles with titles such as 'The use of the telescope in viewing the heavens'.

Unfortunately, social science is, in many ways, more complex and messy than astronomy or entomology, and we *do* have to think harder about these methodological questions. The trick is to get the thinking just about right: not too little but not too much (many social sciences students spend far too long in a methodology section writing about all kinds of arcane epistemological matters that have no relevance whatsoever to their studies). Because the social sciences are so complex, however, we do need to spend *some* time thinking about this. So many avenues are open to us as social scientists that we need to be clear about our design, why we are using it and where we hope it will lead us. This is especially so with a case study.

What is design?

There's nothing magical about research design. Designing a case study is like designing any other kind of research, which, in turn, is like designing anything at all – a bathroom, boat, website, garden or a poster … anything. You start with a purpose – you have a reason for needing to design whatever it is. Then you go to the drawing board. You have a conception of how to meet your purpose. You look around you and beg, borrow and steal ideas from others. On the basis of this initial desk research, you refine your original conception and think about how you are going to do the work, then progress towards actually doing the task. You then review your work and, if your design has been good, you will not need to go back to the drawing board and start again.

> Designing research is like designing anything else – you start with a purpose and then plan how to achieve it.

I say 'if your design has been good' and there are a number of features to designing a case study that need to be kept in mind to achieve this 'goodness' in design. These features relate to the points that I have just stressed and their interconnectedness:

- purpose
- conception (or question)
- your desk research or literature review
- the approach you decide to take
- the design frame, methods and analysis you decide to use
- the process you will use in the case study – your modus operandi.

You should be aware, though, that it is not a simple question of ticking off one bit after another in this checklist. To do that is to take what is sometimes called a *linear* approach to research and, although it works in certain kinds of research, a piece of social science research is almost always different – it needs to be *recursive*. That is, it needs to go backwards and forwards, with twists and turns; there will be a toing and froing as you find out new things and refine your questions and your decisions about your approach in the light of these revisions.

So, the checklist for design becomes – looking at it as a recursive process – rather more like Figure 2.1. It involves each element influencing the others.

Figure 2.1 Do purposes, questions and decisions about the case study design hang together?

Does it all hang together? Is each part informing the others? In other words, are there good reasons for doing a case study? Does a case study design follow logically from your research questions? Can those research questions be answered by doing a case study?

I'll look at these issues in the sections that follow, using examples that I hope will make things clearer.

First things first: your purpose

Research begins with a purpose and a question, not a research design. You have a reason for needing to find something out (your purpose) and this leads to a question. It is this question that will be at the heart of your research. The design follows on from that, rather than the other way round.

Investing time and thought in your research question *will* yield a design solution. But because of all the initial uncertainty about where the research question might lead, sometimes people will be tempted to start by thinking of a design route *before* they have given their research questions more thought. This means that they will approach their research problem from entirely the wrong direction – looking for a method first or going in with a favoured technique – while giving relatively little attention to the research issue.

You must do the opposite: you must put the question *before* the method and let the question determine the method you use to answer it. You cannot say, 'Here's a great method. I'm sure I can use this in my research.' So, you should not, if you are sensible, begin by saying, 'I want to do a case study'.

This mistake of putting the cart before the horse in research design reminds me of the famous story of a man who lost his keys. He was desperately searching the gutter under a street lamp. A friend came along and, seeing him hunting around, asked, 'Have you lost something?'

'I've lost my car keys. I've been looking for them for half an hour', the man answered.

The friend joined in to help him, but after some time she couldn't see any sign of the keys. 'Are you positive that it was here that you lost them?' she asked.

'No,' he replied. 'I lost them over there in that dark alleyway.'

'Well, why on earth don't you look over there, then?' the friend asked incredulously.

'Because this is where the light is, of course!' the man answered.

The moral of this story is that we should *not* concentrate our research and all of our analytical effort on where we have good research instruments, good light, as they will tell us nothing on their own. The main issue must be 'What do I want to find out?' ('What am I trying to find? Oh yes, my keys!') The issue cannot be 'What is the best instrument for finding things out?' until we have decided on that first question.

Next, your question

As just noted, it's easy to get hypnotised by the idea of methods in research – almost as if these methods were at the core of the research. They're not. Methods are a way of answering a question, but the key – at the very start – is to think about the question you want to answer and consider how it can be answered.

If someone asks you a question in real life, such as, 'Do you know the way to San Jose?', your immediate response will surely be to think briefly and then try to answer to the best of your ability. If you are in Fremont, California, a little way up the road from San Jose (the legendary one), you will say, 'Take Route 880 south for 10 miles, and you're there, my friend!'

If, however, you are asked the same question in Fremantle, Australia, 3000 miles from San Jose, your response will depend on your mood and your assessment of the intent of the questioner. Is the questioner teasing you? Is she drunk? Is she genuinely confused? If she is giggling with her boyfriend and you think she is pulling your leg, you might laugh – grudgingly. If in a good mood, you might clear your throat, smile and, in your best Dionne Warwick, trill out, 'I've been away so long I may go wrong and lose my way'. If you assess that she is drunk, you might just ignore her. If you think she is confused, you might call for help.

Whatever the question, you will assess it on the basis of your immediate context and respond to it in a way that accords with that context and to the best of your ability with the tools available to you at the time. You are not a computer, programmed with stimulus–response contingencies, so your immediate reaction to the San Jose question will not be, 'Ah! This is a question about directions. What do I know about *methods* to do with solving directional questions? Maps! Now, do I need a map with a Mercator projection, a transverse Mercator projection, a Collignon projection, a Mollweide projection or, let me see, I really ought to check out the benefits of the Lambert conformal conic projection.'

No, you don't do any of this. You think straight away about how to answer based on your intelligence and common sense – and this must be your first response to your research question. One thing it is important to remember is that, because you are studying something in its completeness in a case study (that is, you are not just studying one or two relevant variables), it is all too easy to try to do too much in both the setting and the answering of the question. If you do this, though, you just end up with a mushy heap.

The key to avoiding mushy heap syndrome is to find a storyline through the general topic in which you are interested – one that is relevant to your particular interests. In Chapter 3 I shall go on to note the importance of seeing the whole situation as an *ecology*, and one of the pioneers of the ecological psychology movement, Barker (1968: 12), makes the point well. He highlights the legitimacy of alternative forms of inquiry and analysis by invoking an example of alternative, but equally valid, explanations of the same event. He asks us to imagine the movement of a train of wheat across the Kansas plains. How is this movement to be explained? An economist will explain it in one way, while an engineer will explain it in another. 'Both the laws of economics and the laws of engineering are true; both operate in predictable ways on the train.'

In Chapter 6 I shall go on to examine the kinds of case studies that can be undertaken once you have addressed your question in detail. I suggest that you use the categorisation in Chapter 6 as a kind of check once you have made decisions about how you will answer the question. That menu of different kinds of case study will enable you to say, 'Oh, I hadn't thought of that'. It will set in front of you the options, the possibilities for your study. First, though, it is important to think about the channels open to you for answering your question.

In sum, you shouldn't start a project assuming that you are going to do a case study. Rather, you should go into it with a question that the research study will answer. The case study may or may not be the design form that you choose once you are clear about your question.

Kinds of questions

So, it is the research issue – your question – that is the starting point for your design journey. It is the pivot for your research: everything rests on it. Your first port of call in doing your research is not to say boldly, 'I'm going to do a case study!', but, rather, 'What do I want to know?' or 'What do I want to find out?' It is the research question that leads you in the direction you need to go.

Your question does not need to be fixed in concrete right at the beginning. It proceeds from a prima facie question to one that is a more refined, final question. When I talk about your 'prima facie' question I mean your first not-very-well-thought-out question. This will nearly always change in the course of your inquiry. It is quite difficult to get your question right, but you have to start somewhere when you are doing your research, which is where your prima facie question comes in. It lets you

> A question is the starting point for your research. Begin with a question, not a presupposition that you are going to do a case study. A case study should follow logically from your question, or else you should not do one.

make a start without unnecessary dithering about whether or not you have got your question right. It allows you to get going. Go boldly with it; be unafraid, on the understanding that it will change. It will get better as you think more about the subject and do more reading.

So, isolating a bit of Figure 2.1, let's, in Figure 2.2, see where your prima facie and final questions lie in the design trail.

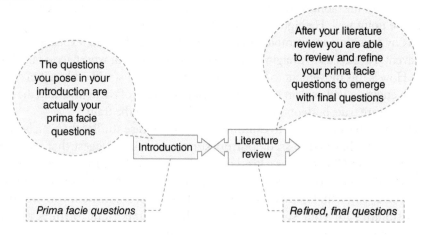

Figure 2.2   Prima facie and final questions

Literature review

I think the best policy is to state your prima facie questions at the outset, in the introduction to your dissertation or thesis, then refine these in the light of your literature review and state them again, rethought out and reformulated, at the end of the literature review.

The literature review is a specialised topic in its own right, so I am not going to cover it here (see my book *How to Do Your Research Project*, 2013). Suffice it to say here that, following the setting of your prima facie question, the literature review will give you a wealth of new information, a treasure trove, and you will almost certainly want to revisit those first questions in the light of it. It may be, for example, that someone has already done exactly the project you had intended to do or you may find interesting paradoxes in the existing literature to which you wish especially to direct your work. Whatever, your ideas will change and you can reformulate your questions at the end of the review. Write them here, at the end of the literature review or at the beginning of your methodology section.

All of this is true of any research. It is particularly important in this case, however, to understand how the reformulated, refined question that crystallises out of your reading and thinking at the end of your literature review will lead to a case study – or some other design framework. Let's have a look at an example of how an initial idea is translated into a prima facie question, which is then shaped into a better idea with the benefit of a literature review, which leads to a well-informed case study.

How to go from idea to question to case study

I draw here on a case study undertaken by the investigative journalist Rageh Omaar. In a Channel 4 film about race and intelligence, Omaar (2009) started with a set of puzzling and troubling findings about race and achievement. In essence, his study concerned the significantly worse performance at school of young people who are black or Hispanic than those who are Caucasian.

Idea

It's a well-established phenomenon, but why should it occur? This was his prima facie question and was the basis for the analytical frame he would employ in his inquiry.

Prima facie question

Omaar first outlined traditional explanations for this poor level of achievement. Intelligence was (and is often still) taken to be at the root of achievement – that if you have a high level of intelligence, it is assumed you will achieve; if you have a low level of intelligence, you will not do well. He looked back through psychological accounts for differences in intelligence, too, and was able to locate a powerful stream of thought in the early twentieth century that had settled on a supposedly hereditary basis for differences in ability. At that time, there was a keen desire to calibrate people's abilities, and this found its expression in the development of intelligence testing and the IQ test. All this happened at roughly the same time as a flowering of interest in Darwin's ideas, summed up in the idea of 'the survival of the fittest'. This came to be used by 'social Darwinists', in a terrible distortion of the theory of evolution, as an argument for sterilising people of lesser ability in a movement that came to be known as eugenics (Thomas and Loxley, 2007: 34–7).

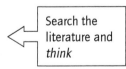
Search the literature and *think*

Although eugenics and the social Darwinism on which it is based are now considered wholly objectionable, their legacy resides in a strong undercurrent of belief about the heritability of intelligence. This is still at the core of many people's

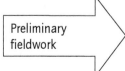
Preliminary fieldwork

(Continued)

(Continued)

attitudes to success and failure. In fact, it is probably still the received wisdom. Omaar interviewed some key psychologists who took this view. The attitude they hold extends to beliefs in differential intelligence for different ethnic groups, with the assumption that people of black and Hispanic ethnic origin tend to be of inherently lower intelligence than white and Asian people.

Omaar's study was now beginning to take shape and harden. He was able to refine his research questions with the benefit of wider reading and new ideas. One of the ideas he took forward was that of the so-called 'Flynn effect'. James Flynn is a researcher who has noted that intelligence, which is supposed to stay fairly stable in both individuals and populations, is, in fact, rising. The rise is disguised by the fact that average IQ scores always stay at 100. This maintenance of the score resolutely at 100 happens because of a standard practice in psychometric science – a periodic 'renormalisation' of the data from which IQ scores are calculated. This 'normalisation' is key to the way our understanding of intelligence is distorted, and it was normalisation that Omaar used to lever his way into the debate.

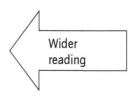

Wider reading

So, what is normalisation? IQ scores are based on the idea that the values of most things in life (height, weight and so on) are normally distributed. In other words, there are the most occurrences in the middle of the range (most people are of average height, for example) with relatively few occurrences at either end of the range (relatively few people who are very tall or very short). In between are intermediate numbers of people and the distribution can be set out in graph form to produce the curve shown in Figure 2.3. This 'normal distribution curve' describes the way in which most attributes in nature are dispersed among a population. Following on from this, the assumption among the early psychologists was that this should also be the case for intelligence.

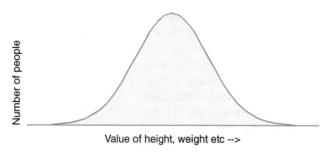

Figure 2.3   A normal distribution curve

This assumption about normal distribution is all very well for height and weight, which are unproblematically measured, but – as I've been at pains to point out throughout this book – things are rather more complicated in the social sciences and, as far as intelligence is concerned, we cannot just measure it with a ruler or weighing scales. In fact, the idea of intelligence has been *constructed* – made up – and, in its construction, because

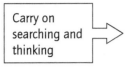

of the assumption that intelligence is a normally distributed phenomenon, there has had to be a correction of the raw scores people get on tests to produce revised scores (called 'standardised scores') that conform to the normal distribution curve. The standardised scores make it look as though what people are achieving is normally distributed and, because of normalisation, that this distribution is staying constant over time.

What Flynn (1987) showed, in an article called 'Massive IQ gains in 14 nations: what IQ tests really measure' (note also his later work: Flynn, 1998, 1999, 2003; Dickens and Flynn, 2001), was that 'intelligence' is *not* stable if you go back to the prenormalised, raw figures. People's ability to do 'thinking tasks' is rising. Amazingly, Flynn was the first person to make any kind of a song and dance about this and what it meant for the notion of intelligence.

Interest in Flynn's work has centred on why the rise should be taking place, but more interesting – certainly as far as Omaar's developing research question was concerned – is the light that it throws on the construct of intelligence. 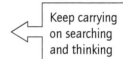 If intelligence is not the stable, normally distributed phenomenon it was once thought to be, it cannot be used as the basis for explanations about why people of different ethnicity fare better or worse at school. It is more satisfactory to use the far simpler explanation that we get better at the things we practise. If our lives at home give us no chance to practise the things that are demanded of us at school, then we are almost bound to do less well there. Given that black and Hispanic children are disproportionately from poorer families where there is likely to be less of that kind of school-related activity going on, the explanation for their poorer performance can be explained straightforwardly by background rather than genetics.

The literature review of this theoretical background – this analytical frame – provided the backdrop for the case that Omaar was making – a theory-building and 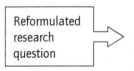 picture-drawing case about the influence that school can have on countering expectations about achievement. He could reformulate his prima facie question to ask a completely new one: 'What influence can school have on countering expectations about achievement?' In answering this, he would need to draw on the analysis conducted as part of his literature review and he would draw also on empirical work: the case study.

Omaar's next step was to go on to identify a school that had bucked the trend – an outlier case that had shown that a catchment of entirely black and Hispanic children could achieve extraordinary feats given favourable circumstances at school. The school he chose was Hostos-Lincoln Academy of Science in the Bronx, New York. This is one

(Continued)

(Continued)

of the poorest and toughest areas in America, with 80 per cent of its students eligible for free or reduced-price school meals.

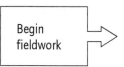

Seek out 'outlier' case

Hostos-Lincoln Academy is one of 36 schools in its locale. It is a public school (that is, a state school), serving 534 students in grades 6–12 (final year of primary school until end of secondary, staying to do school-leaving exams). All of its students are black (23 per cent), Hispanic (73 per cent) or of Asian/Pacific island (4 per cent) origin.

Begin fieldwork

Despite the problems of poverty and deprivation, Hostos-Lincoln Academy is getting its students into some of the best colleges in America. This achievement cannot be explained by better resourcing, for the school has 17 students for every teacher, whereas the average for New York is 13 students per teacher.

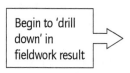

Begin to 'drill down' in fieldwork result

Assessment results show just how well the school is doing with its students. Of the school's students, 52 per cent met or exceeded the standards in English language, while the average for schools in the same district of New York is 31 per cent. In maths, 77 per cent of Hostos-Lincoln Academy students met or exceeded the standards, while the average in the district was 51 per cent. In science, 38 per cent of students met or exceeded standards, while the average for schools in the district was 29 per cent. It was like this in subjects right across the board – social studies, chemistry, Earth science, living environment and so on.

This demonstration of difference, however, is not what is at the heart of this case study. Just showing that the school is different is of no interest without what follows. The heart of the research lies in the in-depth analysis of what happens in the school that means it achieves the results it achieves.

More drilling down

Omaar concentrated on what was going on in the school that enabled it to help its young people so effectively. He interviewed the principal of the school, Nicholas Paarlberg, visited classrooms, made observations, talked to students and teachers and took particular interest in one 13-year-old student, Kwan, who became a nested case within the larger one of the school (see page 177 for a discussion of nesting).

Omaar's conclusions relate high expectations, affirmation and students being given access to a culture outside their own. When the students graduated, they were allowed a portion of the main corridor wall to write their name on to show that they had graduated (see Figure 2.4). In the nested case study of Kwan, Omaar showed that this student lived, ate and slept in a tiny one-bed apartment, but at Hostos he was 'transported to another world, and he is thriving on it'.

This was a well-designed piece of research. Omaar linked important elements to produce a nicely integrated case study. He had:

1 noticed something worth investigating – namely, the consistently poor performance of black and Hispanic students at school

2 read around the area and developed a hypothesis, or theory, as to why this should be

3 looked to find a counter-example, or outlier case, where the usual (that is, the poor performance of these students) did *not* happen

Figure 2.4 The 'graduation wall' at Hostos-Lincoln Academy

4 undertaken a case study of the outlier case, by means of which he sought to explain the better performance of the black and Hispanic students in the context of the theory he had developed on the basis of his reading

5 used the case study as both an explanation and illustration.

Your question, and the analytical frame associated with it, will evolve, as Rageh Omaar's did. It will progress from a prima facie question to a final question. On the way from A to B it may become transformed as you read, conduct pilot work and develop new ideas. This process is not unique to case study – it's there in all investigative work in any field. Einstein famously did it using his 'thought experiments' (Norton, 2004). Becker et al. (1961/1980: 33) describe the way that one relatively simple question led to another, more complex and analytical one in their classic case study on the training of medical students, *Boys in White*:

> We had first the descriptive question: How much effort did students put forth and in what directions? Then we had the analytic question: Why were the students' level and direction of effort what they were and not any of the other things they might have been?

Questions and different approaches to research

Beyond understanding that questions *develop* – they may cultivate 'forks' or 'layers' – it is important to understand that there are various kinds of questions, which lead to different kinds of research. I like to think of these questions being of four basic kinds.

1 *What's the situation?* You are describing something.

2 *What's going on here?* You are trying to understand what is happening in a particular situation.

3 *What happens when ...?* You introduce a change and look to see its effects.

4 *What is related to what?* You examine how one thing is related to another.

Typically, people think of these questions leading to different kinds of research approach and research design – and they do. What is interesting about the case study, though, is that it can encompass different kinds of approach to research. It is like an umbrella: it covers a range of ways of doing research. It does this because, as I have said, it is about a focus rather than an approach. Nevertheless, I like to think of the case study as a design frame in its own right, even though it does cover this range of approaches and methods, which I look at in more detail in Chapter 8. I like to think of it in this way because it has integrity as a way of going about research, as a way of approaching the singular. Let's think a little more about the case study as a design frame and how it interconnects with your research question.

Questions and design frames

Oranges are not the only fruit, and the case study is not the only design frame. It is one of a large number of research design frames that can be adopted in an inquiry to answer the four kinds of questions I have just laid out.

So, there are many design frames that can be used and – just to make things confusing for the first-time researcher – they are not wholly separate from each other, they can nest into and envelop each other. In this sense, it is not very easy to map kinds of research questions on to kinds of design frames.

With this caution in mind (and I'll try to sort out the confusion in a moment), let's outline a few of the design frames most commonly used in small-scale research:

- action research
- case study
- comparative research
- evaluation
- experiment.

Let's also consider what they are good for, because they all have their advantages and disadvantages. Each is better or worse when focusing on different questions. For example, if you are concerned with one of the 'What happens when ...?' questions – that is, if you are looking to see whether or not X causes Y, you will probably want to use some kind of experiment. If you want to discover whether or not some new method of management has had an impact on industrial relations in a particular factory, you will embark on an evaluation. If you want to improve your practice, doing this through research, you will set off on a piece of action research. If you want to compare phenomena in different countries, you will embark on comparative research. It's horses for courses. Let's match up some of the design frames to kinds of questions and kinds of study.

Table 2.1   Questions, purposes and design frames

Design frame	Purpose – especially good for ...	Kinds of questions
Action research	Helping to develop practice	What's the situation?
		What's going on here?
		What happens when ...?
		What is related to what?
Case study	Understanding the details of what is happening	What's the situation?
		What's going on here?
		What happens when ...?
		What is related to what?
Comparative research	Looking at different situations and making comparisons	What's the situation?
Evaluation	Seeing if something is working	What happens when ...?
		What's the situation?
Experiment	Establishing causation – does X cause Y?	What happens when ...?

You will note from Table 2.1 that certain kinds of design frame, such as the experiment, are limited to one kind of question (does X cause Y?), while others, such as the evaluation, are appropriate for more than one kind of question. Others, such as the case study and action research, may cover all of the kinds of questions that I have outlined.

This is because a case study is defined by 'singleness' rather than procedure. There are no procedures that are associated exclusively with the case study, for, in its examination of the singular, the one thing, it is 'allowed' to use whatever procedures and methods it wishes in doing this. The emphasis when doing a case study is on the singleness. In other words, the *case study is not a method, nor is it a set of procedures*. Rather, it is a focus.

Design frames and methods

Inside the design frame, you will be using one or more of a variety of methods to answer the questions that you pose. As far as this is concerned, the case study has broad and capacious arms: it loves all methods. It's perhaps going too far to say that it is promiscuous, but it is, shall we say, *generous* in its affection for methods – observation, diaries, questionnaires, tests, statistics, interviews, whatever … the options are limitless.

Likewise, with different elements of the case study, you may use *other* design frames under the umbrella of the case study – in this sense, we are talking about frames within frames.

The important thing is that you are using a case study to examine your case in detail. In doing this, you choose whatever methods and subsidiary design frames you can think of to help answer questions about your singular case. If you look at some informative and important case studies – such as Ball's (1981) *Beachside Comprehensive* or, in a completely different field, the investigation of the variant Creutzfeldt–Jakob disease (vCJD) cluster in Leicestershire following the 'mad cow' epidemic (outlined on page 127) – you will find that a broad range of methods is used and a catholic attitude is taken to the use of methods. It is not as if just one or a few methods are 'allowed' in the case study. Rather, when we think about methods, it is an issue of looking to see what is best in terms of answering the questions that arise. Observation? Questionnaires? Sociograms? The choice is yours.

> The case study is like a scrapbook or portfolio of sources and information.

It may help to think of your case study as a scrapbook or portfolio. The case study is everything that you choose to put in it.

Using storyboards to help you design your case study

Always, though, there is a problem to be solved and I return to the point I made at the beginning of the book: there is no substitute for *thinking* to solve the problem. Method is not a proxy for thinking, and I make no apology for recalling Rodin's *The Thinker*. It is thinking that will provide the analytical frame for your case study.

To give you a sense of the kind of thinking that needs to go on when designing your case study, I think that the *storyboard* is invaluable. It enables you to brainstorm initial ideas and trace a path through the good, the bad and the ugly in these initial musings. With it, you can sift out the bad and the ugly ideas – or just the not-so-appealing ones – and proceed with those that promise most fruit. You can add to your storyboard as you get further into your literature review and gain information in your initial inquiries. Eventually, a path in which the design elements outlined on page 27 emerges. I cover the processes that are involved in operationalising the design in Chapter 9.

In the following example, I try to give a flavour of the kind of thinking that needs to go on as part of the design process and how the storyboard can help in this.

Designing a case study: an example with brainstorms and storyboards

Let's assume that you are a political science student and interested in the cultural conditions that existed in Eastern Europe during the 1980s. Your purpose, then, is to study this.

This may lead you to a prima facie question such as 'What led to the fall of the Berlin Wall?' This is fine as a prima facie question, but it will need some work to make it interesting as a research question for, at the moment, it is too broad. It could be answered a thousand different ways. Imagine it. I offer some starting points in the brainstorm illustrated in Figure 2.5.

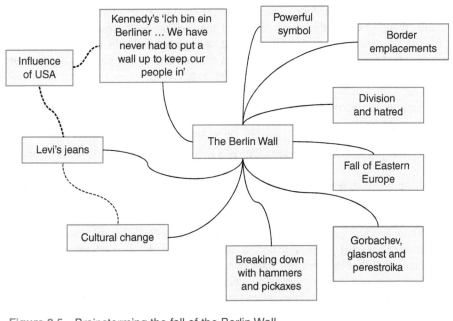

Figure 2.5   Brainstorming the fall of the Berlin Wall

(Continued)

(Continued)

Anything can be considered in brainstorming, and this particular session might lead you to think in more detail about a number of possible reasons that could be explored more fully:

- the interest of the USA and the West in the survival of West Berlin over decades
- the bankruptcy of the Soviet Union after four decades of the arms race
- the conspicuous differences in standards of living in West and East Germany
- the assumption of power by Gorbachev and his liberalisation of politics
- the damage to the economy caused by the black market in Levi Strauss jeans
- the Soviet political hierarchy's refusal to support Erich Honecker, the East German leader at the time
- and so on.

For each of these possible starting points for an answer – each of these analytical frames – there are many potential ways to proceed to examine things further. You could look at statistics and official records, examine newspaper reports, interview those who lived through it and so on.

For a piece of small-scale research of the kind done as part of an undergraduate or postgraduate programme of work, these potential avenues will be narrowed by the options that are open to you. You may have limited time, money and access to information. More importantly, though, as far as this book is concerned, the questions will fan out into a broad range of potential design frames – and the one that we are interested in here is the case study.

So, what marks out the avenue of inquiry that leads to a case study, as distinct from some other design frame? It will be a question that:

- leads to a study of one thing, one phenomenon, one situation
- focuses on a situation that is marked out as special or interesting in some way
- enables you to look at the relationship of a variety of different factors in the situation.

Thinking about it, reading about it (for your literature review) and talking with tutors and fellow students, you may realise that, from the various avenues of inquiry open to you, what you are really interested in is the role of popular culture in Eastern Europe at that time and how far this contributed to the fall of the Wall. This still does not tell you whether or not what you need to do is a case study, though. What will tell you this?

Remember that the defining characteristic of a case study is the uniqueness of your subject. So, if you are choosing to do a case study of the Berlin Wall, you are in some way identifying the Wall as special (see Figure 2.6). Clearly, we have to be sensible here. It is not unique in the sense that it is different from your back garden wall or the wall of your house. (Well, it is, I guess, but not in any interesting way – unless you are a builder or a bricklayer, in which event you might take a special interest in its straightness or the quality of the mortar.) It is interesting perhaps as:

- a definition of territory by an invading power
- a symbol of authority
- a partition
- a national border
- an object on which graffiti are drawn
- an object of state violence.

With any of these phenomena you could take the Berlin Wall as a *case*. You would then be looking at the Wall as an especially interesting example of one of these phenomena – one of these analytical frames.

Taking a slightly different slant, you could choose to look at the *fall* of the Berlin Wall as an especially interesting example of a rather different set of phenomena, such as:

- the collapse of authority
- the victory of the people over autocracy
- the power of bulldozers vis-à-vis the weakness of humans
- the unassailable integrity of the German state
- the success of the Western propaganda machine in the Cold War
- the power of popular culture and mass media in contemporary governance.

Given your interest in popular culture, you decide to take the last of these. You may be interested in how the fall of the Wall in some way exemplifies the influence of popular culture on national and supranational affairs. Your starting point – the germ of your thesis, if you like – may be that politics as it is practised by politicians operates only as a superficial gloss, as a kind of leitmotif on the 'natural politics' of a nation. Your view may be that there is always a deeper political current which will make itself felt and come to the surface to defeat autocracy. (Incidentally, this is not a view I hold, but it is a perfectly respectable starting point for exploration in a piece of research and would lead to an interesting study.) With this starting point, you could identify the fall of several such autocracies, pointing to the role of popular culture in each, then make the point that you are going to concentrate on the fall of the Wall as an especially interesting case and one about which there is a great deal of documentary evidence on which you can draw. Here, then, is the start of your case study.

(Continued)

(Continued)

Figure 2.6   The Berlin Wall: a case study of what?

Having established your grounds for using the fall of the Wall as an example of the influence of popular culture, you need to keep in mind the whole time that it is the fall of the Wall that is the event on which you are concentrating. In other words, don't slip into a discussion merely of the influence of culture on the decline of Soviet influence on Eastern Europe. What is *iconic* in the fall of this huge symbol of division? How can its fall in some way exemplify the power of popular culture? You need to make this connection.

Let's imagine that you brainstorm again and think of connections with culture and how those connections can be linked with the Wall. How can a story be made? I hope you can see something clearly emerging from the brainstorm diagram in Figure 2.7.

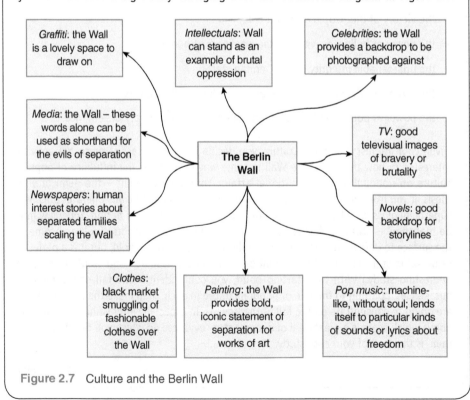

Figure 2.7   Culture and the Berlin Wall

What I'm hoping you can see is that, from the forms of popular culture I have identified here – media, painting, graffiti, TV, newspapers, pop music, novels, intellectuals, clothes, celebrities – there are many elements to the structure of the Wall, culturally speaking. With a spark of insight, you may see that these make it especially fertile ground for these various cultural forms. It's big; it can't be ignored; it is screaming out to be painted on; it stands as a conspicuous symbol of brutality in its scale by comparison with the buildings on either side. It is bounded by stark, empty space; it stands also as a symbol of the seeming hatred of human scale and humanity held by the regime that built it – it's an icon of a rejection of individualism.

It is in all of these areas that you can make a special distinction of the Wall – a reason for it to become a case study that makes it stand out as different from or similar to other borders.

Now you can draw a storyboard (see Figure 2.8) in which you 'join the dots' about all of this thinking. You connect the relevant and important bits of your brainstorming.

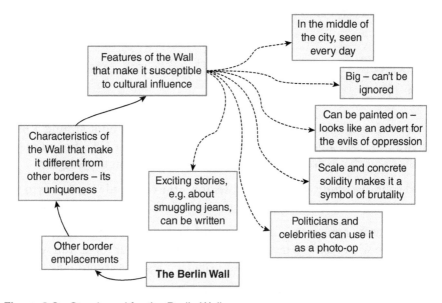

Figure 2.8   Storyboard for the Berlin Wall as a case

The Wall is a symbol of separation and oppression. Here, in Figure 2.8, the story-board concentrates on its unique features as far as culture is concerned. It points to the Wall's special features vis-à-vis others where separation and/or oppression may be involved – think of the separation of North and South Korea or of Lebanon from Israel. What makes them less (or more) iconic cultural symbols than the Berlin Wall? For a start, those barriers are of barbed wire rather than concrete and are separated from ordinary folk by demilitarised zones that effectively sterilise them from contact with people and, necessarily, culture.

(Continued)

(Continued)

These latter features automatically make other border emplacements inert as far as their cultural impact is concerned. By their very nature, they are insulated from people, whereas the Wall was very much 'in your face'. People saw it every minute of every day and it was ripe for use as a cultural icon, eventually working against the very purpose for which it was constructed. It was, we might say, its own worst enemy.

The storyboard shown in Figure 2.8 enables you, I hope, to see how you can go from a loose collection of ideas to a starting point for singularity and specialness to, eventually, an exploration of that specialness, that uniqueness, as a case study. I describe the nuts and bolts of drawing a storyboard in Chapter 11.

If you take only one thing from this chapter, take this ...

- A piece of research is built around a *question*, it is not built around a *method*. Anyway, the case study is not a method – it is a wrapper for different methods. It's the focus that is special to the case study – a focus on the singular.

- Build your case study around your question – the case study is a means to an end (that is, answering a question), not an end in itself.

- Do a literature review early on in your research to find out as comprehensively as possible what research has already been done on your topic. You will then be in a position to adapt or modify your original questions accordingly.

- Remember that case study is not a method. Rather it is a design frame – a scaffold for your research. Within this frame, this scaffold, you can use a wide range of research methods.

- When building your case study, always keep in mind the need to establish a storyline. The key is to draw rich, interconnected information from your singular focus and derive unique insights from the analysis that follows. You can use storyboards to help you do this – to move from what might be a loose collection of ideas to a clear narrative.

FURTHER READING 📖

Ball, S. (1981) *Beachside Comprehensive: A Case-Study of Secondary Schooling*. Cambridge: Cambridge University Press.

Lacey, C. (1970) *Hightown Grammar*. Manchester: Manchester University Press.

These are classic examples of the case study. Each gives a detailed analysis of what goes on in one school over a period of time. They exemplify the kinds of very diverse data gathering that can be done in a case study and the ways in which the case study work can be linked intelligently to national policy.

Becker, H.S., Geer, B., Hughes, E.C. and Strauss, A.L. (1961/1980) *Boys in White*. Edison, NJ: Transaction Publishers.

Another classic. This is about American medical students and the way that they work. It's a good read and tells you as much about the process of the case study as it does about the training of the medical students.

3

THE WHOLE IS MORE THAN THE SUM OF THE PARTS: SEEING A COMPLETE PICTURE

This chapter offers an intellectual history of the case study – a pedigree, showing its scholarly ancestors. This may not help much with the nuts and bolts of doing your case study research, but it will help, I hope, in understanding where the case study has come from and where it currently stands as an approach to inquiry. You do need to know this if you want to get a good mark for your research project. More importantly, you need to know it if you want to understand why the case study is appropriate and meaningful for your work. One of the important chapters in your dissertation or thesis will be your methodology chapter, and if you understand what is in this chapter (that is, this chapter in *this* book), you will write a better methodology chapter of your own.

Looking at the whole represents something of a new – or at least a reawakened – worldview. It is one that emerged during the twentieth century with the purpose of understanding phenomena not as so many disconnected parts but, rather, as interconnected elements. Anyone wanting to do a case study implicitly shares this worldview, though it should be said that the case study does not boast an intellectual allegiance to any one strand of thought but many. I shall review some of these in this chapter.

Break things down or see them as wholes?

That the case study is not superglued on to one of these schools of thought may make it seem like a bit of an intellectual orphan, which is part of its problem as it attempts to establish its credibility. While it may not adhere to a particular stream of thought or school of thinking, its emphasis on the whole – the holistic – puts it in some respected scholarly company. All of this company shares a wish to see things as wholes.

The wish to see things more as wholes does present a number of challenges, however, since the thrust of most scientific inquiry since the Enlightenment (that is, since the beginnings of rational and scientific thought in the mid-seventeenth century) has been about breaking things down. It has been about reducing them and understanding them in terms of their constituent parts. It has, in other words, been about reduction, so is known to philosophers as *reductionism*.

Reductionism has done wonders in the natural sciences and the technology that springs from it – people on the Moon, refrigeration, antibiotics, computers, to name but ... er ... four. Viewing the world from this position, phenomena are nothing more than the sum of their parts.

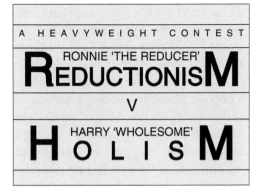

Figure 3.1   Reductionism and holism: each has its own advantages

The starting point taken in the case study, by contrast, is that certain phenomena are *more* than the sum of their parts and have to be understood as a whole, rather than as a set of interrelating variables. How has this holistic position fared next to the super-successful reductionism? Also, given that reductionism has been so successful, why would anyone want to study things differently?

This chapter is really about the attempt to view and analyse phenomena as *more* than the sum of their parts and about the intellectual traditions, mainly in the twentieth century rather than before, that have competed against the highly productive reductionist tradition. This has, of course, been a bit of a David versus Goliath contest. There are a number of themed but unrelated elements to this understanding of things-as-a-whole that I shall look at briefly – each in its own different way about the importance of wholeness in inquiry.

The issue is more complex than simply seeing the world as indivisibly complete versus the world as necessarily divisible and reducible. Associated with the assumptions being made here are beliefs about the purpose of inquiry. In other words, why are we doing the research?

Some have said that the purpose of research is to develop laws and theories with which we can explain the world and predict what is likely to happen next. Others have said that this is fine and dandy in understanding the things of the natural sciences (and it has got us to the Moon and so on, as I mentioned before), but it is less adequate in understanding the things of the social world. Here, reductionism is of less value.

The issue about whether or not reductionism is of value is as old as the hills – the Athenian hills. Plato, Socrates and Aristotle had major disagreements about this. It was pistols at dawn. Well, it would have been, except that pistols weren't to be invented for another 2000 years, so they probably had naked wrestling. Not a pretty sight, but, if your imagination will allow, I'd like you to imagine the ring. In the blue corner, will you welcome Mr Plato, from Athens, who thinks that universal truths developed from generalisation are the bee's knees – they are what we should all be searching for if we want true knowledge. With his friend Mr Socrates, also from Athens, he says, 'I am looking for the *simile in multis*.' He is looking, in other words for the *essence* that captures the truth evinced by many cases – for example, I've only ever seen white swans, so *all* swans must be white.

And in the red corner, will you welcome Mr Aristotle, also from Athens – clearly a popular place for budding intellectuals. Mr Aristotle disagrees with Messrs Plato and Socrates on the value of *simile in multis*. For many kinds of knowledge, says Mr Aristotle, we progress only by using our practical reasoning, craft knowledge or tacit knowing – the stuff we know because of our experience. It's the stuff we learn 'on the job' or by simply being alive and it is explicable only in terms of the particular – the case. It cannot be communicated by reducing it to general princi-ples. 'You are wrong, Mr Socrates and Mr Plato,' says Mr Aristotle, 'to dismiss the value of cases in the production of knowledge.' (I made up this quote, by the way, using artistic licence, but he *might* have said it.) Seconds out … and let's have a good clean fight, boys.

The punch-up on this theme continues to the present day. It proceeded through into Base Camp 1 of the Renaissance, with Francis Bacon – the first scientist, some would say – averring that the generalisers and regularisers, the followers of Plato, 'hasted to their theories and dogmaticals, and were imperious and scornful toward particulars'. Today, the argument has unfortunately come to be known as the 'paradigm wars' (Oakley, 1999) and shows little sign of abating. Any argument that goes on for 2500 years has clearly got legs and we are not going to resolve it any time soon.

It was the occupants of the blue corner, Plato and Socrates, whose ideas won (broadly speaking) and whose thinking took hold so successfully for the natural sciences. Poor old Aristotle sat dejected in the red corner, disconsolately staring at his feet and licking his wounds. This was a big defeat and a big loss for our ways of understanding, asserts an astute commentator on these issues, Bent Flyvbjerg (2001). Flyvbjerg says that the mistake led humankind on two millennia of false starts in understanding social phenomena. The mistake was in the failure to dis-tinguish between different kinds of inquiry for different purposes and it leads us, in extremis, to the absurd position that it is inappropriate to argue or learn from particular examples for fear that this might be thought 'anecdotal' and, therefore, unscientific.

The distinction, then, has been on a long journey intellectually. In essence, it is about the relevance of particular individual events to a larger picture and the extent to which we can use separate events to establish laws or theories by which we can explain and predict. Some say that it's legitimate to generalise in the natural sciences, but not in the social sciences. In the former, physics and chemistry, the stability of the events studied is such that laws and theories can be worked out in a way that they will prove useful for explanation and prediction. In the human sciences, however, events follow such random twists and turns that any attempt at establishing stable laws and theories that will reliably explain and predict is meaningless.

The classic argument here has been posed by the philosopher Alasdair MacIntyre (1985) in his book *After Virtue*. If you are interested, read Chapter 8 in that book, 'The character of generalizations in social science and their lack of predictive power'. It's as entertaining as it is enlightening.

> *Holism* is seeing things as a whole. (Why hasn't it got a 'w'? Don't ask me.) There is an assumption that the whole is more than the sum of its parts. It's about seeing things in their entirety, their totality.

I've said that this argument about reductionism versus holism has been going on for 2500 years and reductionism has certainly won as far as the main method used for the natural sciences is concerned. In fact, it's only in the last 100 years or so that protagonists of Aristotle's views have come to the fore again in thinking about the human sciences.

Earlier, right at the beginning of the book, I mentioned the idiograph – a drawing or figure that stands not for a sound, as do symbols in the Roman alphabet, but for an idea. It was the philosopher Wilhelm Windelband who, at the cusp of the nineteenth and twentieth centuries drew on the notion of the idiograph to separate what he called the 'idiographic' and the 'nomothetic' (from the Greek *nomos*, meaning 'law') in social inquiry.

I personally think that it would have made life easier if Windelband had called the 'ideographic' the 'pictographic' since 'pictograph' is a perfectly acceptable alternative to 'idiograph' and it more straightforwardly explains what he was trying to get at. A pictogram is a small picture that has become stylised, so that it represents the thing in written form. The Chinese pictogram for 'person', for example, looks a little like a matchstick person, with a trunk and two 'legs'. (Interestingly, these picture representations eventually take on sound-like representations as well, developing into our modern system of alphabetic writing.)

With the idiographic, the approach is to specify and study individual phenomena in detail – we have a 'picture' in front of us. With the nomothetic, by contrast, the approach is to generalise from many cases and derive laws from such generalisation.

Windelband was not the first to notice this difference but, as is so often the case in the history of ideas, he encapsulated something nicely in his separation of the idiographic from the nomothetic and the distinction he drew has stuck.

It has proved enormously helpful in summarising the differences between these kinds of inquiry.

Gestalt psychology

Not long after Windelband, one interesting avenue down which this discussion travelled was that of Gestalt psychology early in the twentieth century. This was key for the case study since the essence of Gestalt thinking is that things should be seen in their totality, as we try to do in a case study. The key idea to emerge here was that the mind works not by perceiving things in isolation, separately, but, rather, as wholes – as integrated units. We humans, alone among animals, invest meaning in what appear to be unrelated phenomena and make patterns, make sense, out of these. It is almost as if our minds are patternmaking or sensemaking machines.

The key figures here – psychologists such as Max Wertheimer and Wolfgang Köhler (and, later, the great social psychologist Kurt Lewin, the inventor of action research) – suggested that the methods psychologists use to study psychological phenomena distort our understanding of them. By always reducing, atomising the subject matter of psychology into constituent variables, the end result is a misunderstanding of the way the mind works, they said. The mind works not in the convenient building blocks of psychological science – variables such as gender, age, reaction speed, time, class – but *wholes*.

It is certainly true that *Homo sapiens* is a pattern-finding animal. The fertility of our brains in divining patterns is boundless – it requires only the mildest encouragement for shape and form to crystallise out of what may seem at first to be chaotic stimuli. Look at Figure 3.2. After looking for a while, you will see a Dalmatian dog. (Can't see it? Its nose is in the middle of the picture and its backside towards the top right.) In fact, perhaps dangerously for certain kinds of inquiry, we even seem to be predisposed to preferring to see form where there is none rather than not see any form at all.

The philosopher Karl Popper suggested that this facility may be inborn. It may be due, he proposed (1977: 270), to 'mechanisms which make us search for regularities'

Figure 3.2 We have a wonderful capacity for seeing shapes and making meaning

and be responsible for what he called 'the dogmatic [ouch] way of thinking'. In a similar vein, Barrow (1997) points out that the human brain has an evolutionary imperative to *over*-see patterns – that is, occasionally see patterns where they don't exist (as 'false positives', for instance 'seeing' slender shadows as tiger stripes) – as this has historically given us an evolutionary advantage over the opposite state of not recognising patterns where they in fact exist (where the slender shadows are actually the stripes of a tiger).

The bottom line is that we must be cautious about this precious ability to see pattern since, today, harbouring a predilection to make shape and theory out of that which is shapeless may not be quite so useful. We may overdo generalisation, tending to generalise from insufficient information. It is this tendency that has to be guarded against in all of the sampling procedures that have been developed with what has been called probabilistic research (of which more on page 63).

If we are looking at idiographs (that is, cases) rather than representative samples, however, we are not expecting to generalise. Rather, we are expecting to employ to best effect our ready-made excellence at making sense *without* generalising. It's back to the naked wrestling again and not getting the two kinds of inquiry mixed up.

No, you can't generalise from a case study, but you *can* use your ability to put things together, to draw from experience, make informed judgements about cause and effect in this particular case. It's what the human brain is good at. It's what got us out of the trees. It's what Newton, Darwin and Einstein did. We shouldn't be ashamed of it. It's about connecting ideas, like the ganglia between neurons.

There are a number of superstructures that have been used to accommodate wholeness, intellectually speaking, and I shall look at these in the sections that follow.

Dramas, theatres and stages

> All the world's a stage,
>
> And all the men and women merely players;
>
> They have their exits and their entrances

This quotation is from Shakespeare's *As You Like It*, the words spoken by the character Jaques, and it sums up several streams of thought about how the world – the natural as well as the social world – should be seen. So, it's worth saying a little more about the stage analogy.

In fact, the *As You Like It* quotation could perhaps be the motto of the case researcher because the ways of thinking about social situations that I am going to review in this section are all characterised by seeing the person in context, where the action is defined by interactions between people and situations, which, of course, is the sine qua non of case study research. Each person is affected by the environment around them: no one is an island.

There's no better place to begin to explore this idea than with the work of sociologist Erving Goffman, who actually called his view of social life *dramaturgy*. In the dictionary definition, 'dramaturgy' is the art of writing and producing plays and, for Goffman, life is a set of dramatic performances in which people take on roles and change the way they behave depending on their interactions with other actors. I am a different person with different folk. I take on a different character with my sister Adrienne from the one I take on with my friend Peter, from the one I take on with my boss Edward. The core perhaps is the same, but if ever I were to be faced with the three of them in one room (heaven forbid) I would suffer from an acute case of triple personality implosion syndrome – or PIS[3], as it is known in the psychiatric literature (that's meant to be a joke, by the way).

> Interpretivists say that there is no 'objective' social world 'out there'. Rather, it is *constructed* differently by each person in each situation they face, so it is useful sometimes to see the world as a stage on which we play out characters.

Goffman differentiated between the kinds of situations in which such performances are necessary, noting that there is a 'front stage', where the 'act' is always used in order to 'impression-manage', and a 'backstage', where people can be more 'themselves'.

Goffman's dramaturgical perspective was itself an offshoot, an important one, of a branch of sociology known as symbolic interactionism. Here's how one of symbolic interactionism's main proponents, Herbert Blumer (1992: 82), presents what he calls the 'basic premises' and 'methodological consequences' of this school of sociology:

> human beings interpret or 'define' each other's actions instead of merely reacting to each other's actions. Their 'response' is not made directly to the actions of one another but instead is based on the meaning which they attach to such actions. Thus, human interaction is mediated by the use of symbols, by interpretation, or by ascertaining the meaning of one another's actions.

Symbolic interactionism is, in turn, a tributary of a wider stream of thinking known as *interpretivism*. The basic assumption here is that the social world is *constructed* by each of us differently, with words and events carrying different meanings for each person and in each situation. Interpretivism started, broadly speaking, with the American sociologist George Herbert Mead, and I'll examine it in more detail in Chapter 8.

Though not directly linked, a forerunner to these lines of thought was the phenomenology of Edmund Husserl, which emerged at the beginning of the twentieth century. This is generally thought of as a philosophical rather than a sociological movement, but it is connected to the thinking of the interpretivists and the symbolic interactionists in its emphasis on meanings. Actions, Husserl would say, cannot be broken down into their constituent elements to understand them. They are understandable only in terms of the meanings that actors impose on them. They are understandable only, in other words, in terms of the wholeness of the context in which they occur.

In fact, a clutch of philosophers, and those in the infant disciplines of sociology and psychology, were saying much the same kind of thing at this time. Wilhelm Dilthey came up with the idea of *Verstehen* (meaning 'understanding'), more adequately to demarcate between the stuff of the natural and the human sciences and our ways of inquiring into them. We cannot, he said, ignore the historical context and the context of meaning in all that human beings do and say.

Ecological psychology

Another manifestation of the need for wholeness is seen in ecological psychology. In its 'green' sense, ecology refers to the relationships between living things in the environments that they inhabit. It is the study of the complex interrelationships that take place in those environments.

A starting point here is that the lives of organisms inhabiting these environments are inextricably intertwined with the nature and quality of those environments. Changes in any small aspect of the environment will have knock-on effects that will affect the lives of the organisms populating it. An important aspect of this is that there will be an equilibrium in this environment and it will be maintained. If foxes become blighted, their main meal, rabbits will breed like ... er ... rabbits, with few predators, so the remaining foxes do well, eating the superfluity of rabbits, so then rabbits decline, causing foxes, in turn, to decline, then rabbits breed ... and so the cycle goes on (see Figure 3.3). Thus, the equilibrium is maintained, and the same happens in the environments (family, school, factory) that we inhabit as people.

So, ecological psychologists would say, people – that is, humans, persons, *Homo sapiens* – live in a multicoloured world. It's an ecology where an increase in one stimulus invokes not an automatic reflex or a tropism, but a thought-out reaction or an overreaction.

The difficulty is that it's not as if you could set up a meaningful research study to assess the effect of turning up the volume of music on the volume of people's conversation. Of course, you could do it physically – you could get some volunteers conversing in a room where rock music is playing quietly and start turning up the

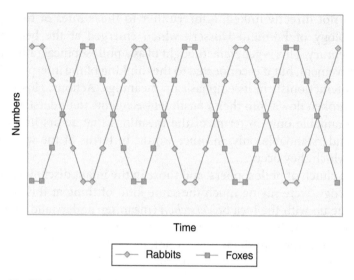

Figure 3.3   Equilibrium is maintained in an ecology

volume and measuring the volume of the volunteers' voices. I guess that you would find that the volunteers' voice levels rose (much psychological experimentation is of this kind). An ecological psychologist would say, however, that the real world is not like this. In the real world, people would just leave the room to talk or someone would go and turn the volume down again. Then someone would go and turn it up again and perhaps there would be an argument, then maybe a fight, then someone would be taken to hospital, and so on.

The real world, then, is complex, and it is the real world in which we are interested. The understanding that ecological psychology offers is that the way people behave in a psychological laboratory, with its tight control of a small number of variables, does not remotely represent the way people behave in the real world.

The basic idea is the same as the one behind symbolic interactionism, which is that no behaviour occurs in a vacuum; it occurs in the context of others' activity, in the context of the family, place of work, school or community and in the context of the linguistic, cultural, legal and physical environments. Because of the way that psychology and its inquiries typically proceed – by isolating variables, controlling important ones and manipulating one or two – we can get into a rut of thinking that they, using these controls and manipulations, are valid representations of what happens in our everyday lives. We come to think that the world in which we live is really like this – like a psychological laboratory with a simple set of variables that are all more or less inert in their relationships with one another.

The traditional focus on the individual in psychological endeavour permeates the applied field, where interventions also often take place in a vacuum, with scant consideration of the physical and social environments within which individuals learn and behave. The ecological metaphor used by some psychologists since the mid-twentieth century enables an understanding that things are not that simple. Behaviours may emerge in an environment that are a consequence of conditions outside the narrow ambit of the individual. Changing one or two features of this system may have unanticipated consequences or may have no effect at all.

Adopting an ecological model is like using a wide-angle lens, enabling an examination of the wider situation that surrounds the target and encouraging analysis in the wider situation. In essence, an ecological view enables a recognition that people inhabit a variety of contexts, each one impinging on the other. Any attempt to oversimplify the richness of the ways in which these contexts interplay is bound to have shortcomings. An ecological view says that it is impossible to disentangle the functioning of a constellation of phenomena simultaneously interrelating in any social arena.

It is Roger Barker (1968) who has generally been credited with introducing the notion of ecological psychology. He suggested that behaviour settings have both static and dynamic attributes. On the static side, the setting consists of one or more standing patterns of behaviour and milieu – the latter comprising elements such as house, classroom, a windy day. On the dynamic side, the setting comprises the interpersonal relationships among people and groups. Science, Barker says, attempts to keep apart the static and the dynamic, the physical and the behavioural, but their interaction is the central focus of his attention. He gives the name *synomorphs* to the settings in which these interactions occur.

> *Ecological psychology* is about the complexity of the psychological world. Everything is connected, so it is difficult to assess the effect of changing one variable. Things tend to stay in equilibrium.

Barker clearly intended his model to be useful in the real world rather than the laboratory. By taking as a starting point the integration of behaviour and environment, he intends to be able to predict real-world events and solve real-world problems. Unfortunately, as you will realise if you follow up his work, the Byzantine complexity of his model and the impenetrability of his language render his aims pretty well unachievable – his aims are on a different numbered bus from his model; in fact, the buses are going in opposite directions, one going to Moscow, the other to Timbuktu. This is a pity, since his central thesis is as powerful as it is important.

Amidst Barker's complex analysis is a continual reiteration of the influence of the physical environment and its interaction with a range of other influences, such as the ideologies of the participants, and the procedures, practices or rituals associated with certain synomorphs. It is notable that Barker and others, such as Gregory Bateson (1972/1999), who promoted an ecological thrust to understanding people in their environments, had a multidisciplinary scholarly background themselves and promoted intellectual interchange with different fields.

Another important figure in this area is Kurt Lewin, whom I mentioned earlier. Lewin was a bit of a psychological polymath – brilliant ideas came sparking off him almost as if he were a human Van de Graaff generator. He was just a fizzing lightning ball of brilliance and, among other things (in his spare time, probably), he invented action research.

In the current context, he came up with an idea that he called 'field theory', which is linked as much to Gestalt psychology as it is to ecological psychology, but I'll mention it here. Lewin (1951; 1997) suggested that the 'field' of an individual's psyche comprises a range of social and psychological factors and changes with the person's experience. An alternative term he uses for fields is 'lifespaces' – home, job, school, sports club – that we occupy at different times and in different ways. All are joined by 'vectors' that operate at different levels of strength.

Lewin, with his mercurial (and maybe slightly manic) mind, perhaps tried to make things too mathematically precise, but he offered another stratum to the developing bundle of ideas about holism.

One of the main proponents of ecological thinking was Urie Bronfenbrenner, but since he developed his model from a hybrid of ecological and systems thinking (covered next), I shall deal with the latter before going on to talk about his ideas in more detail.

Systems thinking

Systems thinking is a way of viewing the world that lends itself naturally to the case study since it aims to see the system as a whole, in much the same way that you aim to do in a case inquiry. The difference is that systems theory and its various branches are bounded by some quite firm frameworks about viewing the interrelationships that exist.

With the case study, there are no methodological prescriptions. By contrast, systems theory proffers methodological tools and route maps to assist analysis. It's a *particular* way of studying the whole, unlike the case study. That is not to say you can't use the methods of systems thinking in a case study – you can and they may prove to be very useful for structuring your thinking. For this reason, I go into some detail on a branch of systems thinking in Chapter 11.

Systems theory was developed in a variety of contexts, from biology to engineering, and thus can be relevant for a range of foci and adapted for use in each of these. If your interests are in engineering or biology or an applied science or if you are interested in the interrelationship between one of these and the social world, it may well be worth you exploring aspects of systems theory.

The models for understanding that have been advanced in systems thinking were developed specifically to address the need for holism in getting to grips with complex dynamics. As with the parallel trains of thought in psychology and sociology that I have just looked at, the finger is pointed at the barrenness of attempts to understand complex behaviour by reductionist methods. Our understanding, systems theorists say, has to push that complexity to the front: we have to try to understand the ability of the complex system to adapt, change and 'learn' from experience. Systems theory used ideas from biology, such as *negative entropy* (the ability of a system to make sense, re-form itself and maintain an equilibrium), and from mechanics, such as *feedback* (the effect of a signal going back into a loop and magnifying itself each time it returns). These are characteristics of *systems* that are not seen in *individual parts* of the system.

One of the first proponents of systems theory was Ludwig von Bertalanffy (1950) with his *general systems theory*. At the risk of getting repetitive, the same theme emerges – one of complex interactions – though von Bertalanffy didn't leave it at that.

He made an important distinction between what he called open systems and closed systems. A *closed system* is one such as an engineering system (think of a diesel engine) that has very little in the way of a change to its movement once it is working, aside perhaps from a movement of the throttle by the operator. By contrast, an *open system* is one such as a biological system (think of any living thing, even a bacterium) that seeks to maintain itself in equilibrium by responding to its environment.

Apart from features such as feedback and negative entropy, von Bertalanffy spoke about features such as *isomorphism* (that is, being the same shape) between biological and social systems. So, a beehive could be seen (from some points of view) as being a bit like a town.

His thinking led naturally to interdisciplinarity, with insights from one field providing clues for thinking about how things work in another. In fact, von Bertalanffy expected to see more of an integration of the work of science – natural and social. Sadly, there is not a huge amount of evidence that this is occurring today, despite attempts to promote it by all and sundry. He said that the human sciences were too often atomistic, they were a kind of 'social physics' of the worst kind.

Beyond all of this, systems theory has been taken forward by others in some interesting ways that may be quite useful to the case researcher. One of these is the development of *soft systems theory*, expounded by Peter Checkland (1981) and his colleagues at Lancaster University.

Checkland tried to incorporate the basic tenets of systems thinking while offering a framework for seeing the ways that the elements interconnect. He thus advanced a model that was simpler than the one promoted by Barker (see page 55), but still offered a framework of a more holistic understanding of social environments. Developing his 'soft systems' within the context of industrial psychology, he suggested that the matters with which we are concerned are complex wholes that maintain themselves in a changing environment. They do this by means of adaptation and control action.

Although the concepts used in Checkland's model are borrowed from biology and engineering, he does not explicitly use the ecological metaphor, but his aims are congruent with those of the ecological psychologists. He suggests a model that draws a distinction between the 'real world' and 'systems thinking' and forces an analysis of both. He asserts that the 'soft, messy problems of human beings in their everyday lives' are not amenable to the methods of the 'hard' systems tradition of engineering. He suggests that the hard systems tradition can handle natural (that is, biological) systems and designed systems (such as bicycles, computers, mathematics), but cannot cope in situations dominated by human perceptions. He calls the latter 'human activity systems'.

His soft systems method suggests a sequence of events and processes for analysing social settings. I describe this in detail in Chapter 11, which is on forms of analysis.

Ecological systems theory

I've already mentioned Bronfenbrenner (1979) in the context of ecological psychology, but his work is also interesting as a fusion of ecological psychology and systems thinking. Being a psychologist rather than a sociologist, Bronfenbrenner was not so fond of theatres and stages as metaphors (with which sociologists seem fascinated, if not mildly obsessed). No, rather than seeing human behaviour and activity as a drama, he saw it as an ecology. The metaphor was biological rather than theatrical (or 'performative', in sociological jargon).

Bronfenbrenner has perhaps contributed most systematically to furthering the ways in which the ecological approach can be used practically. It is he who could also be said to have been the most assertive proponent of ecological approaches, with some quite direct attacks on the more narrowly scientific approaches to psychology of his contemporaries. For him, a parallel track was not sufficient. He saw psychology's traditional methods actually doing harm to our understanding of people and he wanted to force a reappraisal of its traditions, habits and methods. It could almost be said that Bronfenbrenner was aiming for a paradigm shift in the way that psychology proceeded as a form of science.

For him, culture and society provide a set of 'instructions' for how social settings are made and he conjoined all of his ideas about context into a formal framework that he developed as a form of 'systems theory' (Bronfenbrenner and Morris, 1998). He saw ecological environments as being composed of what he called micro-, meso-, exo- and macrosystems. A *microsystem* is a pattern of activities, roles and interpersonal relations of an individual in a given setting. A *mesosystem* is a system of microsystems. An *exosystem* is a setting where the individual is not involved but events occur that affect or are affected by the individual's setting. A *macrosystem* comprises the belief systems or ideology that structure other, lower systems (see Figure 3.4).

So, taking an ecological and Bronfenbrenner-type view, if Samantha decides not to get up and go to work today, how can we explain this? Looking at the situation in just one-dimensional terms, we might see it in terms of depression. Looking more widely, we might see it in terms of friendships and Sam's lack of contacts, having just moved here from Australia. Looking out even more widely, we might find a

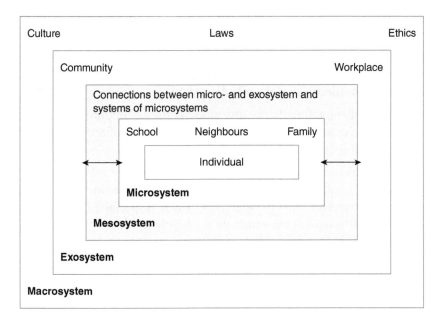

Figure 3.4 Bronfenbrenner's ecological systems

problem that she has been having at work. Even more broadly, she may be affected by an overdue tax return and a demand to her employers from HM Revenue & Customs to take tax directly from her salary, leaving her mortified with shame.

This kind of understanding is a million miles from traditional psychological inquiry and is now encouraged by a new wave of clinical psychologists such as David Smail. Indeed, in what sounds like an echo of Bronfenbrenner, Smail (1993: 13) asserts that: 'There is certainly no evidence that the wider availability of psychological theories and techniques is leading to a decrease in psychological distress.' It is the oversimplifying models that are used to approach distress that are to blame, says Smail.

Thinking particularly about children, Bronfenbrenner's comment on traditional psychological inquiry was that it sacrificed far too much to gain experimental control and led to 'the science of strange behaviour of children in strange situations with strange adults for the briefest possible periods of time' (1979: 19). The links with symbolic interactionism are manifest. There's nothing new in the world.

If you take only one thing from this chapter, take this ...

I hope you can see that the stress on the context and the 'wholeness' of behaviour is many-stranded and is particularly suited to the case study. A number of points came through in this chapter:

- Reductionist science has concentrated on breaking things down to the smallest units, manipulating variables and looking for the effects of such manipulation.

- Holism, by contrast, assumes that the whole is more than the sum of the parts – that psychological and social phenomena cannot be understood without an examination of the whole system.

- At the heart of the rationale for case study is the assumption that holism provides an effective and fruitful way of addressing many of the questions that are posed in social inquiry.

- Several streams of thought have emerged from a holist understanding: Gestalt psychology, dramaturgy, ecological psychology, systems thinking. Throughout the twentieth century such perspectives gained respectability as it was recognised that they provided the rationale for highly productive methods of social and psychological inquiry.

- Figure 3.5 summarises some of the schools of thought that have led to today's more eclectic attitude to inquiry. It's an attitude that accepts the relevance and utility of the idiographic and provides ways of addressing wholeness by emphasising rather than denying the interconnectedness of the strands of psychological and social life.

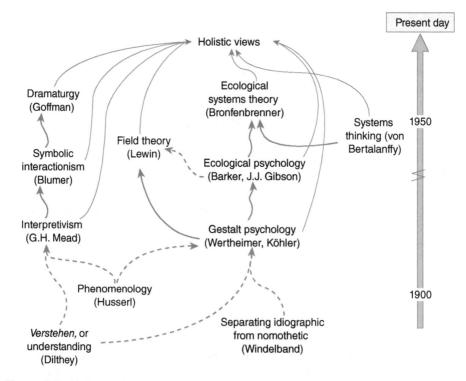

Figure 3.5   Holism and its schools of thought

FURTHER READING 📖

Barker, R.G. (1968) *Ecological Psychology*. Palo Alto, CA: Stanford University Press.
One of the most important pioneers in the movement to make psychology more respon-sive to the whole, Barker insists that behaviour is always *situated* – in other words, it doesn't exist in a vacuum. A useful platform for the case study.

Bateson, G. (1972/1999) *Steps to an Ecology of Mind*. Chicago: University of Chicago Press.
A collection of Bateson's essays and lectures. Really, his thesis is about *ideas* rather than the 'mind' of the title, and the book is about what he calls 'an ecology of ideas'. It's rather mysterious and enigmatic, but good for thinking further about the ways in which ideas interact – and we must make them interact in a case study.

Becker, H. (2014) *What About Mozart? What About Murder? Reasoning from Cases*. Chicago: University of Chicago Press.
An excellent discussion of what case study is, and what it can do.

Burgess, E.W. (1927) 'Statistics and case studies as methods of sociological research', *Sociology and Social Research*, 12: 103–20.
A classic article that presages many of today's debates about the distinctions between research involving small and large numbers.

Checkland, P. (1981) *Systems Thinking, Systems Practice*. Chichester: John Wiley.
Checkland's original thinking on soft systems.

Flyvbjerg, B. (2001) *Making Social Science Matter: Why Social Inquiry Fails and How It Can Succeed Again*. Cambridge: Cambridge University Press.
See especially Chapter 6, 'The power of example', for a comparison of case study with methods that seek to establish generalisation.

MacIntyre, A. (1985) *After Virtue: A Study in Moral Theory*. London: Duckworth.
Chapter 8 is the key one in this book: 'The character of generalizations in social science and their lack of predictive power'. This is taken to be a key critique of the methods of social science and their attempt to establish generalisation.

Travers, M. (2001) *Qualitative Research through Case Studies*. London: Sage.
This is essentially about the interpretative tradition and the case study and has a good chapter (Chapter 3) on Goffman's dramaturgical analysis.

RIGOUR AND QUALITY IN YOUR CASE STUDY: WHAT'S IMPORTANT?

Rigour is important in research: judgements about rigour frame much of our assessment of the quality of research. But what do we mean by 'rigour' when we are talking about case study? And, given the flexibility in the form of case study, what can 'quality' mean with this kind of research? If rigour is spoken about, I imagine the first things people think about are accuracy, precision, thoroughness and strict attention to detail. While these features of research are always important (for it would be strange to accept inaccuracy or imprecision in any circumstances) they are far from being the whole story when it comes to doing case study. And it may be that some of the chief structural characteristics of social research – the characteristics via which rigour is judged – may distract us or mislead us, for we may be judging accuracy, for example, using the criteria by which we measure it in very different kinds of research.

Let's have a look at some of those structural characteristics of research – sample, reliability, validity, quality, generalisability – and think about their meaning and relevance in case study. My purpose in this chapter is also to take a look at features of research such as theory and positionality, which are especially important in this kind of research. Much has been written about these dimensions of research quality – some elements of the methodological discussion being quite contradictory – so I intend to take a critical look at this in the context of case study.

Is the 'sample' important in case study?

When thinking of the *sample* in research, the emphasis should, I believe, be on it being a sample *of* something. It is a sample *of* a wider population (the total figure of all the people in whom you might be interested is called the *population*, and the sample is a slice or selection drawn from this population).

You might, for example, be interested in alcohol consumption among students nationally. Clearly, it would be impracticable to issue a questionnaire to each and every student in the country (the population) so you have to find a way of getting a representative sample of the students to whom you *are* able to gain access. This smaller sample from the whole population is intended to *represent* this population and, clearly, the bigger the sample, the better the chance of representing it accurately.

You can, of course, imagine all of the things that can go wrong in sampling of this kind. A sample from one university is unlikely to be representative of all universities; a sample from one group, such as your lecture class, even less likely, and 11 students in the bar on Tuesday night even more unlikely accurately to provide a representative sample of the wider population – especially if you are interested in students' more usual drinking habits.

I said 'the bigger the better' for a sample, but there are ways of sacrificing size by doing clever things such as 'stratifying', which means making sure that you get the important parts of the population (by sex, age, type of institution attended and so on) properly represented in your small sample.

Now, *none* of this is relevant to a case study. The reason why I have devoted several precious paragraphs to it is to try and hammer home the point that those 'samples' and all of the assumptions behind them are not necessary for a case study. In fact, 'sample' is the wrong word for what is wanted in a case study. In textbooks, to separate out the representative kind of sample (of which I have just given an example concerning alcohol and students) from all others, the term 'sample' is sometimes divided into *probabilistic samples* and *non-probabilistic samples*.

I personally think, however, that to make such a distinction is confusing. In a case study, the choice that you make regarding your subject is nothing like a sample, probabilistic or non-probabilistic. In fact, with *any* research, not just a case study, I would go so far as to say that there is no such thing as a non-probabilistic sample – or, at least, there might be, but we could just as easily and with less confusion call it a 'bad sample' or, more generously, a 'quick and dirty sample'. A *sample* has to be 'a portion that shows the quality of the whole', in the dictionary definition. If it isn't that – if it doesn't accurately show the quality of the whole to you as a researcher – it is at best a convenience, purposive or pilot sample.

The point of a case study is *not* to find a portion that shows the quality of the whole. You are looking at your selection of subject – a marriage, country or whatever, with one, two or a few being focused on – without any expectation that it represents a wider population. So, it's not a sample; it's a choice, a selection. It is

> A sample should show the quality of the whole. A 'sample' is not what is wanted in a case study. (Yes, 'not'.)

this *selection* that is vitally important for your study. In Chapter 6 I examine the way in which you can make that selection.

Do I have to worry about reliability and validity in a case study?

As with many topics in research methodology, there is a variety of views on reliability and validity, and the views are different for very good reasons. Those different reasons usually concern the different 'takes' that people may have on what research is about. I explore this in more detail in Chapter 5 of *How to Do Your Research Project* (2013). Let me summarise my argument for advising you that reliability and validity are not your principal concern when doing a case study.

Reliability is a concept imported into research methodology principally from psychometrics – the branch of applied psychology that is about testing people's mental faculties. When giving tests, it is important that those tests are reliable as instruments. It is important, in other words, that they give accurate data on different occasions and in different circumstances, like a ruler or a weighing machine will do. This is also true for certain kinds of applied social research, where, in some kinds of inquiry, there are the same expectations of consistency of findings in different circumstances. This applies *only* in certain kinds of inquiry, however. In a case study, where there is one case, expectations about reliability drop away. They drop away because, with just one case, there can be no assumption from the outset that, if the inquiry were to be repeated by different people at a different time, similar findings would result.

> The notions of *reliability* and *validity* have been imported from particular kinds of research. Their meaning in the case study is far less clear.

Now, I should make it clear that this is my personal position and, while it is shared by many others (such as Smith and Deemer, 2000) it is by no means shared by all (Silverman, 2010). A common approach is to hold on to the notion of reliability as a criterion for the assessment of all research, even research that could never achieve (and would never want to achieve) findings that are consistent from one time to another or one researcher to another.

Validity is similar to reliability when it comes to making judgements about its value in case study research. Everything that I have said about reliability applies also to validity. In many kinds of research – in those, for example, where probability samples are used – validity is about the extent to which a piece of research is finding out what the researcher intends it to find out. (It's not quite as simple as this, and I tease apart some of the ways in which the word validity is used in *How to Do Your*

Research Project.) In the kind of research we are looking at here, however, where there is no probability sample and we may have no idea at all about what we expect to find out from the research, the idea of validity is less meaningful.

This is generally recognised in discussion about the quality of some kinds of interpretative research, but, despite the concerns about the limited appropriateness of validity, it is still felt by some people to be terribly important. There is almost a cult of what Schwandt (1996) calls 'criteriology' – in other words, an obsession with finding criteria. A treatise on methodology is felt to be naked without a discussion of validity and criteria that can then be ticked off as having been (or not having been) achieved. Validity is thus wrenched out of its home in normative research with its samples, variables and statistics and bent and twisted into something quite different for the purposes of interpretative research. The result is that we end up bashing our square peg, validity, into the round hole of case study research.

For example, Whittemore et al. (2001), after having reviewed a range of authors who have written about validity in interpretative research, emerge with a panoply of criteria for assessing it. These include plausibility, relevance, credibility, comprehensiveness, significance, confirmability, positionality, canons of evidence, generalisability, fittingness and auditability.

Now, I know that people read books like this one having got to the relevant section via the index and do not contextualise what they have found. So, if this is you and you are tempted to copy these words down (plausibility, relevance and so on) and offer them in your methodology chapters as criteria for validity in case study research, let me repeat that I do *not* agree with them. Validity is about that which makes the research valid. It is not about plausibility, credibility and all the others.

Looking at the criteria with which Whittemore et al. emerge from their review, I could say that some of the most fascinating and ground-breaking pieces of research would have failed all of the tests of validity above. Let's look at one – Einstein's work leading up to his theory of relativity. Would it have met many of the criteria collated by Whittemore et al.? No. Let's look at some of those criteria.

With the criteria for validity outlined in Table 4.1, an iconic piece of inquiry, key to the development of late twentieth-century science, fails on nearly all counts. We have to be wary of assessing work on the basis of these crude, post hoc constructions. They are the tools of an audit society, not of good research.

I have deliberately chosen Einstein's ground-breaking work in the natural sciences, because it is a clear case of highly significant work – done, interestingly, via 'thought experiments' and case studies rather than the conventional experimentation of natural science – that conforms to none of the maxims of methodological correctness. I could have turned in the other direction and chosen work that *does* conform to the criteria of Whittemore et al., but which was ... well, worthless. I could quote work such as that of the educational psychologist Cyril Burt, who has been shown to have fabricated his results (Hearnshaw, 1979: 245–7), but which, at the time of publication, seemed to conform to all of the conventional measures of validity.

Table 4.1 Did Einstein's work have validity? Or ten ways of *not* assessing validity

Criterion	✓ or ×	Has the criterion been met?
Plausibility	×	No. It was highly implausible (which was why no one else had thought of it)
Credibility	×	No. It was entirely unbelievable that time slowed down as you moved faster. In fact, it was incredible
Relevance	×	No. What possible use could it have had at the time? In fact, applications were not realised until decades later
Comprehensiveness	×	How could it be comprehensive? It applied to one thing: space-time. Why should it, or any piece of research, in the natural or social sciences be comprehensive?
Significance	×	Only a few far-sighted souls could have seen its significance at the time
Confirmability	×/✓	Much of Einstein's work was done through 'thought experiments'. His general conclusions could only be confirmed in a piecemeal way
Canons of evidence	×	I'm not sure what 'canons of evidence' are. Einstein's breakthrough came from *thinking* about things – not from evidence per se. The latter is as dead as a doornail without intelligent thought
Generalisability	✓	If correct (which it was), Einstein's findings were generalisable
Fittingness	?	What is 'fittingness'? Why should it be relevant to validity?
Auditability	×	There was no possibility of 'auditing' mass–energy equivalence at the time this breakthrough was made

In fact, Burt's work amply meets the expectations of *plausibility* and *credibility* that appear in the list from Whittemore et al. It is plausibility and credibility (the first two criteria in Table 4.1) that are usually to the fore when validity is discussed in the social sciences in the context of interpretative work. For me, however, these raise particular problems as indices of any kind of validity, whether we are thinking in a technical or even an everyday sense of the word.

Plausibility (in fact, surely much the same as credibility) seems to me a strange way to assess validity. It is placing responsibility in the hearts and minds of the scholarly community (you and me) to make that assessment of plausibility, but our views of what is plausible will depend on the worldviews that have shaped our own thinking. Our thoughts and ideas are slaves to what we already know and believe (well, mine are anyway). The case of Burt is especially instructive because it is clear that he lied and fabricated evidence to match with ideas about the heritability of intelligence, which he 'knew' to be true. Here is the important point: his conclusions were ultimately embraced *because* they were plausible. That is why they were accepted.

Researchers' audiences (you and me again) – as judges of plausibility – cannot be insulated from the prevailing academic, cultural and scientific orthodoxies in making their judgements. I wonder what is supposed to inoculate us against employing, in any assessment we make of plausibility, the very prejudices and expectations that give shape to plausibility. It was this plausibility that made Burt's views acceptable to his intellectual peers. Plausibility was the culprit, not the knight in shining armour.

That was a long way of saying that I don't think you need to spend a great deal of time worrying about validity and reliability in case study research as a form of inquiry. This is partly also because the case study is not one single kind of research, for it encompasses component methods. In certain of those component methods you will certainly want to ensure that you pay attention to reliability and validity, but remember that there is always a choice involved. You have to look at the constituent bits of your case study and ask yourself whether or not reliability and validity, in fact, are appropriate issues. Overall, though, the case study, as a study of one thing, is not the kind of inquiry in which considerations about validity and reliability should be to the fore since it is the singleness of the subject and the singleness – the peculiarity, even – of the interpretation and analysis of the evidence that is significant.

Triangulation

The term *triangulation* is used in a metaphorical way in the social sciences, based on its original use in geometry and surveying. Triangles don't actually need to be involved, nor do things need to be done in threes. What the term means here is that viewing from several points is better than viewing from one. Given the critical awareness that should be the hallmark of good social science researchers, another viewpoint or another analytical method may make us decide to reject initial explanations.

Of course, this should be what 'case studiers' are all about, looking in from different angles and vantage points. I mentioned at the beginning of the book Foucault's 'polyhedron of intelligibility'. By this, Foucault meant that we can only really understand something – it only becomes intelligible – by looking at it from different directions and using different methods. So, Foucault went one or perhaps several steps further than calling for triangulation. We could (if we wanted to invent yet another awful jargon word for the social sciences) say that he was calling for 'polyhedronation'. It is this that is the starting point for the case inquirer – think small but drill deep, using different methods and drilling from different directions. So, you may use observation in one part of the study, interviews in another, a frequency count in another, perhaps even a small experiment in another. This collation of methods provides the triangulation. I discuss triangulation further in *How to Do Your Research Project* (Thomas, 2013).

Positionality

Oftentimes in case study you will be immersed in the subject and the situation of your research. You become an active, not passive, agent in acquiring knowledge of the processes, histories, events, language and biographies of the research context. You yourself will take a central role in interpretation. In doing this, it is important to recognise that you have an undeniable *position*, and this position affects the nature of the observations and the interpretations you make.

Recognition of this involves an inversion of some of the shibboleths of traditional methodology, such as the supposed imperative to 'objectivity'. There is no attempt to be 'objective' when working interpretatively, but rather an acceptance of the importance of researchers themselves – their likes and dislikes, their backgrounds and their pastimes, their vested interests and expectations – in making interpretations. It is subjectivity, in other words, rather than objectivity, that comes to the fore. Because of the importance of the nature of the relation between the researcher and research participants, the researcher's biography – including class, gender, ethnicity, ideas and commitments – needs to be made explicit.

In presenting an interpretative case study you should accept your subjectivity and not be ashamed or afraid of it. Given that it is central, your case study should be written up in a way that makes clear your understanding of the underpinning principles that guide the conduct of this kind of research. An interpretative case study will therefore be reported in an entirely different way from an experimental study. You should begin – right at the beginning, in the introduction – with a full discussion of positionality: of *yourself*, why you are interested in this topic, what your personal circumstances are, and so on. You will always write in the first person, saying, for example, 'I believe that ...' rather than 'The researcher believes that ...'. This may seem obvious, but it is a common mistake for students conducting interpretative research – research that demands that they put themselves at the centre of the analysis – to report their work as if they have just conducted an experiment and to omit any information about themselves. If you do this kind of research, readers need to know who you are and where you stand, metaphorically as well as literally.

Generalisation

The case study has often been taken to be deficient in the generalisation department, as I discussed in Chapter 1. But its 'poor relation' status exists, I think, only because it is *conspicuously* deficient in its potential for generalisation. Its weaknesses in terms of generalisation, in other words, are not disguised. Other design frames in social science seek ways to calibrate and enable generalisation, but these attempts rest on something of a sleight of hand in the presentation of what generalisation can be.

If, as many have argued (and I shall rehearse the classic case in a moment), little significant generalisation *at all* is possible in the human sciences, arguments about the case study's deficiencies in this department lose force. My point is that, when thinking about inference, generalisation in social inquiry is constrained to remain at the level of what Peirce (Houser et al., 1992) calls 'abduction' rather than induction. I shall explain what abduction is in a moment.

If my argument has validity, then there are forms of interpretation that can come from case studies which owe their legitimacy and power to the exemplary knowledge of these studies rather than to their generalisability. For me, seeking generalisability – seeing generalisation as the first and most important aim of social science – can inhibit or even extinguish the curiosity and interpretation that should be at the heart of inquiry.

Generalisation, induction and abduction

Generalisation is at the core of the natural scientific method. From generalisation comes induction – that is, X happens regularly in certain conditions, so we can infer that X will happen again in those conditions. The process is attempted across the social sciences and is seen across the methodological spectrum.

There are differences between the natural and social sciences, though, that are easily elided when one is thinking about the value of generalisation. The establishment of regularities, generalisations, laws, universals and theory in the induction of natural science is governed by exacting expectations and procedures that enable investigators to deal with exceptions, anomalies and idiosyncrasies and establish their credentials and significance as limiters to the power of the generalisation.

The problem is that, outside natural science, such expectations are unrealisable. Alasdair MacIntyre's (1985) argument here is the classic one – comparing generalisations in the social sciences with those in the natural sciences and noting the role that counter-examples to the development of law play in each. The attitude in the social sciences, MacIntyre (1985: 89) says, is 'tolerant' of counter-examples. Social science's generalisations – all of them, not just those in case studies – are pretty useless, for, 'we cannot say of them in any precise way under what conditions they hold' (MacIntyre, 1985: 91).

He proceeds to argue that social scientists have insisted that what is offered in social science is *probabilistic* generalisation. Nor is this any good, says MacIntyre (1985: 91), for 'if the type of generalisation which I have cited is to be a generalisation at all, it must be something more than a mere list of instances'. According to MacIntyre, then, generalisation is possible in the natural sciences, but its status in the social sciences can never be any better than that of the generalisation of a layperson. Its value will always be limited by the sheer variability of social life and human agency in all of its unpredictability.

The problem here is with expectations of watertight (or almost watertight) induction following generalisation. Perhaps, though, following Peirce (Houser et al., 1992), our expectations should be moderated concerning the generalisations that can emerge from social studies. A number of commentators have queried the reliance on a naïve model of scientific induction (for example, Haig, 1995) and others, such as Miller and Fredericks (1999), point to the lack of 'specialness' of inductive reasoning. The thrust of their argument is that common, everyday induction is better described as 'inference to the best explanation', or Peirce's 'abduction'. *Abduction* is making a judgement concerning the best explanation for the facts you are collecting. It is what we do in case studies.

Hammersley (2005: 5) suggests that 'what is good evidence for abduction is different from what is good evidence for induction', proceeding to describe abduction as 'the development of an explanatory or theoretical idea, this often resulting from close examination of particular cases' (see also Hammersley, 2007). It could, perhaps simplistically, be thought of as 'conclusions drawn from everyday generalisation', whereas induction concerns conclusions drawn from a special kind of generalisation – a kind, if MacIntyre is right, that is impossible in the social sciences.

Thinking about all of this, it seems to me that any argument about the weakness of the case study resting on its lack of generalisability fails to recognise the limits of induction in the social sciences generally. It also fails, simultaneously, to acknowledge the significance of abduction. It fails, in other words, to recognise the offer that can be made in local circumstances by particular kinds of looser generalisation, whatever one calls these. I have chosen to use Peirce's term 'abduction' for these to foreground the distinctions to be made with *induction* in discussing the supposed weaknesses of the case study, but they have been framed in many other ways – from the 'common interpretive act' (Schatzman, 1991), to 'bounded rationality' (Simon, 1983), Bourdieu's 'thinking tool' (in Wacquant, 1989: 50) or Althusser's Generalities II (Althusser, 1979: 183–90) – all of which describe much the same kind of process. That process is a fluid understanding explicitly or tacitly recognising the complexity and frailty of the generalisations we can make about human interrelationships.

They describe our processes of garnering and organising information to analyse and deal with our social worlds. Abduction connects all of these, providing heuristics – that is, ways to analyse complexity that may not provide watertight guarantees of success in providing for explanation or predication, but are unpretentious in their assumptions of fallibility and provisionality.

All of these forms of generalising to regularity – these kinds of abduction – seem to be the appropriate 'inference form' for the case study.

Theory

Developing or testing theory can be thought of as being at the centre of case study, and I examine how you can develop theory in Chapter 11. Here, though (and in the context of rigour and quality), I want to take a sideways, critical look at theory and what it is.

In the traditional account of the process of science, the end point of the inductive process results in theory. Seen in the way that Peirce presents it above, abduction generates ideas, tentative 'theories', which serve as hypothetical explanatory concepts. This abduction is then followed by deduction (the connecting of ideas), which is followed in turn by systematic data collection in pursuit of verification of the initial explanatory concepts. This last is induction, via which the speculative theory is or is not verified.

The assumption that this is the course things invariably take seems to me to lead always to the dead-end identified by MacIntyre. In other words, the assumption of theoretical validation from inductive inference necessarily implies a firmness to the structure and reliability of theory that is unachievable in the inquiries of social science. Because of both the contingency of social life and the necessary limitations on the kind and quantity of confirmatory evidence that can be disclosed, theory, in any kind of technical sense, is surely unattainable.

There is an elision of expectations here in the discussion of theory. As I have noted elsewhere (Thomas and James, 2006; Thomas, 2007), a reading of interpretative inquiry scholarship from Glaser and Strauss (1967: 1) onwards (Mouzelis, 1995) reveals an insistent theme in the expectations of theoretical explanations and predictions from induction.

Of course, something is attainable, but the question is, 'Is it really theory?' It can be theory only in the sense that *everything* is theory. Fish (1989: 14–15) suggests that much discourse about theory in the academy generally is not really about theory at all, but, rather, 'theory-talk' – that is, 'any form of talk that has acquired cachet and prestige'. He also notes (1989: 327):

> Am I following or enacting a theory when I stop for a red light, or use my American Express card, or rise to speak at a conference? Are you now furiously theorizing as you sit reading what I have to say? And if you are persuaded by me to alter your understanding of what is and is not a theory, is your new definition of theory a new theory of theory? Clearly it is possible to answer yes to all these questions, but just as clearly that answer will render the notion 'theory' and the issue of its consequences trivial.

In other words, 'theory' has come to mean almost anything – *any* generalisation, *any* thought, *any* structured reflection (or, indeed, *un*structured reflection) may be called a theory. It is unhelpful in our deliberations on inquiry, however, for looseness to exist about the terms we use – in this case, 'theory' – particularly when separating abduction from induction and looking to the end point of induction.

The process of induction is supposed to lead us to a theory of a particular character – a theory that summarises and generalises in such a way that we can use it to explain and predict. It confuses our deliberations on inquiry to call *any* kind of summative or generalising process 'theory'. When a theory has been used as part of the reasoning to validate a case study (Eisenhart, 2009; Vaughan, 1992; Walton, 1992), it has indeed been as part of this summative, inductive, or quasi-inductive, process.

It is worth returning to MacIntyre's analysis here, since it speaks to the central problem with generalisation and theory in the social sciences. He notes that there are a number of reasons for the failure of theory (that is to say, theory as part of a quasi-inductive process), all resting on the 'systematic unpredictability' of the social world. Because of these, he suggests, unpredictability will always win over predictability as far as the matters of social science are concerned. It is only the trivial things that are predictable, and we don't need any kind of sophisticated methodology to tell us about these.

Theory and phronesis

If this critique has any legitimacy, and it surely does, we have to make a distinction, in response, between *theory* and *phronesis*.

Aristotle's notion of phronesis is about practical knowledge, craft knowledge, with a twist of judgement squeezed into the mix. As it has been used more recently – particularly in the discussion of the applied social sciences (for example, Back, 2002) – it has come to have more of a sense of 'tacit knowledge' (Polanyi, 1958) about it.

Phronesis is practical knowledge. It is a model based on personal experience. It is personal, and it helps us to make sense of particular situations. Sometimes, confusingly, it is called 'practical theory'. It is judgement made on the basis of experience and has no pretensions to lead us to the kind of external guide that theory is supposed to provide. It is in practice that phronesis is developed and in practice that it comes into play.

Back goes on to provide a contrast between phronesis and theory, explaining that, in Aristotelian terms, 'theory' exists as a way of establishing absolute laws that can be laid out in an organised framework which can explain. It must be able to withstand tests as to its validity and it needs to be consistent. By contrast, in the practical (or tacit) knowledge of phronesis, there are none of these expectations as to consistency – phronesis is about understanding and behaviour in particular situations.

Fish's (1989: 317) explication of practical learning analyses the contrast well, for he explains how practical learning varies with the *context* of a practice – that is, as circumstances change, so 'the very meaning of the rule (the instructions it is understood to give) changes too'. The phronesis that we acquire and accumulate is always malleable and corrigible. So there is, in talking about phronesis, a recognition of the provisional, the tentative in interpretation and analysis.

There is, in other words, a need to move away from the expectations of *generalisable* knowledge that go alongside the inductive process. Correspondingly, there is a need a move towards the '*exemplary* knowledge' of abduction and phronesis. With the discussion of 'exemplary knowledge', I am talking about an example viewed and heard in the context of another's experience, but *used* in the context of one's own. The example is taken to be neither representative nor typical, nor is it exemplary in the sense of being a model to follow. Rather, it is taken to be a particular representation given in context and understood in that context. It is interpretable, however, only in the context of one's own experience – in the context, in other words, of one's phronesis, rather than theory.

If the case study is concerned with phronesis rather than theory – if it is decoupled from the inductive frame of theoretical analysis – what are the consequences?

We are left with a view of a case study's validation coming no longer from reference to a body of theory or generalised knowledge. Rather, its validation comes from the connections and insights it offers between another's experience and your own. The essence comes in understandability emerging from phronesis – in other words, from the connection to your own situation.

This is based in what Abbott (1992) calls colligations of occurrences, involving the making of narrative – the development of stories with which one can connect. This is a characteristic, he notes, of all social science, intelligently done.

Finding or regularising

Having had this discussion about induction versus abduction and theory versus phronesis, I think it's worth noting again that this discussion is not new. I outlined in Chapter 3 the difference between Plato and Aristotle on the desire (or not) to establish laws. That debate influences even now our attitude to the ways in which inquiries should be conducted. You could say that the contrast is between those who could be called the *finders* and those who could be called the *regularisers*.

Another way of putting it would be that it is an intellectual battle between the *narrators* and the *theorists*, and it exists not just in the social sciences. The great historian R.G. Collingwood (1946/1994: 30), in *The Idea of History*, compared the approaches to history of Herodotus and Thucydides and concluded that Herodotus contributed so much more, because 'what chiefly interests Herodotus is the events themselves; what chiefly interests Thucydides is the laws according to which they happen'. Thucydides' problem, Collingwood (1946/1994: 31) suggests, is that he 'is constantly being drawn away from the events to some lesson that lurks behind them'. Collingwood favours Herodotus' critical questioning of narrative as a way of doing history. He notes (1946/1994: 29), 'In reading Thucydides I ask myself, What is the matter with the man, that he writes like that?' He answers (1946/1994: 29) that

Thucydides abandoned history for a kind of pseudo-psychology: 'It is not history at all, but natural science of a special kind. It does not narrate facts for the sake of narrating facts. Its chief purpose is to affirm laws.'

Collingwood seems to be speaking straight to those undertaking case studies here since he seems to be saying 'be more like Herodotus'. Herodotus asks us to look with him at the facts. He may tell us what *he* believes, but he also invites readers to make their own judgements. The lawyer Thomas Geoghegan (2007) puts it this way: 'we should also spend more funds to get our young people out of the library where they're reading Thucydides and get them to start living like Herodotus – going out and seeing the world'. Again, a motto for the case inquirer.

Quality

I have used the term 'structural characteristics of research' for many of the concepts I have discussed in this chapter, and, as I hope I have indicated, these concepts (reliability, validity, generalisation and so on) take on different meanings in case study from those they might assume in other kinds of research. It's difficult, in other words, to judge the quality of a case study via the criteria that are often used in judging other kinds of research.

There are characteristics of research, though – very general ones – by which we can unequivocally judge quality. Assuming for a moment that we are concerned principally with the interpretative aspects of a case study, Hammersley (2005: 3–4) has offered some useful indicators as to this quality, which I have adapted as follows.

- The clarity of the writing
  - Is there consistency in use of terms?
  - Are definitions provided where necessary?
  - Are sentences well constructed?
- The problem or question being addressed
  - Is this clearly outlined?
  - Is sufficient rationale provided for its significance?
- The methods used
  - To what degree, and in what respects, was each of the methods chosen (as regards selection of cases for study, data collection and data analysis) likely to be an effective one?

- The account of the research process and the researcher
  - Is there sufficient, and not too much, information about the research process?
  - Is there sufficient, and not too much, information about the researcher?
- The formulation of the main claims
  - Are the main claims made clear?
  - Are the relations between claims and evidence made clear?
  - Is the nature of each claim (as description, explanation, theory or evaluation) indicated?

Hammersley (2005: 6), however, proceeds to give a health warning about the criteria he has offered, and this chimes with the 'criteriology' warning that Schwandt (1996) issued. Hammersley says of the points that he makes about quality:

> these are lists of what we might call issues for threshold judgment: they remind the reader what to take account of, what they need to make a judgment about. However, they are not operationalised in such a way that anyone who did not already know how to make the judgments concerned would be able to apply them, nor do they tell the reader what would be sufficient in each case. And they do not tell us whether all of the thresholds have to be met for a positive conclusion to be reached, whether high scoring on one can counterbalance a lower 'score' on another, and so on. Moreover, I do not believe that they *can* be operationalised in this way, or that attempting to do this would be desirable.

Put differently, how could you know that you have met these criteria? How could readers apply such criteria if they weren't aware of them implicitly in the first place? Further, it would be impossible for researchers or readers to weigh up the importance of one criterion versus another if they weren't already steeped in the discourse of the field of study.

For me, the issues boil down to the choice of your case, the choices made concerning analysis and the robustness of your argument. In other words, your answers to the following questions:

1 How well has the case been chosen? Decisions should have been made appropriately about the approach and the processes to be adopted in data collection and analysis.

2 How well has the context for the study been explained and justified? Including justification for decisions about how analysis has been undertaken.

3 How well have arguments been made? Have rival explanations for the same kind
   of observation been explored? This is where the storyboards that I have drawn
   for some of the examples in this book can help – providing space to think about
   alternative storylines for the same plot. Is it justifiable that, on this evidence and
   with this reasoning, these conclusions have been drawn?

If you take only one thing from this chapter, take this …

The quality of a case study depends less on ideas of sample, validity and reliability
and more on the conception, construction and conduct of the study. It depends on

- your initial idea
- the ways that you choose your case
- the thoroughness with which you describe its context
- the care you devote to selecting appropriate methods of analysis
- the nature of the arguments you deploy in drawing your conclusions.

The case study offers the opportunity to bring evidence together from many and
varied sources to support arguments in ways that would not be possible using other
forms of inquiry that are fenced in by different considerations. Concerns about
how far we can generalise from a case study are neutralised when we realise how
tentative *any* generalisation might be in social research. Conclusions drawn from
case study research become less pronounced when we realise that, to a greater or
lesser extent, all forms of inquiry, especially social inquiry, produce knowledge that
is *provisional* – in other words, good only until we find out something else which
explains things better.

FURTHER READING 📖

ESRC/TLRP Seminar Series: Quality in Educational Research, available at: www.education.
    bham.ac.uk/research/seminars1/esrc_4/index.shtml
This is a series of seminar inputs on quality in educational research, giving transcripts
and articles from the series. The seminars cover issues to do with quality of evidence
and how quality differs in quantitative and qualitative research.

Schwandt, T.A. (1996) 'Farewell to criteriology', *Qualitative Inquiry*, 2: 58–72.
Critiques the idea that quality can be assessed by reference to a series of criteria.

Thomas, G. (2010) 'Doing case study: abduction not induction; phronesis not theory', *Qualitative Inquiry*, 16 (7): 575–82.
Thomas, G. (2011) 'The case: generalisation, theory and phronesis in case study', *Oxford Review of Education*, 37 (1): 21–35.
Thomas, G. (2013) *How to Do Your Research Project* (2nd edn). London: Sage.
In Chapter 6, I go into more detail about issues such as reliability, validity and samples.

Thomas, G. and Myers, K. (2015) *The Anatomy of the Case Study*. London: Sage.
Tobin, J. (2007) 'An anthropologist's reflections on defining quality in education research', *International Journal of Research and Method in Education*, 30 (3): 325–38.
Good on the problems of defining quality in social research.

5

ETHICS

Ethics are principles of conduct about what is right and wrong. But deciding on what is right or wrong can be a complex business in social research. What is right for me may not be right for you, and what is right for the researcher may not be right for the participant. The consideration of ethics may encourage us to look at the nature of what we are doing in the name of furthering knowledge.

> It's especially important to consider ethics in case study research since you may be very closely involved with the research participants.

Obviously, we all want to do what is right and avoid what is wrong. Although the matter seems simple, there are many examples in social research where a questionable action may have been taken in the name of doing right. Researchers have had as their purpose the idea that they are pushing back the barriers of knowledge or helping humankind in some other way and have used this as a reason for employing intrusive or distressing procedures in their research. Several high-profile examples, such as the 'Milgram experiments', where volunteers were instructed to give stooges what they were told were life-threatening electric shocks, have caused decades of debate about the rights and the wrongs of such studies (Milgram, 1963, 1981).

You are most unlikely to be contemplating anything as dramatic as the Milgram experiments. However, there may be ethical issues of which you were not aware or which you had not considered. Many of these will present questions of the kind that confront us now looking back at Milgram, albeit on a smaller scale. Who is the research benefiting? Do you have the right to take up people's time and energy? Is there any possible discomfort that participants will have to experience? Are you invading their privacy?

Your participants

Your case study may not involve you dealing with people. It may be a paper-based study, looking at one historical case. However, in most of the studies in which we become involved we will be working with people. In the bad old days, when social scientists did research with people, they called those people 'subjects'. Now, especially in applied social science, we think of the people with whom we research more as 'participants' or even 'partners', rather than 'subjects'. Thinking with ethics to the fore, we have to see the people with whom we are involved as participants in our research and part of it, rather than simply objects from whom data can be extracted.

In working with our research participants, we have to recognise that these participants have rights and they should have a stake in the process of research: it shouldn't be a question of simply 'using' people and then walking away. To be genuine participants they have to be involved to some extent in the planning, execution and write-up of your work. You will need to think about their particular kinds of contribution and their particular needs. Especially, you will need to think about the needs of people who are vulnerable for any reason.

Vulnerable groups

For those who may not understand the ins and outs of consent or who may be susceptible to pressure to cooperate because of their social or economic position there will need to be special considerations. These will include:

- children/legal minors (anyone under 16)

- people from non-English-speaking backgrounds

- anyone with a physical disability

- anyone with learning difficulties

- patients, or clients of professionals

- anyone in custody, or for whom a court has responsibility.

Some people are especially prone to become drawn into research projects because of their 'ready availability in settings where research is conducted', as the US government's Belmont Report (1979) put it. Careful thought should be given to questions about why and how they are being involved, and they should be protected against involvement solely for the sake of convenience, or because they may be easy to persuade or even manipulate.

Lewis and Porter (2004) urge that the following questions should always be asked

> Children, patients, employees and people with special needs are all vulnerable and you will need to consider carefully the ethics of working with them.

with any kind of vulnerable group, including children and those with learning difficulties:

- Has the participant's ability to give fully informed consent been assessed and discussed with others such as parents, caregivers or teachers?

- Have ways of checking for understanding of confidentiality/research purposes been explored?

- Will participants, at appropriate intervals, be reminded of their right to withdraw?

- Have all possible steps been taken to ensure anonymity, given that this may be particularly difficult to achieve with minority populations?

- In giving feedback, have steps been taken to ensure the intelligibility of the information? This can be done through, for example, asking a person who is well known to the individual to talk with them, or offering pictures with simplified text or case study material.

- How is the end of the research relationship with participants to be managed? It is easy for close relationships to be forged during research, and these should not be terminated abruptly.

Participants' activity

When relating with your participants – and we are now thinking about all participants, rather than specifically those who may be vulnerable in some way – you should think about issues such as:

- Administration of any questions or procedures which may cause mental or physical discomfort during or after the research – these may include questions which appear at first sight to be quite straightforward. Always think about the effect that questions may have on your participants.

- Performance of any acts (such as role-play) which might diminish self-esteem or cause embarrassment. The more extravert among us sometimes, I think, fail to appreciate how mortifying and disabling procedures such as role-play can be to those of us who are more introverted. Not only are such procedures questionable on ethical grounds, they also may give misleading findings.

- Involvement of participants in any illegal activity. Definitely a no-no.

- Whether the participants will be in receipt of any substance or agent – this is likely only in health-related research and there will be very strict professional codes of conduct on issues such as this.

Deception or concealment

The default position on doing research is that you should be honest and open in all your dealings with research participants. Sometimes, though, as in the Milgram experiment I mentioned earlier, you will need to be less than 100 per cent open because you may be researching something where the participants' knowledge of your aims would invalidate any findings that you may make. If this is the case, you must be prepared to argue convincingly for the need for concealment, and you must build into your plans a debriefing session with your participants after the research has finished wherein you explain what you were doing in your study and why you could not be fully open at the outset.

The codes of conduct from professional associations usually recognise that an element of concealment or even deception may sometimes be necessary. Indeed, the US government's landmark Belmont Report (1979) recognises it, but says that:

> Always put respect for your participants centre-stage. As far as possible be open about your aims, and avoid subjecting people to any kind of discomfort.

> In all cases of research involving incomplete disclosure, such research is justified only if it is clear that (1) incomplete disclosure is truly necessary to accomplish the goals of the research, (2) there are no undisclosed risks to subjects that are more than minimal, and (3) there is an adequate plan for debriefing subjects.

So, if any degree of withholding or misrepresentation is involved, it will be important for you in gaining ethical clearance to:

- explicitly acknowledge what is being done
- justify fully the reasons why it is being done
- note that you will be explaining to participants following the research the purpose of the research and why it was necessary to withhold information from them.

Confidentiality and anonymity

You should always treat any information provided to you as confidential, taking care at all times not to breach or compromise that confidentiality. Maintaining the anonymity of your participants is a key part of this, in your everyday dealings and conversations with others, in your storage of data and your reporting. Anonymity can be ensured by changing participants' names as well as the name of any institutions (such as schools) to which they are affiliated and the regions in which they are situated. You can either give pseudonyms or code numbers to achieve this. You'll need to be especially careful in working with participants whose identity may be hard to disguise, for example those in minority groups. Where appropriate, you should make it clear to participants that your commitment to confidentiality as a researcher may be overridden given your legal or moral duty to report incidents of harm. Circumstances such as these will be most unusual, but if you do come across them you should discuss them with your supervisor and/or the appropriate services (such as child protection services) immediately.

Confidentiality is not secured simply by paying attention to anonymisation, important though the latter is. More broadly, it is about a commitment to respecting the wishes of informants, who may not want the information which they have given you to become public. While engagement in research should involve, of course, an understanding that findings will be published, your informants may expect that you will disguise or hide information which they take to be confidential – perhaps using it in drawing your conclusions, but keeping the details off the record.

You should always be sensitive to this possibility and even proactive in asking about it, moving on to negotiate with your research participants how much – and how – you intend to use, analyse and disclose your findings. They may ultimately decide that they do not wish you to publish certain facts or opinions, and this is a wish you must respect. In cases where it is unclear whether you have secreted or masked data to the satisfaction of your informants you will need to give them the chance to read through your final report to allow them to make suggestions about how to edit it. You can find an excellent discussion of all these issues in Wiles et al. (2008).

> As a default position, all data should be treated as confidential and names coded or otherwise anonymised. Data should be kept secure and deleted after analysis.

Occasionally, research participants may ask to be identified and not anonymised in research outputs (see Grinyer, 2002). You should respect any such requests while ensuring that you discuss fully with all those involved, including caregivers, the potential consequences of disclosure. And remember that if one person's name is revealed, this increases the risk of a breach of confidentiality for other participants who wish to remain anonymous. Having carefully weighed up all the pros and cons, you should, if you decide to agree to any request to disclosure, obtain written consent that an individual wishes to waive the right to confidentiality.

Data security and stewardship

You have a responsibility to keep the data you collect about people or institutions secure, even though you will have taken every effort to anonymise that data. Various exemptions exist in the UK Data Protection Act to allow research-ers to collect data without the need to inform the Data Commissioner, but this does not mean that you can ignore principles of good stewardship of data. You should:

- Only use data for the purposes for which it was collected – not for other purposes.

- Keep data for an appropriate length of time. What counts as 'appropriate' varies according to the circumstances: for most undergraduate research it will be appro-priate to destroy raw data immediately your project is completed and marked; however, for some research (for example, that which is part of a clinical programme, which a postgraduate project may be part of), professional codes of conduct specify that data must be kept for several years following the close of a programme.

- Keep data secure. You should use passwords on any files that contain pre-anonymised names. For Microsoft Office documents, this means clicking on the Office button (top left of the screen), clicking on **Prepare**, then clicking on **Encrypt document**. (If this doesn't work, click the F1 button for help, and enter "password".) You'll be asked for a password, which you must remember. If you don't remember it, there is no way to get back your data.

- Don't pass the data on to anyone else – obviously, since it wouldn't then be secure.

- Keep the data anonymous (see previous section).

Consent

Because of the harm that might be caused during research involving people, an important issue to think about when considering the ethics of research is that of *consent*. Consent is about the agreement of people to take part in the study. More than simple agreement, however, is needed, given the issues I have already considered. *Informed* consent is needed. In other words, potential par-ticipants should understand what they are agreeing to. Informed consent is centred around the following points:

(a) The information participants need to know; this will include:

- the nature and purpose of the study, including its methods

- expected benefits of the study

- possible harm that may come from the study

- information about confidentiality, anonymity, how data will be kept and for how long, with details of when data will be destroyed

- ethics procedures being followed and appeals

- your full name and full contact details

(b) The presentation of (a) in a meaningful and understandable way, explaining any unusual terms simply, in non-technical language

(c) The option for a potential participant to choose to take part or not

Opt-in versus implied consent

An important distinction exists between *opt-in* consent and *implied* consent:

- With opt-in consent, participants have to make an active choice about becoming involved and signal their willingness to take part in the research. You would have to offer an invitation to participants to become involved, preferably in writing, requesting that they return a form indicating willingness to participate. This could be done directly and orally if written communication is not possible. Alternatively, some other active choice of the participant would have to be involved, as would be the case in returning a questionnaire. It must be made clear that the participant's consent may be withdrawn at any time and that if the participant chooses to do this there will be no further collection of additional data, no further analysis of data initially collected and removal of existing data from your records.

- With implied (or opt-out) consent, you tell participants about the research and assume that they give their consent unless they tell you otherwise. Information about the research can be distributed by a range of means, for example by a letter from a school to all children who would be personally involved. The letter would include the information you would give as for opt-in consent, but would be accompanied by a phrase such as 'I am assuming that unless I hear from you, you have no objections to Ellie's participation'. Depending on the degree of risk assumed to be involved, information might also be communicated by announcements or leaflets, as long as it can reasonably be assumed that the intended recipients will receive the information. There should, of course, in every case be a clear explanation of the provisions for opting out and people should be given the easiest possible way of doing so – by text, letter, telephone, social media or email, or face-to-face with you.

> Always seek the consent of participants, through either asking them actively to opt in to the research, or, if there is less risk, giving them the option to opt out – in other words, you assume acceptance of participation unless the participant actively contacts you to indicate otherwise.

There are pros and cons to opt-in versus implied consent. If there is any degree of significant risk, then opt-in procedures are clearly to be preferred. Opt-in consent involves more work for the researcher than does opt-out or implied consent. However, there is some evidence also that samples may be skewed by the use of opt-in procedures (because only really willing people opt in, and this may exclude important subsections of the population). Junghans et al. (2005), working in a medical context, therefore suggest that 'the opt-out approach should be the default recruitment strategy for studies that pose a low risk to patients'.

Low risk or high risk

The key phrase in the previous paragraph is 'low risk', and what constitutes low risk is a matter of judgement. If you are unsure about this you can discuss it with your supervisor or your local ethics representative.

Potential risks include:

- the possibility of causing psychological or physical harm to participants or others
- concealing information about the project from participants, or deceiving them about its objectives
- the possibility of damaging the standing or reputation of participants or others who may become involved, peripherally
- impinging on the privacy of participants or others
- the possibility of breaking the law
- the possibility of harming a community in some way (for example, by drawing attention to differences within it).

If there is judged to be any significant risk concerning any of these matters, you should consider its extent and duration. You may need to consider also the extent to which any risk can be 'undone', either naturally or through steps taken by you. You will also need to weigh any risks against benefits or scholarly merit, which may include particular advantages to participants or others or any potential advance in knowledge. You should be prepared to expand on all of these and make a good case for your research when you seek ethics clearance.

As a guide, Table 5.1 offers a selection of different kinds of study so that you can get an idea of the dimensions on which ethics judgements may be assessed and the conclusions that could be drawn about whether these are high risk or low risk.

Table 5.1 reveals, I hope, that judgements about risk are difficult to make and that the conclusions are never definitive. For example, while I have suggested that unintrusive observation in a teacher's own class may be low risk, others may disagree, based on the potential obtrusiveness of observation and the dangers of class students realising what the teacher is doing. However one chooses to categorise it,

Table 5.1 Ethics: low risk or high risk?

Risk level	Case study: subject and object	Methods used	Why this risk level?
No risk	Subject: The Cuba missile crisis Object: Understanding the role of militarism in American foreign policy, 1960–70	Documentary analysis of contemporary media commentary, government records and interviews with key individuals.	There is no direct involvement with people (that is to say, research participants) in the data collection.
Low risk	Subject: A child who 'freezes' when asked to take a test in class. Object: Insight into the consequences for school students of a test-led curriculum.	Observation over a term of the circumstances of each occurrence of 'freezing' in the teacher's own class.	While this could be high risk if any direct involvement with the child were to be planned, risk is much reduced providing observation and note-taking are discreet. This is quite possible, given that the study is to be done in the teacher's own class.
Medium risk	Subject: A week in the life of an art gallery. Object: Understanding responsiveness to the public in museums and galleries	Observing; interviewing staff, guides, volunteers, groups and members of the public attending the gallery.	Museums and galleries are unlikely to give rise to much embarrassment or discomfort in respondents. However, with this particular case study delicate issues may arise because of emerging information about tensions or disagreements among staff about the running of this gallery.
High risk	Subject: An intensive study of a young woman with *anorexia nervosa*. Object: Understanding the phenomenon of 'taking control' in *anorexia nervosa*.	A three day intensive stay with one young woman in the young people's unit of a psychiatric hospital, 'shadowing' her, talking with her and talking with staff and other patients.	While much good could come from this study, there are serious potential dangers here for a vulnerable young person. Handled insensitively, the young woman could become upset or disturbed and treatment could be disrupted.

it would be necessary in this example to inform parents and child in broad terms of the intended research, with the opportunity given to veto the activity.

If, in seeking ethical clearance (see 'Getting clearance – ethical review', below), you are asked about risks and benefits, you should spell out:

- the physical, psychological, social, legal or economic risks that may be associated with the research and outline the arrangements that you have put in place to manage that risk
- if there are likely to be any immediate benefits to participants
- if there are any specific risks to researchers
- if any degree of concealment or deception are felt to be necessary, and if so why
- how potential benefits to participants outweigh any risks
- any arrangements that you have put in place for support after the study.

Issues of consent are particularly important if you are working with children. There is an unequal power relationship between any adult and any child, and your position as a researcher heightens the perception of authority held by the child. Good discussions of the ethics of working with children are provided in Lewis and Lindsay (2000), Alderson (2004), Kellett (2005) and Simons (1989, 2009).

Information sheets and consent forms

When you write or talk to your potential research participants you will have to do so after having thought about all of the issues above. If it is a complex case study you will need to produce an information sheet for participants which explains the details of your project and what you expect to come from it. If the project involves any degree of discomfort for participants, they should also be asked to sign a consent form. Either – information sheet or consent form – should include:

> It's helpful to write an information sheet for participants, explaining what the project is about.

- the title of project and the name(s) of researcher(s) and their institution
- an explanation of what the research is about
- confirmation that involvement in the project is voluntary and that participants are free to withdraw at any time and/or withdraw data supplied

University College, Badlands
24th October 2016

Dear Parent

My case study in your child's class

I am a student at University College, Badlands, and as part of my course I am doing a case study research project on the way in which teaching assistants help children in school. In my spare time I work as a volunteer helper at Badlands Primary School and Mrs Tumbleweed, Headteacher, has kindly agreed to allow me to contact parents to ask for their permission to allow their children to be involved in my project.

Say something about you

We know that teaching assistants provide a great deal of help to teachers. In my research I want to find out how teaching assistants work with teachers and children. I hope this will contribute to our understanding of the ways in which teaching assistants work, and I hope that I will emerge with suggestions about how they may work more effectively.

Briefly explain your project

I will be observing the work of the teaching assistant in your child's class and I may be asking children about their work.

If you would prefer that I avoid observation of your child and that I do not talk to him/her, no questions will be asked and there will, of course, be no consequence for your child.

Say what the participants are being asked to do

I will not be sharing any personal information I gather with anyone, even school staff. No names will be recorded: any information about individuals will have a code on it instead of a name. After my write-up, all information I have collected will be destroyed.

If you are happy for me to undertake my project as outlined in this letter, you don't need to do anything. However, if you would prefer that I do not observe or talk to your son/daughter as part of my research, please complete the tear-off slip below and return it with your daughter or son to give to their teacher. Or, if you have any questions at all, please complete the sheet as appropriate.

Explain anonymity, data security and feedback

Many thanks

Lucy Bloggs
Student in educational studies

✂--

If you do **not** wish your son/daughter to be involved in my project or if you have any questions at all, please complete the following and return to your child's teacher:

Consent is implied

I'd rather my daughter/son is not involved

I'm not sure: I have some questions

} *Delete as appropriate*

My son's/daughter's name _____

My name _____

☐ *phone me on* _____

☐ *text me on* _____

☐ *email me on* _____

Figure 5.1   An example of a letter seeking participants' involvement via implied consent

- an explanation about what involvement will be asked of participants and whether, for example, audio or visual recording will be involved

- details of arrangements being made to provide for confidentiality, such as anonymisation

- arrangements for data security including when the data will be destroyed

- arrangements for debriefing and feedback.

Where involvement is less complicated, a simple letter may be all that is needed, as long as it covers these issues in an intelligible way. Figure 5.1 shows an example of a letter which doubles up as an information sheet and a seeking of implied consent.

Contacting participants

Remember that each situation is different. You will need to assess how best to make contact with potential participants and how to explain to them the nuts and bolts of your research. In written communications with participants, always use straight-forward language. Imagine that you are in a spoken conversation with them. So, for example, write 'my study starts on ...' rather than 'my study commences on ...', or 'Please read through this' instead of 'Please peruse this'. (When has anyone actually said the words 'commence' or 'peruse'? I've no idea why people who devise forms are so fond of words like this.) Use everyday terms such as 'information' rather than 'data'.

A very good website on ways of seeking and gaining consent is that of the World Health Organization (http://www.who.int/rpc/research_ethics/informed_consent/en/), which gives templates of letters, forms and information sheets covering:

- informed consent for clinical studies

- informed consent for qualitative studies

- informed assent for children/minors

- informed parental consent for research involving children (qualitative).

Care for your participants – and yourself

I have discussed the many things you will need to consider in order to avoid causing harm or discomfort to your research participants. If, despite your best endeavours, though, it happens that you uncover something distressing for your participants, or you trigger a response which is clearly painful for them, you should think about whether it is appropriate to offer information to them about relevant support services.

And you should consider, too, the potential for harm to yourself in doing social research. While most situations will not, of course, present any danger, some will. If you are meeting people who are strangers, for example, always take a mobile phone with you and let a friend or family member know where you will be going, whom you are meeting, and when you expect to be back. You might suggest that you will phone at a particular time during or after your fieldwork.

Where do I put discussion about ethics in my case study write-up?

It's a moot point. Your discussion of ethics can come right at the beginning in your introduction, but if you put there it can rather unbalance the narrative about the purpose of your study. It can have a chapter all to itself, but this seems almost to treat matters about ethics as a separate, special concern, bolted on, and distanced from the main body of your work. I think the best place for your discussion about ethics is in a separate section in your design and methodology chapter. Here, you can discuss ethics alongside your deliberations about design and explanations about how you have gone about your work. You may also want to discuss ethics briefly as you actually report your findings and analysis, if this seems appropriate. Put sample copies of any forms, information sheets, letters to participants, guidelines, and so on, in an appendix.

Getting clearance – ethical review

A key element in starting your case study is in getting ethical or institutional clearance. This goes under different names in different places, but may be referred to as ethical review or institutional review. You will have to write an outline of your proposed research which will be looked at by a group known as the 'ethics committee' or, more commonly in the USA, the 'institutional review board' (IRB).

The use of these formal procedures by universities for ensuring ethical practice in social science research projects is relatively recent and still regarded by many researchers, both student and professional, as a bit of a chore. However, this is not the right attitude, and it stems – I speak only for myself – from a less than self-critical belief that I could not possibly be doing anything that would harm anyone with whom I researched. It stems from a belief that my own judgement about the balance of rights and wrongs is naturally the best judgement and that it is an attack on my integrity to question this. But the passage of time and experience have shown me how delicately balanced these matters can be and how necessary it is to have ethical concerns explicitly articulated and systematically checked. In fact, the systematic checking of these concerns with another person often will add insights beyond ethics to the design and conduct of the research.

Your university will have a code of conduct for research, and it will have a helpful webpage outlining procedures for gaining ethical clearance. The relevant professional organisations also have policies and guidelines on ethical research. Those for the British Educational Research Association (BERA), for example, can be found by entering "BERA ethical guidelines" into your favourite search engine. Others are given in the box below. All are very helpful, though some (for example, that of the American Psychological Association) are so long that you may lose to will to live if you embark on them. A very good, well-written one is the Social Policy Association's Guidelines on Research Ethics.

> You'll need to go through your institution's ethics clearance process before you start work. Professional bodies have codes of conduct that may be helpful in doing this.

Codes of conduct and other guidelines

For the codes of conduct or guidelines issued by these professional bodies or government agencies, just enter the words below into your favourite search engine:

- American Psychological Association Ethical Principles of Psychologists and Code of Conduct

- American Sociological Association Code of Ethics

- British Educational Research Association Ethical Guidelines

- British Psychological Society Code of Ethics

- ESRC The Research Ethics Guidebook

- General Medical Council Good Practice in Research and Consent to Research

- Social Policy Association Guidelines on Research Ethics

- US Department of Health and Human Services Office for Human Research protections

The World Health Organization's forms and guidelines on ethics can be found at: http://www.who.int/rpc/research_ethics/informed_consent/en/

The key thing to remember in looking at any of these protocols is that it is the consideration of ethics that is important – not the protocols themselves, helpful though these can be. A reflection on ethics should be integral, and not seen as a bolt-on or a chore to be squeezed into your timeframe.

Undergraduate-level ethical clearance

For undergraduate research, ethical review usually happens at school or department level. Getting clearance will involve completing a form which gives in a nutshell details of your plans. You will need to think about this right at the beginning of your project, as soon as you have decided what to focus on and have discussed the topic with your supervisor. Don't be intimidated by this form or by the procedure surrounding it. It shouldn't take too long and it may help you to get down your early thoughts on paper to give structure to your work. In most universities, this will usually be looked at in-house – that is, in your department or faculty – for approval.

Postgraduate-level ethical clearance

For postgraduate projects there are more complex arrangements. These usually entail a process that will involve completing an online form first in which you are asked various questions about your research. Your answers to these determine whether the research is 'low risk' or otherwise. If you have been able to answer 'no' to a series of questions, the project is taken to be 'low risk' – and that, for you, is then happily the end of the procedure. You can proceed with your plans.

However, if you have not been able to answer 'no' to all of the questions you will have to proceed to the second stage, which involves scrutiny of your plans by a university-wide committee. The process of ethical review must happen before the start of any active empirical work, including any pilot studies.

For your own university's exact procedure, take guidance from your department, or just enter "University of [name of your university] ethical review" into your search engine, or, in the US, "University of [name of your university] IRB review".

Ethics is a specialised and increasingly important topic, and all universities will have detailed procedures for ensuring that you consider ethical issues appropriately (my university's procedures – accessible to anyone – are at: http://www.birmingham.ac.uk/Documents/university/legal/uob-code-of-ethics.pdf). If, in your planned work, ethical issues seem to loom large and you wish to think about them in more depth, then you may wish to look at the further reading listed at the end of the chapter.

If you take only one thing from this chapter, take this ...

Ethics is more than just a process to be gone through. It is essential to consider carefully the ethical dimensions of a case study, given the intensity of involvement that may happen in this kind of research. You have to consider especially ...

- *Your participants.* Make sure that they know what is involved and that you give them ample opportunity to participate or withdraw, as they wish. Consider especially the needs of vulnerable groups – in other words, those (such as children) who may not fully understand what is being asked of them, or those who feel that they have to accede to a request because of their social position (for example, employees).

- *Gaining consent from participants.* In doing this, you'll need to provide as much information as possible about the project.

- *Openness and sharing of information.* Some withholding of full details may be necessary in some circumstances, but this will shift a project into 'high risk' and will need to be explained fully to an ethics committee.

- *Confidentiality.* There may be exceptions, but the default position is to treat all data as confidential and anonymise names.

- *Data security.* Keep data secure and destroy after your analysis.

- *Getting ethics clearance.* All universities and large organisations will have procedures to be gone through. Ensure you do this before your case study starts.

FURTHER READING 📖

Alderson, P. and Morrow, V. (2003) *Ethics, Social Research and Consulting with Young People*. London: Barnardo's.
Good on the ethics of working with children and young people.

British Educational Research Association (2004) *Revised Ethical Guidelines for Educational Research*. Nottingham: BERA.
Grinyer, A. (2002) 'The anonymity of research participants: Assumptions, ethics and practicalities', *Social Research Update*, 36: 1–6.
Discusses the value of anonymity and whether in some cases disclosure is to be preferred.

Malone, S. (2003) Ethics at home: informed consent in your own backyard, *Qualitative Studies in Education*, 16 (6): 797–815.
A critical account of research and its potential impact on participants.

Murphy, E. and Dingwall, R. (2001) 'The ethics of ethnography' in P. Atkinson and A. Coffey (eds), *Handbook of Ethnography*. London: Sage.
A comprehensive review and discussion of research ethics in ethnography.

Shaw, I. (2003) 'Ethics in qualitative research and evaluation', *Journal of Social Work*, 3 (1): 9–29.
Good on ethics and social justice.

Simons, H. (2009) *Case Study Research in Practice*. London: Sage.
See especially Simons's reflections on principles and procedures on pp. 103–10.

Simons, H. and Usher (2000) (eds) *Situated Ethics in Educational Research*. London: Routledge.
See especially Glen's paper discussing 'complex integrity'.

Social Research Association (2003) *Ethical Guidelines* (available at: http://the-sra.org.uk/wp-content/uploads/ethics03.pdf).
A useful introduction and bibliography.

Wiles, R., Crow, G., Heath, S. and Charles, V. (2008) 'The management of confidentiality and anonymity in social research', *International Journal of Social Research Methodology*, 11 (5), 417–28.
An excellent discussion of issues around confidentiality and anonymity.

PART 2

SELECTING A CASE AND CONDUCTING THE STUDY

In this second part of the book, I look at:

- how cases can be categorised
- how you can identify a case
- the purpose of your case study
- the approach you may take in your case study
- the kinds of processes that you may follow when conducting a case study
- and how all of these interrelate to create your unique study.

DIFFERENT KINDS OF CASE STUDIES: SELECTING A SUBJECT FOR YOUR CASE STUDY

In this chapter, I am going to look at different kinds of case studies and the ways in which they can be categorised.

Categories are much loved by textbook writers because, with them, the world can be made to look as if it is neatly divisible into tidy segments within which you can organise your work. This is a dangerous way to think when it comes to research, however, because it encourages a view of the world as neater than it really is. The world is *not* neat – keep this in mind as you read this and the subsequent chapters. The categories I offer are simply intended to help you think about, contextualise and frame your research. I'd be disconcerted if you assumed that I was offering some kind of straitjacket into which you had to squeeze your work.

Offering a framework for design also presents the potential problem of putting the cart before the horse – in other words, the view that you can *start* with your research *design* rather than your research *question*. You think that you can say, 'There are X, Y and Z types of case study – I think I'll use Y.' That's not the way research works. Research starts with a *question* (see Chapter 2), and this is something you must always remember when you are doing your research.

With these caveats in mind, I'll begin …

How do you select your case study subject?

Your question – if it leads to a case study – will be about something in its completeness, looking at a process within your choice of focus and at the *how* and *why* of the process. Once you have established this, your choice will be determined by a number of questions. I summarise these in Figure 6.1.

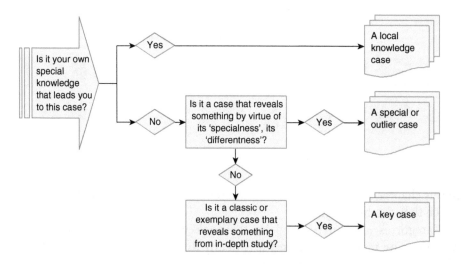

Figure 6.1   Where is the study coming from? Your subject

Your *subject*, your choice of focus, whether it be an interesting or unusual or revealing example, will be critical since it will lead you on to questions about the kind of study that you ultimately intend to conduct. This is particularly important for the student researcher, since, as Figure 6.1 indicates, there are two principal routes that can be followed when making this decision.

The first route may be taken because of your familiarity with it. I have thus called this a *local knowledge case*. Is it, for example, your own work or domestic situation or another situation with which you are familiar? Here, in your own place of work, your placement or even your home, you have intimate knowledge. You know and can 'read' the people who inhabit the arena – you may know it like the back of your hand. This is a ready-made strength for conducting a case study.

Another aspect of this is that you may be obliged to undertake a research project as part of your university studies and have limited access to anything other than your own situation – or, to put this more positively, it may be that, in your own situation, you can gain access to the richness and depth that would be unavailable to you otherwise. This is a perfectly valid reason for choosing your own situation in which to do your research and a good one for doing a case study. Do consider, though, if you are in this situation, that there are other forms of research also well suited to small-scale inquiry (I outline some of these in *How to Do Your Research Project*, Thomas, 2013).

The second route is taken if you are not choosing your study because of your own local or special knowledge. Are you focusing on this subject because of its inherent interest – is it a *key case*? In the examples that follow (see Table 6.1), Hurricane Katrina is a particularly interesting key case by virtue of its size and the extraordinary amount of damage that it wreaked on New Orleans and its environs.

Alternatively, are you examining the case because it is in some way special – in other words, because it is an *outlier* that shows something by virtue of its difference from other examples? An outlier may occur because it is different from the rest, as in the case of Kerala – the state in India that has extreme poverty yet unusually low infant mortality rates.

Table 6.1   The origin of your case

Kinds of case study subject	… which means	Possible choice	How to justify your choice
Key case	A good example of something; a classic or exemplary case	1 Hurricane Katrina 2 Hostos-Lincoln Academy, New York	1 A key case of hurricane damage 2 An exemplary case of high achievement among poor students
Outlier case	An 'outlier', showing something interesting because of its difference from the norm	Kerala	A state in India with unusually low infant mortality
Local knowledge case	An example of something in your personal experience about which you want to find out more	1 Ioan, from a Romanian orphanage 2 Brandon	1 A case of good adjustment 2 Brandon's sudden fall-off in progress in reading and intimate knowledge of Brandon's situation

Let us look at an example of a key, an outlier and a local knowledge case, remembering that the trick in each case will be to find an analytical frame that the case is a case *of*.

A key case

Hurricane Katrina

Having completed a degree in geography, Jake is now studying for a master's degree in environmental management and has to do a piece of research that examines the consequences of a major disaster in which environmental management has played a part. Jake has an uncle and aunt and a brood of grown-up cousins in the New Orleans area, which makes him think that he might be able to get some real-life accounts of what happened in the Hurricane Katrina disaster. So, he decides to focus on Hurricane Katrina and the part environmental management played in the ensuing disaster.

Could Jake simply entitle his project 'Environmental management and the Hurricane Katrina disaster' with a question such as 'What effects did environmental management have on the disaster that followed Hurricane Katrina in New Orleans?'

Well, he could, but it wouldn't make for a very interesting project. It misses the *analytical frame* (see pages 15–17), and without this it would be nearer to a piece of reportage than a research project. Some research would clearly be involved, but it would not be directed at anything very much other than a description, ranging widely around the event, with some superficial speculation thrown in. It could very easily become an account that showed merely straightforward links: the sea level rose, the levees became overwhelmed, the city was flooded.

What, then, is needed to pursue this as a good piece of research? First, a tighter focus is needed. To narrow down the focus, Jake would have to do some brainstorming to come up with ideas about the disaster and what constituted it, both at the physical geography level and at the social level, and how these interrelated. After the brainstorming, Jake might emerge with the following as possible elements. Two of these foci stress the 'front end' of the weather event in itself and the consequences of this; others focus at the

'Front end'	• Hurricane Katrina as an example of the kind of 'storm surge' that is typical of hurricanes. It causes the sea level to rise in the area of a hurricane and is especially dangerous in low-lying areas. • New Orleans as a coastal city with large areas below sea level protected by levees (wall defences).
'Consequence end'	• Gangs were roaming the city, stealing from homes and looting from shops. • Around 3 million people were left for over a week without electricity. • Much of the country's oil-refining capacity was disrupted. • Many people were made refugees by the disaster, having to move to temporary homes elsewhere in the country. Some of these would never return.

'consequence end', looking at the nature of the disaster, how it became a disaster and whether or not anything could have been done to avert it.

Each of the points here relates to a specific aspect of the Hurricane Katrina disaster. For each, Hurricane Katrina can act as a case in its completeness for Jake's examination.

Figure 6.2 shows a simple storyboard that takes the 'front end' ideas forward. It links the disaster that Hurricane Katrina inflicted on New Orleans to a set of cultural expectations and prejudices about planning and the role of government – local and national – in planning. Could it be that these prejudices in some way affected the political climate in which planning and environmental management took place?

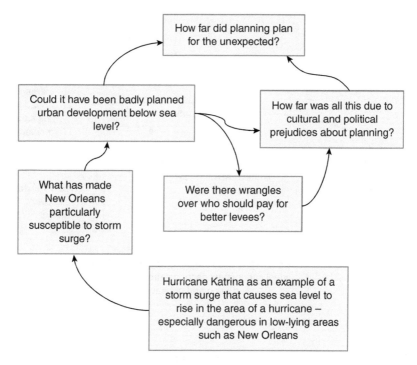

Figure 6.2 Storyboard for the consequences of Hurricane Katrina

This is the basis for a thorough case study. Some pilot exploration, perhaps by examining online local planning records in the local papers or discussions with relatives, could confirm this as a basis for a plausible prima facie hypothesis. If it does indeed seem to be a reasonable narrative that could be explored in depth, then further data can be collected – from news footage, interviews, books, original documents and archives about building plans locally and objections made to them.

(Continued)

(Continued)

Alternatively, Jake could focus on the 'consequence end' and look at the huge upheaval caused by Hurricane Katrina – the looting, lawlessness, displaced people and disrupted power supplies locally and nationally. He may wish to examine the extent to which this was the consequence particularly of a hurricane or how likely it would be for it to happen elsewhere and with different environmental events. Here he would look at the particular features that mark out Hurricane Katrina and New Orleans to see if they interacted in some peculiar way that made for this collection of social consequences. A different storyboard would follow, like that in Figure 6.3.

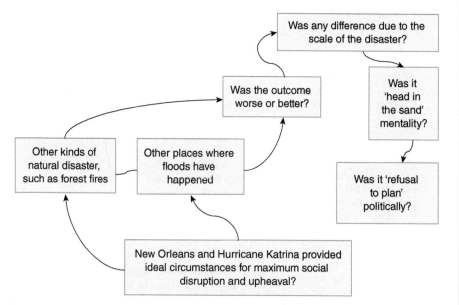

Figure 6.3   Second storyboard for the consequences of Hurricane Katrina

The two storyboards show how different narratives are possible from very similar starting points.

An outlier case

An outlier case is a puzzle. It's a case that is conspicuously different from the norm, and the question is why. You may have an idea as to a reason (or reasons) and this will offer a 'way in'. It may also offer a possible analytical frame (see pages 15–17).

Kerala: puzzling longevity

An interesting outlier case comes from the work of Caldwell (1986), who examined the correlation between gross national product per head in a country and the average life expectancy of a person in that country. In other words, he was looking at the association of average income with the age a person could be expected to live. A high correlation was expected and revealed – that is, as income goes up, so life expectancy goes up. Caldwell's great inspiration was to focus on the exceptions – countries (or states within countries) that bucked the trend, were outliers.

A shining outlier is the Indian state of Kerala. The state has extremely low levels of income – at the time of Caldwell's study, it had a gross domestic product per person of $160, which placed it higher than only four other countries in the entire world. Despite this, it had a life expectancy of 66 years – well up with the best performers, including industrialised states in the West. How could this be explained? What analytical frame could be put around this phenomenon? Caldwell's focus was on how Kerala and two other similar outlier states – Sri Lanka and Costa Rica – achieved such good life expectancy and if similar routes could be followed by others.

Looking back to the original statistics, which came from a Rockefeller Foundation inquiry, Caldwell noted that its author had suggested Kerala's achievements had resulted from a combination of 'political and social will'. He was left with a series of questions, which included the following:

- In what ways do countries with exceptionally good health records contrast with those with exceptionally bad ones?

- Under what circumstances can political and social will be exercised? To what extent has the political leadership been uniquely shaped by the history and nature of its society?

- For countries with vastly different histories from those with success stories, are there lessons to be learned or policies that can be put in place to accelerate mortality reduction?

His research design route in answering these questions was to conduct a case study. He had to use available statistics and knowledge of culture and history to arrive at potential explanations for how Kerala, Sri Lanka and Costa Rica had been able to manage such extraordinary accomplishments in the health and longevity of their citizenry.

The first job he set himself was to isolate from the statistics not just the best but also the worst, to see if this offered any opportunity for contrast (see Figure 6.4). In doing this, he was struck by what appeared to be a cultural difference between the best achievers and the worst achievers. The worst achievers happened to be Oman, Saudi Arabia and

(Continued)

(Continued)

Iran, with incomes 15 times higher than the poor states with good life expectancy, yet life expectancy down in the fifties. What could the differences be between the achievements of Kerala, Sri Lanka and Costa Rica on the one hand, and Oman, Saudi Arabia and Iran on the other? Caldwell hypothesised that cultural and religious differences were at the root of many of the contrasts between these two groups of states. In the cases of Kerala and Sri Lanka, the Buddhist tradition stresses 'enlightenment', which can be interpreted in Western terms as education. By contrast, the wealthy poor achievers – Oman, Saudi Arabia and Iran – were characterised by cultural and religious traditions that separated women, giving them limited access to education. Not only were there low levels of female schooling in these countries, but also low levels of family planning and limited access to employment for women outside the household.

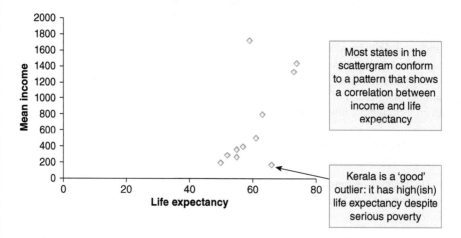

Figure 6.4   Life expectancy in years against mean income ($)

The link with female education is striking, notes Caldwell (1986: 177): 'For most countries in both lists the 1982 infant mortality rankings are very close to the 1960 female primary school enrolment rankings' – as education of females goes up, infant mortality goes down.

He concludes that there are some remarkable parallels between these states. These parallels include a substantial degree of female autonomy, dedication to education, open political system, largely civilian society without a rigid class structure, history of egalitarianism and radicalism and national consensus arising from political contest.

In a fascinating and wide-ranging analysis, Caldwell suggests reasons for the importance of the position of women in society, from the likelihood of girls becoming nurses to the position of children in society being higher where that of women is higher.

He reports that an early anthropologist, John Davy, noted the Sinhalese treated their children with 'extraordinary affection', attending to them when sick in the way that other groups he had studied did not.

Caldwell's conclusion was that women's education may be important not just because women may know more about, say, nutrition and development to help their babies but also because then women are valued and included – something more intangible but nonetheless seemingly just as significant. Thus, the provision of education for all seems to be operating at two levels: it is providing for individual knowledge but is also symbolic of society's affirmation of once-marginalised groups and its endorsement of those groups' participation and inclusion. So, in some way, this provision seems to be endowing added value. Perhaps this added value comes in the form of a boost for identity, status, belonging and self-belief. Inclusion, and the status it brings, breeds not only health but also the conditions for learning and growth to occur.

He looks also at historical and cultural investment in health and hygiene, noting that the high performers had a record of valuing these matters and investing powerfully in them since the nineteenth century. Education is important, too, but not just as education per se. It is linked with an active and participatory political system that in some way enables the hearing of the people's 'voice'. Caldwell (1986: 202–3) puts it thus:

> All evidence suggests that continuing political activity is important, especially if there is a dominant populist or radical element, and that such activity hastens the emergence and the spreading throughout the community of adequate educational and health systems. However, such politics are often encouraged by educating the electorate, and this has an impact at the grassroots as well as at the upper level.

He compares this with what happens elsewhere in India: 'The inefficiency of much of the health infrastructure in rural India is explained by both the low educational levels and the political passivity of the poor' (Caldwell, 1986: 203). There appears to be a symbiosis between education and health.

Although Caldwell's work is at no point called a case study it emphatically is one – of this limited set of countries. In doing work with such a small number, he cannot definitively assert that factor X or factor Y is, in fact, the cause of the good life expectancy figures in these outlier countries, but he can make a good, informed guess. This guess can be buttressed with evidence from historical records, other statistics, anthropological studies, reasoning about cultural difference. In fact, while Caldwell's study starts off as an epidemiological inquiry based largely on statistics, it ends more as a comparative history. The inclusion of all the forms of data, argument, reasoning and analysis is a form of triangulation that should not be downplayed in its importance.

The outlier case is always a puzzle, so Caldwell amasses all of this evidence – he brings them together to form Foucault's 'polyhedron of intelligibility' (see page 4) – to emerge with intelligent potential solutions, informed guesses, about the puzzle.

Caldwell's *informed* guessing – we could also call it 'hypothesising' – is the foundation stone of good analysis and attempting to understand. As long as it involves the intelligent putting together of evidence, it provides the basis for finding solutions and solving problems.

Always, though, we should have at the front of our minds the importance of the need to be critical in this or any other kind of thinking when conducting an academic inquiry. We should keep to the fore the need to be our own most strident critics of the explanations we propose. Done in this spirit of critical inquiry, there is nothing wrong with informed guessing.

If you were doing Caldwell's study today, you would be able to draw on a wider range of studies that have used Kerala as an example of something extraordinary. For example, the Nobel Prize-winning economist Amartya Sen (1999: 45–8) describes the process operating in Kerala as a 'support-led' approach to improvement in life conditions: 'The support-led process does not operate through fast economic growth, but works through a program of skilful social support of health care, education and other relevant social arrangements.' You could draw on Sen's notion of 'capability' among a nation's citizenry, which he takes to be more important than imposed top-down measures designed for the good of the people. In other words, this is about giving the people the opportunity to be involved – a concept similar to the one Caldwell identified in the participatory political system.

Nowadays, if doing this kind of study, you can draw on some extraordinary banks of data that are bundled together with miraculous software that enables you easily to draw comparisons of the kind that Caldwell would have had to spend weeks putting together. For example, Gapminder (http://gapminder.org) can instantly draw a sophisticated set of international comparisons of everything from national per capita income to life expectancy, oil reserves and quality of teeth (see Figure 6.5). Not only this, but it will also show how things change over time. In the example in Figure 6.5, life expectancy is shown against income per capita for 2004. This is the sort of information that enables you easily to see outliers.

If I were doing a 'Caldwell-type' study now and looking at Gapminder, I might choose to focus on the 'best' and the 'worst' African countries using the same measures as Caldwell. These turn out to be Cape Verde and Swaziland, respectively: Cape Verde has a life expectancy of 72 years with a per capita income of $3283, while Swaziland's life expectancy is 40 and its per capita income $4595. There will be different forces at play for these two countries, but ones that will reveal fascinating outlier case studies for comparison. A storyboard might include factors such as:

- insulation from continental Africa, in Cape Verde's case

- stability of post-colonial government and its nature

- consequences of AIDS

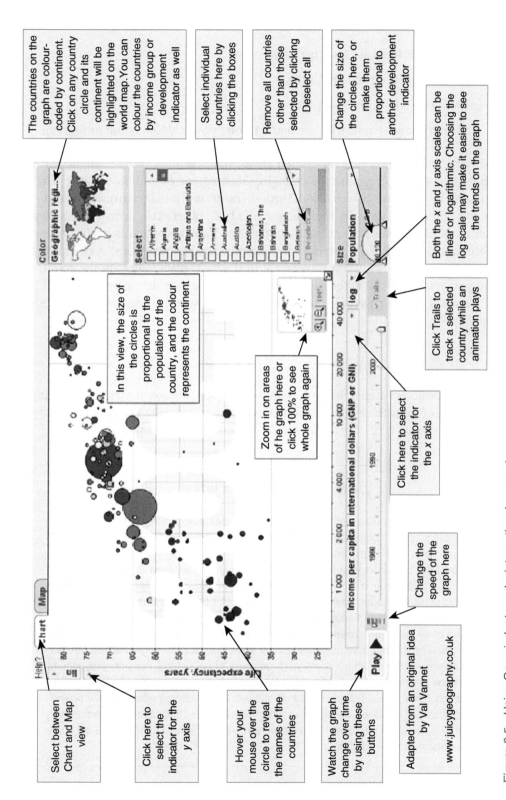

The countries on the graph are colour-coded by continent. Click on any country circle and its continent will be highlighted on the world map. You can colour the countries by income group or development indicator as well

Select individual countries here by clicking the boxes

Remove all countries other than those selected by clicking Deselect all

Change the size of the circles here, or make them proportional to another development indicator

Both the x and y axis scales can be linear or logarithmic. Choosing the log scale may make it easier to see the trends on the graph

Click Trails to track a selected country while an animation plays

Click here to select the indicator for the x axis

Zoom in on areas of he graph here or click 100% to see whole graph again

In this view, the size of the circles is proportional to the population of the country, and the colour represents the continent

Change the speed of the graph here

Adapted from an original idea by Val Vannet
www.juicygeography.co.uk

Watch the graph change over time by using these buttons

Hover your mouse over the circle to reveal the names of the countries

Click here to select the indicator for the y axis

Select between Chart and Map view

Figure 6.5   Using Gapminder to make international comparisons

- use of international aid for large capital projects
- support from émigré communities
- spending on education and health
- availability of new industries, such as oil, solar power, desalination or tourism.

Using the information that I found on any of these 'leads', I could triangulate my embryonic storyline against the changing scattergram over time, looking back, perhaps, to the time before Cape Verde became independent from Portugal. I could begin to 'drill down' with demographics from other easily accessible sources, such as the US Census Bureau International Data Base (www.census.gov/ipc/www/idb/pyramids.html), which gives instant international comparisons, even drawing population pyramids for you if you click in the right place. Click on the country and year you want, and in the next screen click on the 'population pyramids' tab.

It's not a problem getting data nowadays – it just needs leavening with your imagination.

A local case – *your* knowledge

Research projects often start with some special knowledge, noticing something interesting or unusual, putting two and two together and, with a spark of curiosity, a research project is fired and ready to fly. How might this happen?

Ioan: adopted as an infant

Let's imagine that you are undertaking an undergraduate degree in psychology for which you are required to complete a small research project that you intend to do in your special area of interest – child psychology.

Down the road from your home, there is a family who adopted a baby, Ioan, from a Romanian orphanage in 1990, after the fall of the Romanian dictator, Ceaușescu. Many families in the West adopted Romanian children at this time. Everyone in your neighbourhood knows about Ioan's adoption since the family have made no secret of it.

You know Ioan, now grown up, and his family well – Ioan's older sister went to school with you. The starting point is that you have some special knowledge that you feel may enable you, with the family's consent, to do a useful case study. From reading around, you know the results of research undertaken by Rutter and the English and Romanian Adoptees (ERA) Study Team (1998) that showed these children were typically severely developmentally delayed on arrival in their new families, but caught up impressively thereafter. You know also that those who were adopted before 6 months of age did better than those who were adopted after.

Clearly, you are not able to do a piece of research remotely similar to that of Rutter in his comparison of 111 Romanian adopted children with 52 native adopted children. You are not going to be able to make meaningful comparisons between Ioan and his peers in your neighbourhood. What you *can* do, however, with your special knowledge and the knowledge you have from your reading and wider research, is construct a case study that connects what you know about Ioan – he seems to be a happy, fulfilled young man – with some of the findings of the research, namely that some of the adopted children proved to have serious emotional difficulties.

How can you construct a study here? You can try to interconnect your own information with that from your reading to emerge with a topic that focuses on Ioan's success, noting that success has not always been the picture for some of these young people.

How has success been achieved? In answering this question, you could look at the age at which Ioan was adopted, the nature of the family into which he was absorbed (number of siblings and so on), Ioan's parents' reflections and Ioan's own reflections, including his experiences at school.

You will be using all kinds of data for evidence and analysing it and interpreting it in a variety of ways – see Chapters 9 and 10.

The point is that the case study will enable you to 'drill down' into this one case – it's as if it were *one* of Rutter's sample of 111. Where Rutter, in his huge piece of research, was able to offer some generalisable findings about the progress of children adopted from Romanian orphanages, he was not able to do the kind of study that yours promises to be with your local knowledge.

Brandon: not progressing in reading

Kareena completed her postgraduate certificate in education (PGCE) two years ago and teaches a class of 9–10-year-old children in a large inner-city school.

One of her pupils, Brandon, is a bright boy and has always done well in class, but has recently begun to be truculent and his work has deteriorated in quality. He is laggardly in wanting to engage in classroom activity and, most importantly as far as Kareena is concerned, his reading has failed to progress at the same rate as that of the other children in the class.

Kareena has decided to do an MA in teaching studies at her local university. The main element of this is a thesis, which will involve a piece of small-scale research. From the research methods course that occupies the first part of the MA, she understands the potential of the case study to illuminate puzzling states of affairs in need of in-depth analysis. So Kareena decides to do a case study, with Brandon as her subject.

(Continued)

(Continued)

Kareena realises that the essence of a case study is to 'drill deep' and look at the situation from as many angles as possible – to take an ecological stance (see Chapter 3). She understands, therefore, that she has to see Brandon's behaviour not simply as a function of what is happening in the classroom but also as a manifestation of everything happening in his life.

She decides to frame the analysis that she undertakes in the models provided by systems psychology (see page 58), wherein she is able to draw a picture, literally, of the interconnecting forces that appear to be having an impact on Brandon's life.

She arranges to see Brandon's mother, who arrives at school with her new boyfriend. It transpires that the relationship Brandon's mum has with her new boyfriend is far more intense than was the case in her previous relationships. Brandon's mum realises that this is having an unusually serious impact on her strong relationship with Brandon.

Kareena interviews the school's special educational needs coordinator (SENCO). She also talks to Brandon after class and observes him informally in class, taking notes as she does this. She completes a diary every day about interrelationships in the class and draws a sociogram of the class.

It does not take systems psychology to understand that Brandon is feeling squeezed out by his mum's new relationship. The analysis that it offers, however, placing his life at school in the context of his life at home, is a useful counterpoint to the predominant way of tackling difficulties at school, which tends to seek pedagogical (that is, instructional) alterations that might help to ease the problems.

Kareena's analysis confirms her original suspicions – namely, that directing extra instructional resources to Brandon's new difficulties with reading is likely to be unsuccessful as he is confused, depressed and increasingly switched off from everything that school has to offer. He will also, surely, reject new forms of teaching or additional help organised by the SENCO.

There are two important points for us to note now about this case study. The first is that it is one Kareena has intimate knowledge of. She is part of the situation that she is researching. She could be a participant observer. She has easy access to all of the people involved, with some degree of authority and control over the situation.

The second is Kareena's focus. She was concerned not to undertake a case study just for the sake of doing one. There had to be a reason for doing it – a question that would frame the way that the study and its analysis took shape. So, she did not focus on Brandon, who was failing to learn to read, simply because he was a good example of someone failing to learn to read. What would be the point of that as a piece of research? It would be the verbal equivalent of taking a photograph – you would simply be describing Brandon and his circumstances to the reader. Interesting as this might be, it would not constitute research.

To be research, it needs to have a question and an analytical frame (see page 15) to focus the inquiry. If your question is about why Brandon suddenly appeared to lose focus and drop behind his peers three months ago, you immediately have an 'angle' to focus a piece of research that will benefit from the completeness of a case study analysis.

Same starting points, different paths – there's no right way

In Jake's case study of Hurricane Katrina above (a key study), I indicated how rather different case studies might follow from the same starting point, and this is a natural and inevitable feature of the case study method. A case's uniqueness is defined not only by the core topic, but also, more importantly, by your own interests and circumstances. It's about what you want to find out and the limits of what you can do.

It's as if Pooh Bear were on a walk in the woods. The Hundred Acre Wood is a big place – at least, to Pooh it is. If he were to start out from Piglet's house, he could go east to Eeyore's Gloomy Place (if he was feeling cheerful enough to withstand the blast of gloom) or a little bit north and to Owl's house if he needed some edification and wise advice. If he were tired, he could go straight north, back to his own house, or go north east to Christopher Robin's house.

The physical frame determined by Hundred Acre Wood is like the boundaries of your case – think (suit)case again. Beyond this, Pooh's choices are determined by his mood, needs and predilections, in the same way that yours are when you are framing your case study research. He can take his walk in a variety of directions, as you can when you do your research. He can't do everything, though, and neither can you in doing a case study. If he tried to visit everybody – Owl, Eeyore and Christopher Robin – the quality of his conversations with each would be abbreviated, to say the least. Owl wouldn't even have time to put on the kettle for a cup of tea, never mind give any wise advice.

This is one of the dangers of the case study, when its holistic (holistic means 'to do with the whole') quality is talked about. Because completeness is being emphasised, this does not mean that *everything* has to be covered. The trick is to get a line of inquiry running through the study. This should be determined either at the beginning (in the theory-testing phase), as in the case of Hurricane Katrina, or it should develop as the study progresses (in the theory-generating phase). (I shall look more at testing a theory versus generating one in Chapter 8.) The quality of the case study will be determined by the integrity and the coherence of this line of inquiry and the extent to which you can weave together data from a range of sources in addressing the narrative that you develop. Think of your storyboard as an analytical map, a bit like the one of Hundred Acre Wood.

There are no rules, then, about the *scope* of your study. Its quality is determined by the line of inquiry that you choose to take. As White (1992) points out, the scope can be as broad as Lenin's analysis of peasant social formations or as narrow as one of Goffman's smiles. It's up to you *how* you choose to walk Pooh through the Hundred Acre Wood – how you relate the *subject* to the analytical frame or *object*.

> There is no formula or right way to decide how your study begins or proceeds. As White (1992) suggests, the scope can be as broad as Lenin's analysis of peasant social formations or as narrow as one of Goffman's smiles.

Likewise, it is difficult to say that there are particular kinds of focus for a case study. At least, if we can categorise case studies, we can do this only post hoc – that is, *after* they have been done. As I tried to make clear in the examples of Jake and Brandon above, the choice you make regarding what kind of case study you do has to be for a relevant reason that concerns your research question. It is not something that is imposed on the inquiry at the outset, but has to be arrived at following your thought about your purposes in doing an inquiry, your approach to addressing these purposes and the processes you will use with that approach. I shall come on to this in Chapters 7, 8 and 9.

To close this section, I should reiterate that it's not worth getting in a tizzy if you can't work out whether your case study is, for example, a 'key' case or an 'outlier' case. These are categories into which a study is put for the benefit of understanding what is going on and what alternatives are open. For example, I found it hard to decide whether the Hostos-Lincoln Academy was a key case or an outlier case. One moment it seemed to be a key example of a process and a set of expectations and activities that happen in good schools, and the next it seemed to be an example of something that is different, for not all schools are like this.

Does it matter which category I ultimately put it in? No, not really. Much more important is to know how this starting point sets you on a case study design track that lets you answer your questions in the best, most interesting way. The categorisation of case studies merely provides you with a set of options – a menu through which to look so that you can see what is available and choose from alternative ways of proceeding. You should not be straitjacketed by it.

Kinds of case studies

Finding your case is all about choice of focus – it's about deciding where you are going to shine that searchlight beam. The deciding process involves not just one decision but many. We have just looked at the decision you will make concerning the *subject* of your study. You also need to think about the analytical frame or *object*. Beyond this, we need to examine how it proceeds after having made this choice.

You have to make a number of further decisions here and these define the kind of case study that you undertake (see Figure 6.6). These choices about *purpose*, *approach* and *process* interact variously to produce an array of permutations and, ultimately, each unique study. I'll go into detail about this in a moment, but I want first – just to contextualise my judgement that we should next look at purpose, approach and process – to look at the way some authorities have addressed the issue of kinds of case studies. Table 6.2 summarises categorisations of case studies from a number of experts. It's by no means an exhaustive list, but it captures some of the main views.

You can see from Table 6.2 the perils that come from attempts at defining types. Each of these authors has used different ways to categorise case studies. Let's look at it in a little more detail and see if we can distil something out of it.

First, we have to recognise that there is a mixture of criteria for classification here. Purposes are mixed with methods, which are mixed with kinds of subjects, which are, in turn, mixed with different 'shapes' of case studies. Second, there is duplication – different authorities have said the same thing, but perhaps in different ways.

Figure 6.6 Your investigative path is determined by your purposes, approach and process. These all involve making choices

Table 6.2   Kinds of case studies, as defined by different authors

Merriam (1988)	Stake (1995)	Bassey (1999)	de Vaus (2001)	Mitchell (2006) (drawing on Eckstein, 1975)	Yin (2009)
Descriptive	Intrinsic	Seeking a theory	Descriptive/ explanatory	Illustrative	Critical
Interpretative	Instrumental	Testing a theory	Testing or building a theory	Social analytical	Extreme or unique
Evaluative	Collective	Storytelling	Single or multiple cases	Extended (over time)	Longitudinal
		Drawing a picture	Holistic, embedded	Configurative, idiographic	Representative
		Evaluative	Parallel or sequential	Disciplined, configurative	Revelatory
			Retrospective or prospective	Heuristic	
				Plausibility probes	

Let's first of all extract the *subject*. A couple of the authors have identified subjects in their classifications. I, in the first part of this chapter, looked at this crucial decision, too. We decided (or, to be accurate, I decided) that this involves you choosing to conduct one of these: a key case, a local knowledge case, or a special outlier case. Beyond this, the experts' classifications involve thinking about:

- your *purpose*, in explaining or evaluating or exploring and so on

- your *approach*, in describing or interpreting or trying to build a theory or test a theory

- the nitty-gritty of how you will go about actually doing the case study – the *process* – as in single, multiple, parallel and so on.

In Table 6.3, I have sorted the classifications, taking out the duplication. The important feature of this table is that subject, purpose, approach and process are separated. You need to have the distinctions shown here clear in your mind when designing your study.

Aside from (hopefully) simplifying the categorisation of case studies give in Table 6.2, in Table 6.3 I have also added one or two things and taken some away.

Table 6.3   Kinds of case studies – simplified

Subject	Purpose	Approach	Process	
Special or outlier case	Intrinsic	Testing a theory	Single or multiple	Nested
	Instrumental	Building a theory		Parallel
Key case				Sequential
	Evaluative	Drawing a picture, illustrative		Retrospective
Local knowledge case	Explanatory			Snapshot
		Descriptive		Diachronic
	Exploratory			
		Interpretative		
		Experimental		

I have added an extra 'approach' – the experimental – and two extra 'processes' – snapshot and diachronic. ('Diachronic' means changing over time, and I have used this label in preference to the word 'longitudinal' to avoid confusion with other kinds of longitudinal research.)

For the taking away, I have removed the duplication and I have also removed one of the kinds of case study used by Yin (2009: 48) – namely, his *'representative or typical case'*. You will have to choose whether or not to take my advice here, but, for me, typicality is *not* a reason for studying a case. For a start, even if we know that the case is typical following some empirical work to show that it is typical – a typical Chicago street in terms of the ethnicity and age distribution of its inhabitants, say – what can we legitimately *do* with this typicality in a case study? We can only take a photograph (metaphorically, of course), and this is not research: it is photography. It is not answering a question and we are not finding something out since we cannot say, from having drilled down into this street, that its circumstances will have in any way contributed *by their typicality* to the situation it finds itself in (whatever that situation is). We could talk about the street as a street, and be informed about its problems, tensions, intrigues, hostilities, kindnesses and dynamics, but these would not be of interest by virtue of the *street's* typicality, since the *next* typical street would, in all probability, be very different from this one.

If, however, there was something about this Chicago street that made it worth studying – your familiarity with it or, perhaps, the high frequency of fights or the rise in house prices or whatever – a case study might illuminate that.

It's important not to get mixed up about these categorisations. It's important not to think, in other words, that, because you have decided you are doing a 'multiple' case study (or whatever), this is the beginning and end of your reasoning for doing the study. It's not. This describes only one facet of your study. It does not tell anyone *why* you are doing it or *how* you are going to do it.

Your subject, purposes, approach and process are all related to one another and you should be able to explain how you have connected your *subject* with the *purpose* of the study, your *approach* and then the *process* you intend to use. Each step in the chain should be explicable.

Let's go back to the example of the role of popular culture as a contributor to the fall of the Berlin Wall in 1989 (see page 39). We could say that your subject is a *key* one in the topic (for it is not one that is within your local knowledge). Your purposes are *intrinsic* (since you are interested in this phenomenon in its own right), *exploratory* (since you want to explore something about which you don't know very much) and *explanatory* (since you want to explain – to yourself and others).

From here, we can move on to the approach of your study, given these starting points. Will you be seeking to develop new ideas or test out those of others? Probably you'll be doing both, so the study is both *building theory* and *testing it* and this theorisation comprises your *object*. It is likely that there will not be much simple description going on, but you will be seeking to understand the perspectives and positions of those who lived through the period. In this sense, the study is *interpretative*.

From here, we could say that, while you are doing a single case study (that is to say, of one event, namely the falling of *the* Wall – not the falling of several walls), you are looking at *nested* aspects of it, since (let's imagine) you have chosen to look at popular music, art and the media as *nested* elements of popular culture. We can also say that you are looking at the case *retrospectively* – you are looking at something that happened in the past.

The connections between subject, purpose, approach and process for this particular case study are shown in Figure 6.7. We can say that this case is a *key* case with purposes that are *intrinsic, explanatory* and *exploratory*, approaches that are *testing a theory, building a theory* and *interpretative* and processes that are *nested* and *retrospective*.

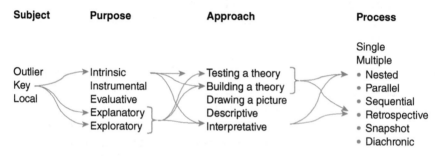

Figure 6.7   Mapping out the design for the case study 'The role of popular culture in the fall of the Berlin Wall'

Let's try this with another example, using one of the case studies from earlier in this chapter – the outlier case of the people of Kerala and their puzzling longevity (see page 103). Here, the subject is one chosen because of its *outlier* status. Its *purpose* is *intrinsic* and *explanatory*. Its *approach* is both to build ideas and test them (*building a theory* and *testing a theory*), and its *process* is through a *multiple* study, taking Kerala as the focal point, but also using contrasting and similar cases in *parallel* (see Figure 6.8).

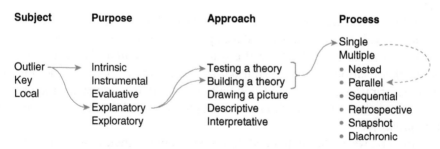

Figure 6.8   Mapping out the design for the case study 'Kerala: puzzling longevity'

I shall use this classification diagram at other points in the book to show the investigative path that case studies may take, depending on how they combine subject, purpose, approach and process. In this chapter, we have primarily looked at your subject, as indicated in Figure 6.9.

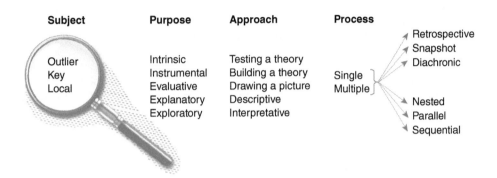

Figure 6.9   First, think about your subject

If you take only one thing from this chapter, take this ...

There are three main routes you might take in selecting a particular subject for your case study. You may choose it because:

- you know a great deal about the case in question and you want to understand some aspect of it
- it provides a particularly good example of something
- it reveals something interesting because it is different from the norm.

Once you have established your reason for doing a case study, there are a number of kinds of case studies for you to choose from. The classification in Figure 6.9 enables you to think about structure in such a way that you can review and select from different design routes for case studies, routes that involve consideration of purposes, approaches and processes. So, in the next three chapters I shall offer ideas on how to think about:

- purposes behind doing a study
- approaches to take when you do it
- processes to adopt to achieve the most fruitful crop of findings.

FURTHER READING 📖

Bassey, M. (1999) *Case Study Research in Educational Settings*. Maidenhead: Open University Press.
Bassey discusses the case study in the context, principally, of educational action research in classrooms. He expounds his idea of the case study producing a kind of generalisation that he calls 'fuzzy'. We can, in other words, be pointed in the right direction by the findings of a case study without being certain about whether or not a generalisation will apply in another setting.

de Vaus, D.A. (2001) *Research Design in Social Research*. Thousand Oaks, CA: Sage.
Useful for putting the case study as a design frame in the context of many other design frames.

7

YOUR PURPOSE: THINKING ABOUT THE OBJECT OF YOUR STUDY

Having considered your subject, we can now move on to the purpose for your case study. So the focus now shifts to the next part of the diagram, as shown in Figure 7.1. This represents a move to the theoretical or analytical side of your work. What is the case – the subject that you have identified – being used to explicate or understand? If you remember, in Chapter 1 I offered the simile of the case, the *subject*, being used like a lens through which to view and examine some theoretical theme, which I called the *object*. It is this object to which we now turn, in order to understand its potential dimensions.

Why are you doing a case study? What is your object? Is it intrinsic interest or is it as a means to another end – perhaps a way of getting a more rounded picture

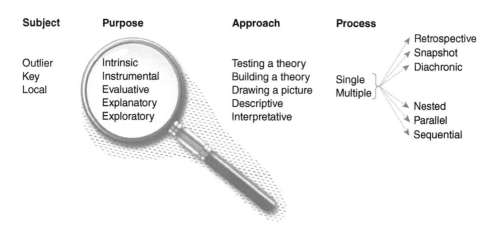

Figure 7.1   Looking at your purpose

of something, such as a medical procedure? Are you doing it to evaluate a process? Maybe you want to conduct the study to explore the field before doing a different kind of study. Maybe you are trying to explain what is going on in a situation.

Stake (2005) uses the words *intrinsic* and *instrumental* to separate the different purposes you may have in your mind at the beginning of a study. Let's look at these first.

Intrinsic

> With an *intrinsic* study, you are inquiring for the purpose of inquiring. It's 'blue sky' research.

In an *intrinsic* case study, the subject is being studied not with a secondary purpose in mind but out of interest, pure and simple. Of course, if we went on to try and analyse our *interest*, it could come from any one of a number of angles, but we'll put that to one side for a moment. Sometimes, when a study is undertaken simply for its interest, it is called 'blue sky' research or 'curiosity-driven' research – blue sky, because you are free to think just of the sky; there are no obstacles or barriers to block the view because there's no ulterior motive – that is, you are finding out for the sake of finding out.

Stake (2005: 445) suggests that the case study is intrinsic

> if the study is undertaken because, first and last, one wants better understanding of this particular case. It is not undertaken primarily because the case represents other cases or because it illustrates a particular trait or problem, but instead because, in all its particularity and ordinariness, the case itself is of interest.

The *intrinsic* label is used to separate a study such as this from an *instrumental* study.

Instrumental

An instrument is a tool and an instrumental study is one that is done with a purpose in mind. You are using the study as a tool; you are not doing it purely for the love of knowledge. Is your research aimed at evaluating something? (More on this in a moment.) Do you have a purpose in trying to understand with a view to making things better? For example, if your case study is about Joshua's persistent difficulty with reading, your ultimate aim is probably going to be something to do with helping Joshua. The case study in this sense is instrumental; it is a means to an end.

Stake (2005: 445) makes the distinction between the intrinsic and the instrumental to emphasise the point that some case studies are

> examined mainly to provide insight into an issue or to redraw a generalisation. The case is of secondary interest, it plays a supportive role, and it facilitates the understanding of something else.

You may notice Stake's use of the word 'generalisation' in this quotation. If so, you may be saying to yourself, 'Hang on. Didn't the bloke who wrote this book say on the first page that you *can't* generalise from a case study?' Well, yes, I did say that and this is where it begins to become a little tricky (strokes beard

> With an *instrumental* case study, the inquiry is serving a particular purpose. So, the case study is acting as an instrument – a tool.

meaningfully), thinking about what the case study can and can't offer. There may be generalisations that each of us holds in our heads – not scientific generalisations, but everyday generalisations – that a case study may help to confirm or refute. You may remember that I discussed this property of case studies in Chapter 4, where I noted their importance for *abduction* and *phronesis*.

Beyond distinctions between the intrinsic and the instrumental, you can divide studies according to whether their purposes are evaluative, explanatory and/or exploratory – or any combination of these. Let's look at each in turn.

Evaluative

Evaluation is framed by the expectation that you are doing the research to see how well something is working or has worked. Something has been changed or a new idea introduced, and evaluative research is carried out to find out what the change has led to. Have things got better or worse – or just stayed the same?

There are, of course, many ways to answer questions such as these, and a case study provides just one avenue into evaluative research. The main thrust of evaluative research will usually involve counting something before the change has been introduced, introducing the innovation, then counting again at the end. Whatever the consequence – an improvement, a steady state or a deterioration – we have grounds for believing that it may have been caused by the innovation. Mind you, I should stress that the key words here are 'we have grounds for believing' since there are many reasons for such changes to have happened. Indeed, much discussion concerning social science method is about the confidence we can have in the beliefs that we hold after research has taken place.

The role of a case study in all of this is a very particular one. It concerns the 'drilling down' that I spoke about earlier, trying to understand about the *how* and the *why*.

If, for example, you are part of a management team that introduces a new rota scheme in your finance office and you find that productivity – the amount of work being got through by each member of staff – drops after the introduction of the new scheme, rather than rises as you expected, you will want to pursue this finding further.

You might do this by conducting some interviews to ask those who work in the finance office what they think is happening. This would be a perfectly reasonable follow-on from your first finding ... but it would not, in itself, be a case study. A case study would involve an in-depth examination – the emphasis here being on depth rather than breadth. The aim would be to gain fine-grained detail about what is going on, looking from many angles at possibly only one person's experience. In looking at one person, you will want to explain his or her personal and professional circumstances in as much detail as you feel necessary, and amplify this with all of the situational detail that you assess to be relevant.

A case study here will contribute to the evaluation, but cannot form the major part of it. Using an outcome measure of some kind, the main part of the evaluation can establish that there has been a drop-off in performance. Then, and only then, can the case study provide insight into *why* that drop-off might have occurred. Given that the case study will be sacrificing breadth for depth, you will probably focus on a limited number of staff to follow up.

You might choose to focus on only one person – say, Jennifer, who has been a member of the finance department for 18 months – to get her impressions of what has happened. You might talk to her in an unstructured interview, asking for her opinions on what happened before and after the change, how she felt about it, what its effects were for her. You might look at Jennifer's Outlook diary and her 'to do' lists before and after the change. You might question her about these (always remembering the need for complete protection of your volunteer informant in a situation such as this, and being fully aware of the need to consider ethics fully – see Chapter 5). All the time, you will be looking for Jennifer's attitudes in this, watching for the nuances in her behaviour that give clues to what she really means, since this was a finding (the deterioration in productivity) that you did not expect and was not expected by the company. You should be alert for subtle messages that Jennifer may be reluctant to articulate.

It is in these subtle clues that you may be able to build a story about what has happened in this case. The key advantage of doing a case study is that you are empowered to do this building job – building from varied sources and using your own knowledge of the world, its intricacies, meanings and webs of understandings. With these, you construct an explanation: a story that knits all of the threads together. The philosopher–educator Jerome Bruner (1991: 2) calls this 'The narrative construction of reality'. In his famous article in *Critical Inquiry*, Bruner (1991: 2) says:

> we organize our experience and our memory of human happenings mainly in the form of narrative – stories, excuses, myths, reasons for doing and not doing, and so on … Unlike the constructions generated by logical and scientific procedures that can be weeded out by falsification, narrative constructions can only achieve 'verisimilitude'. Narratives, then, are a version of reality whose acceptability is governed by convention and 'narrative necessity' rather than by verification.

This is important for understanding what the case study offers. Bruner is making the point that there are different ways of understanding what people do and, if we are assuming that we can use only in a limited way the methods of natural science in social science, we must treat as different the knowledge that comes via building the narrative.

Explanatory

Explaining is probably the most common purpose of a case study. Remember that, in a case study, you are trading breadth of coverage for depth of understanding, and potential explanations based on depth of understanding are what a case study does best.

These explanations may be tentative or context-specific, but it is in the multifaceted nature of a case study that you get the opportunity to relate one bit to another and offer explanations based on the interrelationships between these bits. In being able unselfconsciously to look at these interrelationships, a case study is, thus, the most powerful engine of potential explanations. We must remember, however, that the explanations it offers may be limited to the background provided by the case study's circumstances. Always be aware that you are looking at one among many.

Let's suppose that you are interested in the changing patterns of adult employment in education. In the USA and Europe, these changes have been occurring over the last few decades, with far more teacher aides (teaching assistants in the UK) employed than was the case before the 1980s. Despite the improvement in teacher–pupil ratios provided by these additional adults, there is little evidence that the new pattern of employment actually does the children any good. The outcomes – in, for example, attainment tests – for children in classes with aides or assistants show little or no improvement over children in similar classes who have not had the benefit of this additional resource (Vincett et al., 2005).

(Continued)

(Continued)

Now, this is a finding that merits some thought and, indeed, concern. Why should it be that attainment does not improve *despite* the better teacher–pupil ratios? We can also ask ourselves what the existing research may not be telling us, since it seems obvious that these better ratios ought to be doing *something*.

Storyboarding may help here – it may offer some avenues to pursue, with the aim of developing an analytical frame.

Figure 7.2 shows a very small storyboard. You'll see that there are two directions of travel in the questions that stem from the question at the bottom. Those on the right are about the things that might be going wrong due to the advent of additional people in the classroom – things that might offer an explanation for the findings of research about children's attainment. We tend to think that extra people can bring only benefits, but maybe this brings problems just as big as or bigger than the benefits.

The questions on the left, by contrast, are about our focus in the research. Is the focus on attainment curtailing off some aspect of improvement in the classroom that is unrelated to attainment?

A case study might offer an explanation here. Maybe, though, I should be more tentative and say instead that it may offer some clues to an explanation. How would you construct a case study that might begin to examine this teacher–pupil ratio paradox?

First, we should draw a line around the situation that we wish to study – we should define its parameters. We should be aware that what we are doing is looking for pointers to an explanation, not provide definitive answers. So we will not seek to define this or that variable based on a hunch that it may be important and then test its importance with a study or a series of studies. Rather, we will systematically seek hunches, seek potential explanations.

How can you start on this? Imagine that you are throwing a rope, a lasso, around one situation that in some way exemplifies the area of your interest. By defining the area of interest in this way, you give yourself the opportunity to explain in this small situation. Here, you are thinking of classrooms with extra people working alongside the class teacher, so choose one such classroom. In this classroom, your attention is focused single-mindedly on the problem: why is it the case that research shows additional adults do not seem to help student attainment?

Once the question has been framed and the rope thrown round the situation, you can begin to think around the issue, using a storyboard of the kind shown in Figure 7.2. The boundary of the study here is this class – this teacher with her 29 children in this room in this school. It is not, as would be the case in other kinds of research, this variable isolated and manipulated in this way, judging its effects on that variable. Your aim is explanation – albeit tentative explanation, but explanation all the same – and this involves taking a holistic view.

To get this holistic view with explanation in mind, you will be looking from a number of different directions, and those directions will be determined by the ideas that have emerged from your first storyboard.

First, going back to Figure 7.2 and looking at the left-hand side of the diagram, you might decide to look *not* at attainment but instead at something that seemed not to be examined in the literature on this subject – the children's attention.

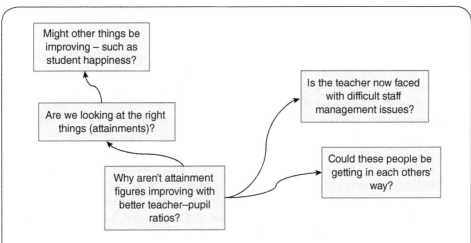

Figure 7.2 Storyboard of questions about the effects of having extra help in the classroom

So, you set up two conditions for observing the children: first, on Monday morning when Mrs Speed, the teaching assistant, is present in the class; and, second, on Tuesday morning when the children are doing the same kind of work but Mrs Speed is *not* present. You look at each child in each situation, video-recording their behaviour. Then you compare the two situations. From this, you are able to say whether or not there was a significant difference in the children's behaviour in the two situations. This on its own, though, is not enough.

For a second view, going back to the left-hand side of the diagram again, moving up, we come to happiness. Even if attainment cannot be shown to change, might the children be happier with an aide or assistant present?

How could you examine this? Could you look at how much the children are smiling? Probably not a good idea since, even if you *could* find a good way to measure a smile (impossible, surely), you could not be sure that smiling was an accurate representation of happiness. Maybe children who appeared to be smiling were merely trying to contain excess wind. Maybe they were smiling because they were laughing and joking in a classroom with little control.

Would this be a measure of happiness? We know that children don't like being in uncontrolled classrooms, so, even though they may be laughing, they may not be happy. (Social research – it's not easy, is it?)

Perhaps it would be better to use some other indicator of happiness, such as a self-report. You could, in other words, simply ask the children, using charts with smileys (☺), how happy they are in the different situations.

Moving to the right-hand side of Figure 7.2, we come to a different set of issues entirely. Here are some quite profound questions about the ways in which people work together, and some interesting ideas have emerged from your storyboarding about the effects that putting two people together in a working environment can have. In fact, academics in

(Continued)

(Continued)

economics and management science know these effects well, summarising them in 'the law of diminishing returns'. This law is that each unit of extra resource – whether it be people or machines – will produce less than the one before it. It may not be 100 per cent appropriate to this situation, but it is a clue as to what might be happening when there are extra people in the classroom. More people equals more confusion if the extra people don't know what they are doing. (They may not know what they are doing since teachers are unfamiliar with having to manage and work with other people in their territory.)

So, how could you, in your case study, try to examine whether or not this law of diminishing returns might be operating? You could do it in a number of ways – perhaps actually observing to see if there are any signs of confusion or irritation. You might ask the teaching assistants themselves, by interview or questionnaire, how they feel about being in this situation. Do they feel unsure? Do they feel directionless? You might ask the teacher if she feels unconfident about how to handle and manage the additional staff. You might watch the children for signs of them taking advantage of confusion between the teacher and the assistant. Are they capitalising on ambiguity?

So, with the case study you would be doing the 'drilling down' into this situation to provide the explanation for the kind of paradoxical finding about attainment.

Exploratory

An exploratory case study will be done where you are faced with a problem or an issue that perplexes you. You need to know more: what is happening and why? You may have little preliminary knowledge of the issue – or, at least, little rounded knowledge of it. You may have some familiarity with it, but what you know may be one-dimensional since you only ever see the situation as one person – in your role as a teacher or as a visiting parent or the school's headteacher or a midday supervisor who helps out as a volunteer during lessons.

Let's take an example.

Imagine that you are a teacher and there is a child in your class, Joel, who freezes when it is time for the annual SATs to be given. Exploring this in a case study, your initial brainstorming will be around the potential reasons for this, which you can follow up with your multifaceted exploration.

Your ideas are likely to be far more tentative and less well formed than they would be with an explanatory study, where you have some clear ideas that you wish to pursue. An exploratory study will therefore be more open-ended. You will be seeking ideas from others using a variety of methods, watching and making notes and conducting interviews. These will give you leads, corridors to follow – some of which may lead to an open door, others to a dead end.

Suppose that the first part of your study is to ask a range of different people about their impressions of Joel. You ask each of them – his teacher, parents, headteacher, the midday supervisor – why they think that Joel freezes when the time for SATs is approaching. Given that the study is exploratory, you will principally be listening for ideas, rather than presenting ideas to test against your respondents' views. It would be inappropriate to say, for example, 'Do you think that Joel has dyslexia?' This would be very much framing the initial ideas of the respondents according to constructs you have suggested – putting words into their mouths.

You might set aside an hour each morning for a week to watch Joel in class at a time when he and his peers are doing more formal work. You would likely observe in an unstructured way, trying to pick up any clues about Joel's behaviour from the contextual antecedents (that is, the things that happened before) and consequences (the things that happened after) of formal work. Did he seem to use avoidance strategies? Did he look anxious? Did he try to remove himself from situations with other students? Did he start messing around when structured work was imminent? Did his teacher or teaching assistant seem to be expressing any anxiety through their behaviour, and could this be transferring itself to Joel?

It is with such exploratory questions, followed by observations and open-ended interviews, that you would begin to conduct an exploratory case study for Joel's situation. As 'leads' appear, you follow them up. Some might seem to have substance, and it is these that you then test further.

Here is another example, from real life. It is a much more complex one, in the arena of public health. It shows, I hope, how useful the case study can be when you have a seemingly amorphous problem. In fact, it shows not just how the case study can be valuable in an exploratory sense but also how these explorations can be taken further, narrowing down the area of search as more data are gathered.

After the arrival of 'mad cow disease' (properly called bovine spongiform encephalopathy, or BSE) in the UK in the 1980s, it was realised, after laboratory work, that the disease had been transferred to the cows from ground-up sheep (including their brains), which had been fed to the cattle as bonemeal. Because cows are, by nature, vegetarians, the eventual assumption about the infection was that they had no evolutionary protection from the diseases that might be transferred to them by eating another creature.

A collateral assumption was that the new disease, found to be caused by an agent called a 'prion' in the cows' brains, could not be transferred to humans (we being omnivores

(Continued)

(Continued)

and, therefore, evolved to eat other animals). The UK agriculture minister at the time, John Gummer, even fed a burger to his daughter to prove to the nation that there was no danger to humans.

Then, worryingly, it was noted that the incidence of a human brain disease called Creutzfeldt–Jakob disease was rising. It was a particular *kind* of Creutzfeldt–Jakob disease – a variant – so the new illness came to be called variant Creutzfeldt–Jakob disease (vCJD). Eventually, the link between BSE and vCJD was established – BSE seemed to be causing vCJD – but it was expected that the risk of contracting the disease was tiny.

In 2000, though, it was noted that there was a cluster of people with vCJD in the Leicestershire village of Queniborough. Between August 1996 and January 1999, five people contracted the disease in the village, all of whom subsequently died. This was now a huge concern for public health. Could it be that this was the beginning of an epidemic? Was it possible that everyone in the UK who had eaten beef was susceptible to contracting vCJD? The cluster had to be investigated quickly to explore if there were particular circumstances that were causing this cluster and if many more clusters were likely to be found across the nation.

The only form of investigation possible here was the case study. The case, defined by this cluster, had to be explored for the circumstances that surrounded it (see Figure 7.3). Were there peculiar circumstances in Queniborough that led to the vCJD cluster? Two researchers, Gerry Bryant and Philip Monk (2001), led the investigation for Leicestershire Health Authority, and their research provides for us a classic example of an exploratory case study.

Figure 7.3 'Mad cow disease' was studied by means of a case study

A number of lines of thought were immediately open to the investigators. Aside from the unwelcome possibility that this was the first of many such clusters to appear, there were also competing explanatory themes that had to be explored.

The disease had a long incubation and the young adults affected had probably contracted it several years previously, at primary school. Might hygiene in the primary school kitchen be to blame? Might a particularly badly infected batch of cattle be responsible? Was it something to do with how the cattle were slaughtered or the meat transported? Yet more potential explanations open to Bryant and Monk included:

- infection via blood transfusions, dental surgery, injections, body piercing and so on in this locality
- baby foods consumed locally, given the youth of the vCJD patients

- lack of manganese in the diet, since preliminary investigation showed that this area of Leicestershire has a particularly low level of manganese in the soil, so manganese elsewhere might be providing some kind of protection.

Any of these lines of thought could provide a promising avenue to pursue ... or lead to a dead-end (see Figure 7.4).

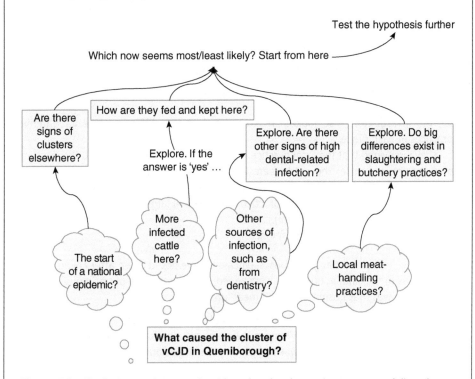

Figure 7.4 Exploring and generating ideas is a haphazard process, so follow the ones that seem most likely first

The first rule is to *think*. The investigators had to think about these alternatives and start with the most likely. They started by looking into cattle-rearing practices locally. They found that:

> Local beef cattle were raised alongside dairy cattle. This meant that beef cattle were fed meat and bonemeal supplements from the age of 6 days rather than 6 months, which is the case for pure beef herds. (Bryant and Monk, 2001: 2)

The upshot was that the cattle raised here had a higher chance of incubating BSE than did cattle elsewhere, having had a longer exposure to the prion in bonemeal than in

(Continued)

(Continued)

many places elsewhere, and this area of Leicestershire did indeed prove to have a high incidence of BSE.

A strong additional candidate for culpability was the nature of the meat eaten in this particular place, which led the investigative trail to butchers' shops. At this point the story gets rather gory, so, if you are squeamish, it is best to avoid the next few paragraphs.

Butchers in the area obtained their carcasses in one of three ways:

- they slaughtered the animals themselves

- they bought them from local, small slaughterhouses

- they bought them from large, wholesale suppliers.

So, the investigators also looked in more detail at the differing cattle-slaughtering practices in each place.

They discovered that the local practice in small slaughterhouses included the insertion of a 'pithing rod' after the cattle were killed with a bolt. The pithing rod is pushed through the bolt-hole in the brain of the cow to prevent the animal kicking, which can occur after the use of the bolt. This practice is not used in large slaughterhouses (and the practice has now been made illegal).

There were two other major differences:

- in large, 'industrial' slaughterhouses, carcasses were hosed down after killing, whereas in the smaller ones they were wiped, because the lore of traditional butchery was that hosing made the meat 'go sour'

- the traditional practice, employed by the small, local slaughterhouses and butchers, had been to split the head to remove the brain, offering further opportunity for cross-infection; this practice was not used in the large slaughterhouses.

Local killing and butchering practices, then, provided a likely candidate for infection. They could actually be responsible for spilling the infective agent out of the brains of the cattle and on to the raw meat. Using the traditional butchers' methods, this material would not be hosed away. In fact, the use of cloths to wipe the carcasses could actually make matters worse, spreading the infective agent around.

Following their initial investigations, Bryant and Monk refined their original 'thought bubble' ideas (see Figure 7.4) to arrive at a hypothesis that:

1 local cattle were particularly predisposed to being infected because, in local rearing practice, consumption of bonemeal happened at an early age;

2 then, given the local slaughtering and butchering practices, the infective agent was spread over the carcasses and, from there, the infective agent was transferred to butchers' local customers (it was known from experimental work that the infective agent – the prion – is not destroyed by cooking in the same way that other pathogens are).

Bryant and Monk tested the second part of this hypothesis by comparing the source of meat consumed by vCJD patients with that of non-patients. Was there a pattern, with the families of patients with vCJD sourcing their meat from traditional local butchers? Using a structured questionnaire, they first of all asked relatives of the infected patients about diet and purchasing patterns for meat during the 1980s. The responses here were compared with those of a set of 'controls', these being comparable people who had *not* contracted vCJD.

The findings were, in short, that four of the five vCJD casualties had regularly consumed meat from one of two local butchers, who had sourced their meat from cattle killed using traditional slaughtering methods. The meat bought by the controls was from a far wider range of retailers (supermarkets, freezer stores and other butchers). The latter – the 'safe' retailers – were questioned about the sources of their meat, which turned out, as expected, to have come from further afield and *not* butchered using the traditional methods.

Using simple statistics, it was then possible to show that the likelihood of this pattern occurring by chance was very slim indeed. The point I keep making, about the impossibility of generalising from case study, however, is still valid and Bryant and Monk (2001: 5) were wisely cautious in their conclusions. They say that the study:

> provides a biologically plausible explanation ... [but] On a national basis, it is unlikely to explain how all of the people who have developed this disease were exposed to the BSE agent.

Enormously helpful information was provided by this case study, however. An unexpected additional piece of information also came from this study:

> Analysis of the exposure of our cases to this butchering practice points to an incubation period for the development of vCJD of between ten and sixteen years. This is the first time that it has been possible to provide an estimate of the incubation period. (2001: 5)

This case study is from the field of public health, but the steps taken by these investigators when doing this exploratory work are common to all such investigations, in any field. They involve:

- initial fieldwork or a reconnoitre to gather facts
- the posing of potential explanations or solutions
- exploratory work to examine the likelihood of any of those potential explanations having substance – having 'legs'
- the testing of those potential explanations.

If you take only one thing from this chapter, take this ...

While the subject, the case itself, is the focus of your direct interest in a case study, it is, in a sense, only a tool you use to examine or explicate some theme or topic. You are using the subject to understand this theme or topic. In this chapter we have looked at the potential shape and dimensions of this theme, this analytical frame, which can be thought of as the purpose or the *object* of your study. We have noted that the purpose of your study may be:

- intrinsic – looking at a subject purely out of interest, to identify or illuminate a theoretical topic

- instrumental – using the case study as a means to an end, better to understand some theme, process or idea.

Beyond this, we can divide case studies into:

- evaluative – where the aim is to find out how well something is working or whether it has worked as expected

- explanatory – where the phenomenon in which you are interested needs 'unpacking', the connections between different parts of the issue need unravelling and the case study offers a route to explanation

- exploratory – where little is known and the principal purpose is to establish the 'shape' of the problem or issue

The issue is about the way in which the analytical frame for your study will take form.

FURTHER READING

Becker, H.S. (1996) 'The epistemology of qualitative research', in R. Jessor, A. Colby and R. Schweder (eds), *Essays on Ethnography and Human Development*. Chicago: University of Chicago Press, pp. 53–71.
This is a fascinating discussion, essentially, of what we mean by 'empirical'. It plays down the distinctions between qualitative and quantitative and makes the case that different kinds of research find common cause in being *empirical* – in other words, in finding out from (our own) experience and analysis, as distinct from what some very important authority tells us.

Booth, W.C., Colomb, G.C. and Williams, J.M. (2003) *The Craft of Research* (2nd edn). Chicago: University of Chicago Press.

Booth and his colleagues give one of the best overviews I have come across of why it is important to look at your purpose. Chapter 14 is especially helpful for establishing the *rationale* for your work. The book looks at research as a holistic, integrated process that, although it *is* integrated, doesn't just 'happen'. You have to think about your purpose, what has been done before and what you have to offer to the area with your proposed research. Although they are not looking at the case study in particular, the stance they take on research is very relevant to the case study, stressing, as it does, the integrity of the complete work. You have to work at making the integrity real for the reader, though, and this is what the book helps you to do.

YOUR APPROACH: THEORY TESTING OR THEORY BUILDING; INTERPRETATION OR ILLUSTRATION

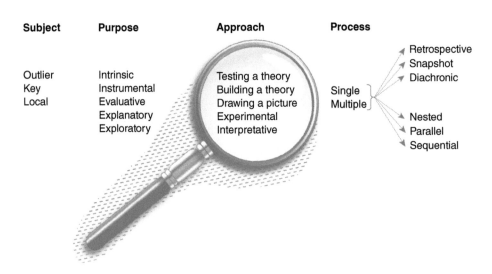

Figure 8.1   Looking at your approach

Having looked at your purpose in Chapter 7, you can think now about *how* you are going to do your study (see Figure 8.1). Are you, for your analytical frame, or *object*, going to try to build your own set of ideas from scratch (building a theory) or are you going to test ideas that you have come across elsewhere (testing a theory)? Are you going to do both of these, as in the vCJD case study in Chapter 7? Is your approach in the case study to illustrate something, perhaps a process that you need to explicate in more detail for some purpose? Will you be seeking to uncover and interpret what is going on in the area of your searchlight beam?

Theory testing or theory building

Let's begin with case studies where the object is to build or test a theory. Presenting these as contrasting is perhaps a little confusing since they are better thought of as being at opposite ends of a continuum of kinds of inquiry. At one end, you are trying to develop shape from data – your mind is open to the shape that it will take, rather like the bits in a kaleidoscope when you twist the barrel.

At the other end of the continuum, the shape is already there, like a template, and the job you set yourself is to see whether or not the template, the theory, in fact provides satisfactory explanations for the data you are collecting. Remember, though, that all research – a case study or otherwise – begins with an inspiration or a hunch and it is this that leads to the journey of your research. You cannot begin without the hunch stage, whether you are building or testing a theory.

Building a theory

'Theory' is a tricky word in the world of research since it has so many meanings. I'll come to this and discuss it a little more in Chapter 11, but, for now, let's assume that theory means an explanatory model. Building a theory is therefore about developing, almost from scratch, a framework of ideas, a model, that somehow explains the subject you are researching.

So, in a theory-building case study, you are aiming to develop ideas, starting off in much the same way that you did for an exploratory case study, but taking the process much further. This is much more than exploration. You build a framework of ideas that has no overt connection to preformulated notions about what is important here. Perhaps that's putting it too strongly, since it is impossible to *not* connect to pre-existing ideas. What I mean is, you have no *allegiance* to pre-existing ideas and no presuppositions. Your pre-existing ideas will always be there – you can't erase them from your mind, after all – but you must have no commitment to them as potential answers. Your mind should be open to new interpretations suggested by your data.

Let's suppose that you are a student of forensic psychology and interested in the way that global terrorism is affecting people's day-to-day lives. Is it influencing the way that people go about their workaday existence? Are there ways in which a fear of terrorism changes what people do? What are the changes imposed by government and institutions in response to global terrorism that have an impact on their lives? These are the starting points for your research and might lead to a case study building a theory that in some way explains people's behaviour.

Let's also suppose that you have begun your inquiries by interviewing some people who are about to go into a London Underground station – say, Oxford Circus. Most of the people you talk to claim that global terrorism has no effect on them at all, but, among the group of people you interview, you come across a few who say that they would be suspicious of a young man wearing a large rucksack and would try to get into a different train carriage from him.

Here is the basis for a theory-building case study. Given that we are focusing on *building* rather than *testing* a theory, the emphasis will be on generating ideas as the research progresses, rather than testing out preformulated hypotheses. While your focus may be on your participants' constructions about danger, race, religion, youth and their interconnection (since you have to have a starting point), you will not have preformulated ideas about how important each of these is, how they were conceived or the nature of any interrelationship. Your aim will be to *build* these as your study progresses.

Your initial interviews give you some pointers. From here you will need to make decisions about the focus for the case study? Will it be:

- the station

- a group of people in a station

- one person who has expressed a fear of a terrorist incident?

Whichever you choose, your focus must be the site of something that is of interest. Remember again Wieviorka's (1992: 160) comment that a case 'is significant only if an observer ... can refer it to an analytical category'. It can't simply be plucked out of the air. You can't simply think, 'I'll do a case study on this station' with no special reason for choosing that station. If you do choose to focus on a station, then, there must be a reason for focusing on the 'station-ness' of this particular station. So, for the case study, there are two issues:

- Why do a case study on a station, in the context of fear about terrorism?

- Why do a case study on this particular station?

What do I mean by the 'station-ness' of a station? Well, if you were to do any other kind of research, you might choose this station because it is in some way typical of a station. You would choose to select participants at this station because it in some way represents stations in central London. Alternatively, you might choose a sample of similar stations or representative groups of contrasting stations. Not so with a case study. With a case study you would choose this station to look at the station environment in the context of potential fear. So you would look at a whole range of matters. You would look at the number of people on the platform and how they enter and leave. You would look at jostling and the distance people stand from each other. You would look at the height of the roof, at the noise made when the train enters and leaves the station. Do the advertising hoardings make people feel uncomfortable or put them at their ease?

So, to choose a station as a focus for your case study, you would have to have a reason for doing so, not just because it is a convenient site for your study. There would be no point in simply choosing a station as a place to interview people since you could just as easily interview them anywhere else. Why would this make a good case study?

This raises an issue as far as building a theory is concerned, since here you are supposed to be starting from scratch. You are, in a sense, expected to clear your mind of expectations and preconceived notions. Is this possible? As I have already noted, probably not, but this is the expectation if you are building a theory.

How, then, can you proceed? The answer is to make a broad assumption at the outset about the importance of your chosen focus – about the station and its 'station-ness' – then follow the usual steps that I have been talking about until now, getting as many different sides of the situation as far as this focus is concerned. These might include starting points about noise, proximity of people, movement, places to sit, presence of concealed entrances, presence of bins and so on. You can then find ways to explore these issues and let the information that you discover speak for itself. You do not go into a theory-building study expecting to *confirm* the significance of these features of the situation – rather, you *explore* their importance.

So, our theory-building case study might be called 'The station: a site of fear about global terrorism'. The weight is immediately being thrown on the station as the core of your inquiry. You are making it clear in the first two words that it is the station that is the focus of your interest. It is this that provides the kernel for your inquiry into terror and why people should feel it. Does the station have any features that exacerbate (or perhaps lessen) people's fears? Your methods need to be geared towards finding an answer to this basic question, then the theory will grow around the data you collect as a result of your inquiries.

I like to think of theory growing, becoming thicker, around productive ideas, while it stays thin or atrophies away completely around the starting points that seem to be going nowhere. So, you might start off with a storyboard like the one in Figure 8.2, which maps out your basic ideas for building explanations for fear in stations. When you have collected your data – completed your interviews, taken photographs, made

(Continued)

(Continued)

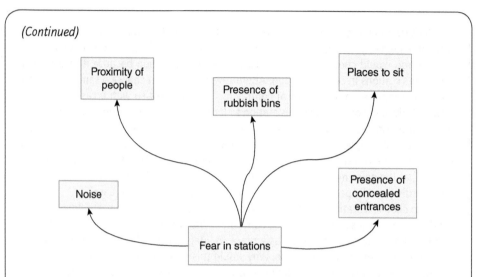

Figure 8.2 Your first storyboard for building your theory

videos, taken sound recordings and so on – you will find that the evidence seems to grow 'thicker' around certain themes, so that you are able to redraw your storyboard, showing the themes that are developing, the theory building, as in Figure 8.3. Here, in this redrawn figure, you can see that the explanation, the theory, is building around the *people* who are present in stations, rather than the physical structures that are there (such as bins and seats).

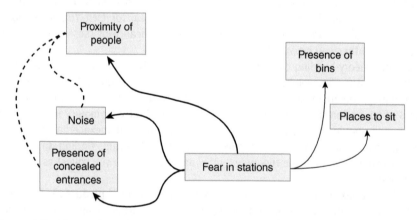

Figure 8.3 Your redrawn storyboard with the beginnings of a 'theory'

So, in the redrawn storyboard, I have moved the boxes around so that the important features are closer together and represented by heavier lines. There are, moreover, connections between the boxes.

Testing a theory

The assumption here is that there is already some sort of explanatory framework available for the phenomenon or situation on which you are focusing. Your case study, then, is being undertaken to test this explanatory framework, this 'theory'.

Imagine that you are a senior nurse in the UK's National Health Service. As a 'clinical specialist' you are an expert in one area of clinical management, so let's imagine that your specialty is infection control and that, in your hospital, infection from the methicillin-resistant *Staphylococcus aureus* (MRSA) 'superbug' is particularly high. You want to examine why this might be the case.

There will already be a great deal of existing 'theory' to explain why levels of MRSA infection are higher in particular places. It is known, for example, that rates are higher in hospitals that have more vulnerable patients and undertake more invasive specialist care, and lower in maternity and paediatric units. It is known also that the frequency of handwashing by staff is negatively correlated with rates of MRSA infection – that is, the more handwashing the better. Furthermore, figures can be affected by the number of patients transferring from one hospital to another.

All of this pre-existing knowledge and theory provides a substantial backdrop for the construction of your own theoretical formulation about the high level of infection by this superbug in your hospital. In fact, it is important to stress that *all* of this contextual information is essential to the conduct of a case study and the 'shape' of your own emerging theory. The fact that you are doing a case study does not absolve you from the task of setting the study in context and finding all that there is to know about this particular situation.

In doing your case study, your first port of call will be this pre-existing theory. Does your hospital fall into one of these categories (for example, more vulnerable patients, such as those who are elderly)? If not, you can move on and assume that there are some other features of the situation that are causing your high rates of infection, and it is these features that may form the basis for your theory-testing case study.

So, the theory that you test will be based on existing knowledge and your own knowledge of the situation. As I noted at the beginning of this section, all research starts with a hunch, and your own hunch will be based on some key observations that you have made yourself as a member of the hospital staff. Imagine that you have heard comments such as:

- 'Everyone knows it's there and everyone in the know realises that the superbug is uneliminable.'

- 'The politicians, public and media are ignorant – we know that this bug can't be got rid of.'

(Continued)

(Continued)

- 'It's about more than washing your hands.'

- 'It's an excuse, a smokescreen, for too little money being spent on the health service on better equipment, better cleaning. They are trying to blame frontline service providers for lack of equipment and shortcuts on cleaning.'

Let's assume that your experience includes working in several hospitals and, alongside these comments, your casual observations suggest that there seems to be less concern about handwashing in this one. You may feel that there is a culture of complacency about this aspect of hygiene, which goes right the way through the system – from the cleaners and ward orderlies right up to senior management.

At the heart of your 'theory' here is an implied comparison with other places and their culture of hygiene, but you have nothing on which to base this comparison other than your own experience. To test this comparison out empirically, you would have to visit other hospitals and collect data that to compare with data from your own place of employment. Clearly, this is not the essence of a case study. What you are hoping to achieve by carrying out the case study is examine this one situation in detail and draw conclusions on the basis of your in-depth, internal examination.

Initially, you might like to look at the kinds of features of this situation that constitute the culture in general, and a culture of complacency about hygiene in particular.

The first question that you need to ask here is about the supposed culture of complacency and resistance. Your focus would be on the presence of this culture in a wider culture – a highly visible and highly audible one – among politicians, health service managers, the media and the public about the importance of top-notch hygiene. No one could claim not to have heard about the need for not just hygiene but *much better* hygiene – all the time, the message is coming through loud and clear about the need to eliminate the superbug from hospitals.

What kind of narrative could be built around this mismatch between knowledge and action? In other words, what can we infer from the fact that there might be a culture of complacency in an environment of excellent knowledge about the danger of this superbug? What does it tell us?

Surely, it says that there is something else going on in the social environment of the hospital that is subverting the message about the danger of lack of hygiene. No one could claim that the message is unimportant, so, if it is being undermined, what is going on?

Your theory – the theory you want to test – is that the 'undermining factor' concerns a resentment about management and new initiatives. This resentment is finding its expression in an oppositional attitude to innovation in this situation. The storyboard for this might be as shown in Figure 8.4.

For the theory-testing that you are doing in this case study, then, you have made a number of assumptions based on the literature and your own knowledge, with a twist of your own analysis. From here, you can go on to test the theory in a number

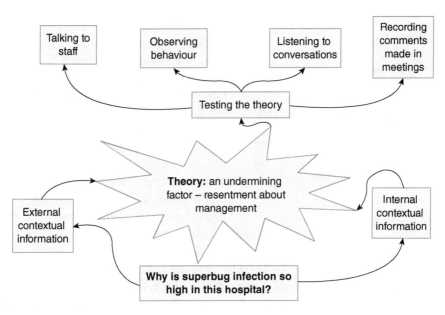

Figure 8.4   Testing the theory

of different settings, as shown in Figure 8.4 – that is, by discussing the matter with staff, watching people's behaviour, listening to them talking and hearing the official and unofficial messages that are articulated during committee, working group and other meetings.

The theory you are testing, in other words, has emerged, has 'thickened around', an idea that you had at the outset, which has been reinforced as you have looked into the issue further.

Drawing a picture – illustrative–demonstrative

Some case studies aim first and foremost to *illustrate* a phenomenon. In the same way that an illustration in a book brings the text to life, so an illustrative case study makes a topic more real for the reader. The subject comes to life.

Clearly, there is more involved than simply drawing a picture, but the picture analogy serves well, for it shows the possibility of making a major difference understandable. The point is made well, I think, in the line drawings here of a cat and dog in Figure 8.5. They are easily identifiable as such, but it would be difficult to put your finger on why the dog is 'doggyish' and the cat is 'kittyish'.

Is it the tongue sticking out on the dog? My cat, Archie, sometimes leaves his tongue sticking out. It makes him look silly, but it doesn't make him look like a dog. Why does the cat look like a cat? Is it the pointy ears? It can't be – many dogs have pointed ears.

Figure 8.5   Pictures say more than words alone

We know from our experience of the world (encapsulated in the word 'phronesis', which we looked at in Chapter 4) what these domestic animals look like. We have some kind of model in our brains that enables us to say 'that's a dog' when our eyes present it with all of the squiggly lines in the dog picture and 'that's a cat' when our optic nerves deliver the cat squiggles. That this is so doesn't bear deconstructing. I recently learned that the best artificial intelligence programs are still highly unreliable when it comes to establishing this kind of distinction. Yet our brains can do it.

We have some kind of amazing picturemaking facility in our brains that lets us fit a new picture with our existing perceptions – here, the cat and the dog. It works for more than just cats and dogs, too. It's ubiquitous in our sensemaking apparatus as the pictures, literal and metaphorical – about cats and dogs, organisations, notions like democracy – are there all the time in our daily sensemaking. A case study, by presenting those 'pictures', enables the connection to be made. It enables readers to share an experience and, drawing from their own models – their own reservoirs of knowledge and experience – to make sense of the new image that is offered.

It's not simply a question of providing illustrations, though. There has to be analysis accompanying it. The great sociologist Erving Goffman (1956), in his book *The Presentation of Self in Everyday Life*, unpacks one illustration after another involving analyses of the ways in which people behave in social life. He notes from these illustrations that people behave as if they are on a stage, trying to convey something with their outward behaviour (see also the discussion of Goffman and dramaturgy on page 52).

Goffman describes a man walking down the street who trips on a loose kerbstone. We already have the picture in our heads, involving not just another person but also ourselves. The man tripping, observes Goffman, will invariably turn round to look at the offending stone. He does this, Goffman says, not out of any deep interest in the kind of phenomena that trip people up, but in order to *convey* something to any

The case study is not an alternative for real experience, but incorporates the ingredients of experience. It illustrates and provides metaphors by which the learner can 'get inside' a problem, thinking about it and connecting with the characters of the story. It enables readers or inquirers to share experience, using their own reserves of knowledge and experience to make sense.

onlooker. The look has a *meaning*. With the turn and the look, the man is saying to any onlooker who might have seen him trip and humiliate himself, 'I am not the sort of dummy who is always tripping over things. Nor am I drunk. What kind of extraordinarily disguised danger could have led me to stumble?' The turn and the look have significance and meaning. By presenting the picture, Goffman lets us share his picture and his analysis.

In his book, Goffman provides a series of annotated illustrations – each one unique – performing work beyond that of *mere* illustration. Goffman works on the illustrations and asks himself what they are saying. It is the reflexive and self-questioning attitude that the well-chosen illustrations bring that is of particular service. Flyvbjerg (2006: 223) offers a good account of what is going on:

> The highest levels in the learning process, that is, virtuosity and true expertise, are reached only via a person's own experiences as practitioner of the relevant skills. Therefore, beyond using the case method and other experiential methods for teaching, the best that teachers can do for students in professional programs is to help them achieve real practical experience; for example, via placement arrangements, internships, summer jobs, and the like.

Importantly, Flyvbjerg connects inquiry and its illustrative capabilities with practical learning here. The case study is not a proxy, an alternative for real experience, but incorporates its ingredients. It illustrates and provides metaphors by which the learner can 'get inside' the problem, thinking about it and empathising with the characters of the story being told. It enables readers or inquirers to share the experience, using their own reserves of knowledge and experience to make sense of its structure and its lineaments. It offers everything that is beneficial in the 'show, don't tell' that Sennett (2009) promotes (I discuss Sennett's ideas further in Chapter 9).

I can give an example from some research I did with some newly qualified dentists who were required to conduct a case study as part of their first year in practice. During that first year, dentists are carefully monitored by both the senior practitioners in the dental practice that employs them and the dental faculty of the university covering the geographical region in which they work. As part of this postgraduate professional development, they attend university one day a week and are supervised in their own dental practice by a mentor (one of the practice dentists), who, in turn, has recourse to one of the university tutors if necessary.

The newly qualified dentists thus have to engage in a whole range of further training and supervised practice. Each element of this postgraduate work has to demonstrate that important activities have been covered and show how professional development will continue so that the dentists in question can prove that they are able to keep up to date as their careers progress. The case study has to illustrate an aspect of this professional development.

The case study is a form of inquiry that is especially well suited to these needs at this stage in the dentists' careers. They have all done the important basics in their undergraduate work at university and shown their competence in these basics. As they start real work on real people, their needs become more individual, with a more individually tailored programme of postgraduate work necessary for each.

So, a starting point was that each case study in the year's cohort of young dentists was always likely to be different from the next one: there is idiosyncrasy in the work of each one. The study could take one of many forms – the use of a particular piece of equipment, a week in the working life of the practice receptionist, the use of X-ray equipment by the practice, a particular patient's experience and so on. The only proviso was that the case study should in some way exemplify and demonstrate the learning that had happened on the course in the postgraduate professional year. Clearly not everything could be covered, so it was specified that the case study should focus on and illustrate two of the five main areas covered in the postgraduate work – areas such as business skills, clinical skills, patient psychology and control of infection.

Nav was one of the cohort of newly qualified dentists. He and his field tutor decided that, in his circumstances, the case study would focus on one new patient's experience following her acceptance by the practice. The purpose of the case study would be to concentrate especially on two aspects of professional practice, as outlined by the expectations of the course. These two aspects would be business skills and patient psychology.

Nav first had to make absolutely sure that his case study of his patient 'Hannah' was ethical, with Hannah giving her informed consent to the use of the information relating to her case (this is discussed more fully on pages 83–5). He planned for the case study to both demonstrate knowledge that had been acquired and illustrate how this knowledge had been used with Hannah. To draw the maximum benefit from this (and to gain the highest marks) Nav would attempt to draw out problematic aspects of the case to exemplify how the problem had been overcome or indicate where there was a systemic problem – that is to say, a problem to do with the system that had been set up in the practice.

Nav started by looking for ways in which he could gain purchase on Hannah's experience. Available to him were the practice records of appointments, letters and e-mails and his own records as a new dentist. He planned to supplement these records with two sets of interviews – one with Hannah herself and another with his mentor, Jayne, who happened to be a senior partner in the practice. As an important part of patient communication, Nav also planned to look at the practice leaflets and other publicity and how these were dovetailed (or weren't) with phone calls and e-mails. With all of these Nav hoped to secure leverage on Hannah's experience and 'drill down' (no pun intended) into this. With the information, he would be able to not only illustrate his own connection with and understanding of the practice but also, if possible, offer signposts for improvement in the practice's work and his own.

Nav started by drawing a storyboard, as shown in Figure 8.6. On the left-hand side of the storyboard are some points Nav planned to address concerning his business planning module, and on the right are some features relating to patient psychology.

Given that he was new to the practice and Hannah was also new, he felt it appropriate to look at the practice's 'front of house' habits, as well as its methods for acquiring new patients and finding out about their needs. Much of this questioning could be done in a structured interview. Richer information – for example, about the demeanour of staff and their willingness to help – could be gathered in an unstructured rather than a structured interview.

On the right-hand side of the diagram are the issues to do with patient psychology and whether or not the practice adequately handles this, offering help and support where necessary, both in the person-to-person contacts that happen immediately on coming through the door and in the general ambience of the place. Are there flowers around? Are there comforting pictures (rather than posters of molars, exposed nerves and adverts for teeth whitening)? Are there large notices about the dire consequences of not turning up to appointments? Is Mozart playing calmingly in the background or can you hear the mosquito-like whine of drills behind doors? That kind of thing.

For both sides of the diagram, the case study is an ideal form of inquiry, for it provides, if it is done properly, the kind of data that will not be gained from other kinds of inquiry. It provides:

- a useful means of addressing the needs of the professional development activity that Nav is undertaking

- a source of rich and valuable information, telling of a patient's experience at the practice in depth and providing temporal continuity (how it was over time) and enabling a connection between different sides of the phenomenon under study (note the dotted line in Figure 8.6)

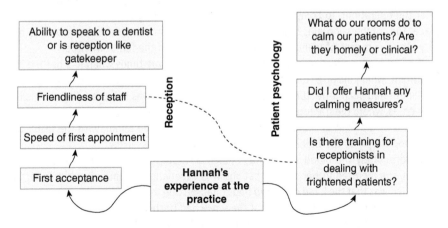

Figure 8.6   Storyboard of Nav's illustrative case study

(Continued)

(Continued)

- a source of readily understandable feedback so people will be able to use the information to improve the service – the case study is on a 'human scale' and, for those working with people, provides access to the kinds of complex emotions and their relationship with each other that other kinds of research often fail to communicate.

It may not be Goffmanesque in the beauty of its analysis or in the depth of its insight, but this illustrative case study did lead to better understanding and development of the dental practice.

A much simpler example of an illustrative case study is that used in medical training or the reporting of unusual medical occurrences. An unusual feature may provide a stimulus for further research or an instructive example for the training of medical staff. Here is a brief example of the latter.

Mrs Smith is a 58-year-old woman who fell and broke her hip. She was admitted to hospital and given the usual treatment for this, which is an operation to install something called a dynamic hip screw. This is, essentially, a long metal bolt that has been bent so that the top part can be screwed into the top of the hip (the ball part), while the end of the bolt is, in turn, screwed in to the top of the femur (the long leg bone) with three, four or five screws. The dynamic hip screw thus holds together the broken bone at the hip. Because it is made to be 'squashable' (technical term), the dynamic hip screw allows the weight of the person's body, when standing (which is encouraged almost straight away after the operation), to compress the fracture, while holding the whole arrangement in place. The compression aids healing, and the dynamic hip screw has been shown to be a very effective means of mending a broken hip or a top-of-the-femur fracture.

While it is very effective in most circumstances, there are times when it is not the best treatment, which include when the hip is broken high up, beyond the neck of the femur. Mrs Smith had such a fracture, yet the dynamic hip screw was still used. The problem in such cases, where the fracture occurs just below the ball of the 'ball and socket' of the hip joint, is that the 'ball' is separated from the main part of the femur, with the result that the blood supply to the ball is disrupted, making healing less likely.

Unfortunately the blood supply was indeed disrupted in Mrs Smith's case. After ten months, she reported to her doctor that she was experiencing pain in her hip. What had happened was that the head of the hip had collapsed due to lack of blood (or 'avascularity', as doctors like to call it) and the end of the screw had pushed through the ball, damaging the inside part of the pelvis – the concave part, known as the acetabulum, into which the ball fits. Because of this, Mrs Smith suffered a great deal of pain and had to have another operation to fix the problems arising from the initial decision to install a dynamic hip screw. The second operation involved something called a hemiarthroplasty – half hip replacement, in which just the ball part of the joint is replaced, not the socket (in a total hip replacement, the socket is also replaced).

The conclusion for this case can be found at www.gla.ac.uk/t4/~fbls/files/fab/tutorial/clinical/orcs2.html, but the key point was as follows:

> This case illustrates why a replacement femoral head (hemiarthroplasty) is the current recommended treatment for a type III subcapital fracture [a break to the femoral neck]. The ... patient in this case study ultimately required a total hip replacement, her second major operation after the initial unsuccessful attempted fixation. With hindsight, a hemiarthroplasty would have resulted in a much more favourable outcome.

This case study illustrates why it is necessary to take into account the location of the fracture when decisions are made about the nature of the remedial action that should be taken to fix the problem. This is, if you like, the analytic frame or object (see pages 15–17). It demonstrates what can go wrong and why, as well as being instructive for practitioners, bringing a theoretical set of issues to life.

In medicine, illustrative case studies can also be used to reveal a new or unfamiliar set of issues, a new syndrome or a promising new technique, yet to be trialled for its efficacy with a larger number of people. With any kind of inquiry, it may also be added to a larger piece of research to exemplify a theme or illustrate an aspect of the analysis.

Case studies are also often used in the teaching or explication of the law. As in medicine, they also tend to be illustrative. A good website for viewing some US legal cases is Stanford Law School's Case Studies Collection (available at: https://www.law.stanford.edu/organizations/programs-and-centers/environmental-and-natural-resources-law-policy-program-enrlp/case-studies).

Another good website for illustrative case studies is provided by the Thames Valley Energy Agency (available at: www.tvenergy.org/case-studies.htm). There you will find a collection of 24 renewable energy projects. Through a wide variety of case studies, it demonstrates how different kinds of solutions can be found to the challenge of providing sustainable energy for domestic, community and industrial premises.

Interpretative

Often, when a case study is written about in the academic literature, what is being discussed is an *interpretative* case study. This is, if you like, the 'classic' approach to doing a case study. This is not to deny the importance and significance of the other approaches I have talked about so far, but the aims of a case study and the style of interpretative inquiry dovetail together very nicely. For this reason, I shall go into this approach in rather more detail than the previous ones.

Interpretative inquiry is a form of inquiry that employs a particular approach to answering questions – an approach that assumes an in-depth understanding and deep immersion in the environment of the subject. You can probably see why, then, I have said that the case study and interpretative inquiry are natural bedfellows, since each calls for rich, intensive understanding. I should go further: they are not only natural bedfellows but also obvious marriage partners. They were made for each other: it's love and marriage – and they go together like a horse and carriage. Each demands a deep understanding of the multifaceted nature of social situations, so they complement each other and seem natural with each other.

This kind of approach is often called *ethnographic*, so a case study using such an approach may be called an *ethnography*. The word 'ethnography' is from the Greek *ethnos*, meaning folk or people, so ethnography literally means 'study of folk'. It was used first in a field of social research that emerged in the early part of the twentieth century as a branch of anthropology.

Before the new ethnographers, anthropologists had done their work by treating people as objects of study, as dispassionately as a biologist might study an insect. Displacing this style of work, the new ethnography aimed to get to the heart of people's understandings of life by doing fieldwork *with* them rather than supposedly objective study *of* them. One could, interestingly in relation to the case study, say that they aimed to reach what is summed up by the Latin phrase *casus anima*, which roughly translates as 'the soul of the case' or 'the heart of the matter'; they aimed to reach an understanding of what makes the person or people tick.

So the ethnographers aimed to get right into the centre of the cultures with which they worked by becoming members of those cultures. They would actually live with the people and try to understand their culture *from within*. It was as if the earlier anthropologists were taking callipers and rulers to measure the people they were looking at, while the ethnographers, by contrast, thought that the best tool for the study of other human beings was themselves, as fellow human beings.

The ethnographers, therefore – people such as Bronisław Malinowski, who in 1914 went to live among the Trobriand Islanders of the Western Pacific – suggested that, instead of trying to distance yourself from your subjects of study, you should, as a social scientist, get as close as possible by becoming a participant in their cultures. Try to understand them as a person yourself, by being a *participant observer*. Forget about any pretence at objectiveness; don't deny that you are a person, pretending that you can see things objectively. This is never possible, said the ethnographers. Not only is it impossible, it simultaneously throws away one of your ready-made strengths as an inquirer among people. That strength is you – yourself – which has to be your watchword in doing the kind of case study that I am talking about here.

The ethnographers influenced, and in turn were influenced by, the thought of a group of social scientists in the 1920s and 1930s who said that the world in which we are interested as social scientists is not straightforwardly perceivable in the way that the world of chemicals is perceived by chemists. We cannot view it like this because it is constructed by each of us in a different way. It's not simply 'out there'; it is different for each of us. It cannot therefore be adequately studied using the methods of the natural scientists (such as physicists and chemists), with talk of variables and quantification – a wholly different mindset and set of procedures is needed for inquiring into it. This view came to be called *interpretivism*.

This approach to social study caught on like wildfire and spawned a range of fascinating, in-depth ethnographies in the middle of the twentieth century, such as *Street Corner Society* by William Foote Whyte (1955/1993). For more than three years, Whyte lived in a slum district of Boston, populated largely by Italian immigrants. He lived among and with the people and documented how young men became either 'corner boys' or 'college boys'. It is interesting to look at the way in which Whyte reflected on *theory* in doing this, because it might be said that this kind of interpretative case study is inherently about building a theory. By interpreting people's words and behaviour, the ethnographer is building theory out of the naked, raw data that is available.

At the time of collection, of data gathering, this data has no 'theory': it is rough and crude, without shape or form. What the interpreter has to do is *build* a theory and an object from it. Whyte (1985: 21), in his own reflection on the process, is quite guarded about this building of theory or 'theorisation', putting it this way: 'what kind of theory can one develop – or to what existing body of theory can one contribute? I have found myself focusing on the *concrete behavior* of individuals, groups, and organizations' (emphasis added).

By talking about 'concrete behaviour', Whyte is drawing a distinction between this and theory, for the latter may seem removed from the real, practical world. He clarifies by going on to say that he seeks a 'conceptual framework that will strengthen my power of understanding and interpreting behavior and organizations across a wide range of social situations'.

It is important to keep this 'framework' notion in mind when thinking about the theory that you develop as part of an interpretative

> Interpretative researchers assume that the social world is indivisible. It is complex and we should study it in its completeness. In this sense, interpretative research marries easily with case study, which also prioritises looking at the whole.

inquiry. This 'theory' is something that is used for the purposes of your study. It is not an immovable and immutable thing that you are establishing, forever to be embedded in the canon of social scientific inquiry. Rather, it is what the sociologist Pierre Bourdieu (in Wacquant, 1989, cited in Jenkins, 1992: 67) called a 'thinking tool'. As he put it:

> There is no doubt a theory in my work, or, better, a set of *thinking tools*
> visible through the results they yield, but it is not built as such … It is a
> temporary construct which takes shape for and by empirical work.

So, the kind of theory that we are looking for is more a temporary 'conceptual framework' or 'thinking tool' than it is an abstraction in its own right and for its own purpose. It should not be an intellectual barricade, to be defended against all-comers. Rather, it should help you to think about and understand the subject in hand. It can be held, tested and then discarded or retained depending on its usefulness.

It's important to remember that some social scientists, in the bad old days, wished to develop what has come to be called 'grand theory'. In the words of *The Hitchhiker's Guide to the Galaxy*, these are theories of 'life, the universe and everything'. It is now generally accepted that that kind of theory is unattainable and it is not useful to try and establish it. In fact, the attempt to establish it has probably done social science a good deal of harm, as the grand theory that is set up is often wildly misleading.

I can give as an example of an interpretative case study a piece of work that I conducted while I was a parent governor of the secondary school that my daughters attended:

I was able to be a participant in the situation of being a governor (since I actually was one) and didn't feel the need to try and stand separately from it, observing from outside. I was a governor, feeling what a governor felt, seeing what a governor saw and hearing what a governor heard.

I recorded my reflections on this process in a diary that I kept over a period of several months in the role. Although I also made observations and conducted interviews, it was this diary that was the principal instrument of my data gathering. Here is a sample of my diary, to give a flavour of the kinds of reflections that I was making and the use I made of them in subsequent 'theorisation'.

The Chair pushes us on to the question of minutes – how they should be written and how they should be presented to the full governors' meeting. I think this has been raised because Walter [one of the governors] insists at each full meeting on reading out his minutes in full and adding long, drawn-out embellishments about things like the lintel over the door in the boys' toilets needing replacing. It's extraordinary that he never seems to detect any humour in the absurdity of the trivia he raises. Chair presents a solution to the problem of needing to get through the subcommittee reports more quickly. He suggests that we have items reported in the minutes that have either one star or two stars, relating to whether they need a full discussion at the full meeting or are simply reported on. Walter seems to get the wrong end of the stick and keeps trying to find examples of one-star and two-star items, delivering them portentously to the group as though he's just discovered the meaning of life. Chair looks at him a little limply as he does this, clearly not sure how to respond: whether to put him straight, tell him to shut up or simply let him carry on until he stops. He decides on the last of these options and we're all therefore forced to listen to Walter droning on with more examples of one-star and two-star items delivered at about one word every five seconds. He obviously thinks that the slower he speaks, the more gravitas he has. Chairing for boring, inconsequential, dull or plain stupid people is clearly a problem in this kind of forum (or in most kinds of forum). The trouble is that we're all such nice people, we don't want to offend the feelings of others – and this is especially so when we are fully aware in this kind of setting (that is, as governors) that we're all working voluntarily and out of the goodness of our hearts. You don't want to discourage people or seem to be denying or downplaying the quality or value of their contribution. It's doubly a problem, though, when the body is taking on quasi-management roles and there is the need to be a little more disciplined about the machinery that makes things happen. If that discipline doesn't exist (or exists badly) there's the possibility the machinery will become completely gummed up.

How can this be turned into interpretation and theory? In other words, how can an analytical frame be established? It's important to note that the diary I was keeping was not simply 'this happened ... then that happened ... then this happened ... and so on'. Rather, it was my reflections on the topic in hand, with a critical edge to the commentary. It's not, as the great anthropologist Clifford Geertz (1975: 9) put it, as if I was merely a 'cipher clerk' in making these recordings. Although you cannot perhaps appreciate it from this diary entry on its own, my attempt in doing this case study was to look at the ability of governors to fulfil a role that the government at the time had set them, which was to act almost as managerial overseers – with a slice of 'voice of the people' twisted in. In this particular diary entry, I was saying something about the ability of school governors to fulfil this role. The key idea coming through in this entry is of amateurism, of not being able to fulfil this role. This can perhaps be seen better in the next excerpt from the diary:

The premises subcommittee report is another matter. The report is prefaced by Walter saying that he will be extremely brief – and obviously he intends to be and starts talking quite fast (for him). This only lasts about 15 seconds, though, and eventually he's back on form, talking in his slow overly loud drawl – he obviously thinks that public people should talk like this, as though they are addressing a council chamber. Citizen Kane syndrome. We spiral down into the depths of the lintel over G31 and worse. There is some discussion of the costs of allowing the free use of the hall and gym by the community and Walter produces some figures that purport to show how much it is all costing us. Another member questions the

(Continued)

(Continued)

figures, saying that Walter has completely miscalculated. He's quite right – the calculations are based on the cost of heating and lighting for the whole year rather than the very limited times of community use. This sends Walter into a paroxysm of waffle and as usual there is no decision made.

It isn't just that these are well-meaning amateurs dabbling and making ill-informed decisions. It isn't simply a random collection of members of the community. People join the governing body for a variety of reasons – sometimes because they want to try to improve things since their own children are in the school and no doubt for other good reasons, but sometimes it's because they are self-important and pompous and, wanting to get into public life, they end up on governing bodies. It's these people who can do the damage.

There are some blatant clues here as to the constructs that I was building. For a start, I use the phrase 'well-meaning amateurs', which is hardly a covert or disguised expression of my views. It needs little interpretation. There are, however, more interesting comments about the nature of the enterprise in which governors are occupied.

First, I make a comment about the sort of language and kind of delivery that Walter is using – it is of an innocent amateur playing at being a professional. Then, there is his error in calculating the costs of heating and lighting. The error is serious, not only for the consequences it might have had on policy (excluding community use of the school facilities) but also for the effects it had on the work of senior management in the school.

My subsequent thinking – my 'theorisation' – about the diary commentary was that government policy, by mistrusting professionals, had produced a 'double whammy'. It had not only displaced the professionals from their proper role but also wasted the professionals' time as they then had to intervene and sort out the mess that the amateurs like Walter were creating.

A stronger narrative around trust, professionalism and the audit culture could be made of this. It could even be linked with an idea such as that of Richard Sennett's (2009) in his book *The Craftsman*, where he suggests that much of the lack of purpose, the anomie, of modern life is about the dismissal of the craft of the tradesperson and the professional – whether the craft is that of an architect, teacher, X-ray technician or zookeeper. Too many of today's crafts are made insipid and trivial, argues Sennett, not only as a result of the intervention of machines and computers but also, even more importantly, because of the procedures that remove the care, skill, pride and dedication from our craft.

Using this insight, I could – for theorising my argument – 'step sideways' and look at what enfeebles and belittles the craft of teachers, removes their professional judgement, their trust in themselves to be making the right decision. I could try to show in this case study how the simple policy decision taken at government level filters down and expresses itself on the ground, in the staffroom and the governing body. Thus, a naïve feeling about woolly-minded, progressive, liberal teachers from a politician travels from cabinet room to civil servants' meeting, to regulations implemented at local authority level, to the meeting of a governing body where a pompous and unqualified governor behaves naïvely and endangers community involvement and wastes professionals' time. Thus, a nice circle could be drawn showing the connections from initial high-level naïvety to ultimate ground-level naïvety.

The case study in this circumstance could be either building or testing a theory, depending on how I had framed it at the beginning, but the important point, as far as this section is concerned, is that interpretation is being used. The germ of the idea at the outset could be about policy decisions and their journey from idea (the idea of the politician or whoever) to action. You collect data about this journey and make interpretations about what is happening along the way.

Experimental

When people talk about case studies, the experiment is probably the last thing that comes into their minds. We assume that a case study is about singularity and depth, whereas an experiment is about large numbers, control and comparing this group with that. This assumption, however, while *partly* correct when talking of experiments is *only* partly so.

Certainly, an experiment is a particular kind of research design where ideas are being tested under controlled conditions, but, in everyday language, 'to experiment' has a much looser meaning. It can just mean to try something out, and so 'an experiment' could be simply a little trial of some kind. So, I might say 'I'm going to do a little experiment' if I choose one day to try putting my milk in my tea before rather than after the hot water to see if the tea tastes better the new way. (I did try it and it doesn't.)

When approaching certain kinds of questions for case studies, we can take the systematicity of the experiment and graft it on to our expectations of a case study. This requires a particular kind of experiment, though. Before going into this – into the kind of experiment that might be used in case study – let me say a little more about experiments and how we can think about them.

In the natural sciences (chemistry and physics, for example), to experiment means something more precise than it does in the vernacular. It means to test an idea under controlled conditions to prove or falsify an idea, a conjecture, a hypothesis. Robert Hooke in 1676 had an idea about elasticity in springs and he tested this idea systematically under controlled conditions, stretching the springs with weights and recording the consequences. He was able to emerge from his experiments with what became known as Hooke's Law, which says that how far a spring extends is in direct proportion to the load added to it.

Ordinarily in the social sciences, experiments are rather different from Hooke's in the natural sciences. Usually, social scientists are trying to establish whether or not something causes something else to happen. Does X cause Y? Does the introduction of a new science curriculum cause an improvement in students' understanding of science, for example? The only way to find out with any sort of validity in social science is to do an experiment.

This has to be done using special procedures and having a particular kind of mindset about the social world that is rather different from that adopted when doing interpretative research of the kind described in the previous section. This mindset is that we can look at this world as comprising a set of variables (that is, things which vary), such as age, sex, amount of pocket money, income, credit history, educational background and so on.

This may not seem too contentious, for we have all become familiar with the methods of social science and we have all got used to these assumptions about variables. We realise that they may be related to one another. We understand that clusters of variables tend to vary together, so, for example, income is related to educational background, which is related to educational attainment.

> Though case study is not normally associated with experimental work, you may choose to include some kind of experiment as part of your study. If so, you will probably choose a design that enables you to use the subject as their own 'control' – an '$n = 1$' design.

The mere acknowledgement and observation of variables for some kinds of social science inquiry is different, though, from actually trying to do things with those variables systematically – manipulating them – in the way that natural scientists do. The essential trouble is that the social world comprises such a 'blooming buzzing confusion' – as the nineteenth-century psychologist William James (1890/1981) put it – that it is sometimes impossible to know what the relevant variables might be.

Imagine that you are looking at a classroom full of children, a teacher and an assistant. What are the relevant variables here that you would need to be aware of if you wanted to observe the classroom under controlled conditions (that is to say, controlling for the important conditions)? If I tried, I could think of hundreds of potentially relevant variables: the variation in the ages of the children, the colour of the walls, the direction of the light, the heating in the room, the presence or not of a certain naughty boy, the hungriness of the teacher (depending on whether or not she had to skip her breakfast that morning), the kind of work the children are doing, the educational background of the teaching assistant and so on.

We can potentially change any of these things and, in a perfect world, control for all of the others. The trouble is, though, that we are *not* in a perfect world and we *can't* control for all of them (or even most of them), and we don't even know which ones we *should* be controlling. We can guess, certainly, but there is a strong chance that we may be wrong. There is also the problem, as the psychologist Jacob Kounin (1970) noted, that the classroom is like an ecology: you can't change one aspect of it without some unexpected consequence. So, if you take out the naughty boy – let's call him Kyle – you may find that another member of the class takes over Kyle's role. Playing with variables in a social situation is a bit like squeezing a balloon – it will bulge somewhere else.

So a preliminary, cautionary note is needed when we are talking about a manipulation of the variables of the classroom – and an experiment demands such manipulation. It makes the assumption that all of the variables can be manipulated and, when we manipulate them, we can look to see how this manipulation has had an effect on other variables.

In its simplest form, an experiment seeks to isolate two variables – the one that you assume may cause change (such as the science curriculum) and the one you are assuming may change as a result (the understanding of science, in the example that we have been using) – from the myriad that might be at play in a situation. Beyond this, there is a vast superstructure of kinds of experiments that are built on this very simple basic assumption, but we do not need to go into them here as it would be most unusual, if not impossible, to find some of these designs incorporated into a case study.

What kinds of experiment, then, can be done in a case study? Well, the case study has to conform to the basic idea of what a case study is, which is a study of one thing. Interestingly, research specialists who are clever with numbers have a special way of saying 'one thing', which is '$n = 1$'. I can already feel the adrenaline beginning to flow into the veins of some of my readers as I include an equals sign in the text. I know that you might be saying to yourself, 'I thought by doing a case study that I was going to be able to avoid equations and statistics.'

Well, you shouldn't think that way. The method you choose should be the servant of your research question and if your research question demands an inquiry that uses numbers and simple statistics, it is these you should use. People's fear of statistics is often completely groundless, and the kinds of statistics that you need for this kind of study is actually quite simple. I look briefly at these in *How to Do Your Research Project* (Thomas, 2013).

The usual form, the classic experiment (see Table 8.1), in the social science situation, involves two or more groups being treated in exactly the same way, except for the manipulation of one variable. So, the procedure is to bring in an extra group, as alike as possible to the first group, and give them everything that the first group had so we can eliminate sources of variation between the groups – every source of variation except the one we are deliberately varying. Any differences that then exist between the two groups after the manipulation is made to happen by the experimenter are taken to exist because of the experimental treatment.

Table 8.1   The classic experiment

	Pre-test	Treatment	Post-test
Experiment group	✐ Take first measure	✓ Give treatment	✐ Take second measure
Control group	✐ Take first measure	✗ Don't give treatment	✐ Take second measure

There is another form of experiment, however, that is especially appropriate for case studies since, in this form, you can look experimentally at change within one situation, such as the members of a classroom. This form is called the *repeated measures design.*

Whereas with the classic form of experiment you are comparing the experimental group with the control group, in the repeated measures (or crossover) design there is no second group used. Instead, the control comes from the group itself, with the 'change' being imposed by the difference in one of the variables. I won't go into the technicalities of the design here, since the explanation of how a repeated measures design is used can be quite complicated and you can find more details elsewhere (see, for example, Field, 2013). I shall simply focus on how and why this procedure is appropriate for a case study. You will have noticed that I said 'the control comes from the group itself', so we are back to our one thing. The main condition of the case study is therefore satisfied.

Let me give an example (loosely based on Cremin et al., 2005) of how a case study might incorporate a little experiment of this kind.

Alyssa is interested in the way that additional adults – teaching assistants (or aides), parents and volunteers – are working in her classroom because it seems to her that something is going wrong. The adults are not working effectively with each other, sometimes getting in the way of each other, and certainly not communicating effectively.

Her first task is to set down a question and draw a storyboard that might begin to sketch out some lines of inquiry that could be addressed (see Figure 8.7).

Alyssa has one permanent teaching assistant and two parent volunteers who come in every morning. The management and organisation of this kind of assistance was not part of her teacher-training curriculum, so Alyssa has read the literature and found that there are a number of ways of thinking about how extra assistance of this kind can be deployed. One method is called 'room management' (Cremin et al., 2005) and involves giving each adult a set of very specific tasks to do (such as predominantly helping individuals or groups), those tasks constituting a named role. The roles can be changed from session to session, but the main thing is that each individual knows which role he or she is supposed to be fulfilling.

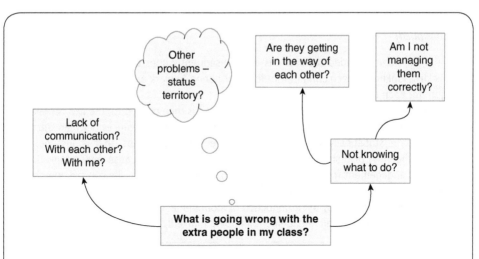

Figure 8.7 Storyboard leading to an *n* = 1 experiment

Alyssa thinks that this method of organisation holds some promise and hopes it will provide some structure for her work with other adults in her class. Rather than simply trying it out and proceeding according to a gut feeling about whether or not the new system of organisation seems to work, she does a small experiment. This involves a repeated measures design where the one group (Alyssa's class) is examined under two circumstances, or conditions – the only change being to the system of organisation in her class. In the first condition Alyssa and the other adults work normally; in the second, the only change is that they will use the room management system of organisation.

To assess the effect of this change, Alyssa decides to measure the children's engagement with their work – in other words, to look at whether or not they do what they are supposed to do, so certain behaviours, such as sitting and writing, will count as 'on-task', while others, such as wandering around the class, will count as 'off-task'. By drawing up a list of on-task and off-task behaviours and observing for these systematically, Alyssa can measure what happens in the class under the two conditions.

The experiment requires organisation that will take many features of the situation into consideration. Alyssa first has to plan when the observations will take place under the two conditions. Because the two conditions must be identical apart from the change in the system of organisation, she has to ensure that the same kind of work is being done by the children and the same people are there with her class for both periods of observation. They also have to be at the same time of day and even, if possible, on the same days of the week, for these are also sources of variation that could plausibly make a difference. Then she has to train the assistant and parents in the room-management system and schedule the sessions. She also has to arrange for observations to take place to test the effect of the system on the dependent variable – children's engagement or 'on-taskness'. She decides to organise this by asking another parent who regularly assists

(Continued)

(Continued)

in the classroom to video the sessions and subsequently goes through the video with a checklist, looking at each child in turn for a set period to work out an on-task percentage figure for each of them.

Each child's overall engagement (or 'on-taskness') is then plotted for the two occasions. Using some simple statistics, Alyssa is able to show that the differences between the two occasions *are* statistically significant. Simply 'eyeballing' the chart (that is, just looking at it intelligently) also shows a number of interesting things. Because Alyssa ranked the children's engagement from lowest to highest in the first condition, she can see how those who are at the lower end of the scale – that is to say, those children who find most difficulty attending – *are* affected by the introduction of room management. The chart clearly shows that, for most of them, their engagement improves markedly over the two conditions.

Such an experimental approach would not be sufficient, in my opinion, for a thorough case study. A thorough case study is one in which we are aiming to gain that polyhedron of understanding mentioned before – looking at a thing from all sides, from the top and bottom. While most of the examples I have used so far do indeed, in some shape or form, take such a multifaceted view, the experimental method *on its own* does not, because it seeks to enumerate and control variables. Added to other sources of information, however, a case study of this kind may well add an invaluable dimension to that polyhedron.

If you take only one thing from this chapter, take this ...

Beyond a subject and an analytical frame for your case study, you will need to decide on the kind of *approach* to take when collecting data and analysing them. The approach you take will be shaped by the firmness of the ideas you have formulated at the outset:

- If, on the one hand, you start with a firm idea or set of premises, you could be said to be *testing* a theory.

- If, on the other hand, you prefer to see what ideas emerge as you immerse yourself in the situation you are studying, you could be said to be *building* a theory.

- Alternatively, you may simply be aiming to *illustrate* something.

Beyond these broad divisions of approaches to case study research, you can pick and mix to create the approach you want to take. So, you may choose to take:

- an interpretative approach as a participant observer, or

- a more formally experimental approach to some aspect of your study, or

- you may decide to do both.

Remember that the case study is like a wrapper: within it, the shape of the study is determined by your question and your purposes.

FURTHER READING 📖

Eisenhardt, K. and Graebner, K.M. (2007) 'Theory building from cases: opportunities and challenges', *Academy of Management Journal*, 50 (1): 25–32.
Despite its recency, this is a highly traditional, but very solid and well-explicated account of theory and the case study's contribution to it, written from the point of view of management science.

Field, A. (2013) *Discovering Statistics Using SPSS* (4th edn). London: Sage.
This really tackles research from the point of view of statistics and, if you do an experiment as part of your case study, it will be invaluable – not least because it is presented via the main software package used in the social sciences, SPSS. If you are doing a study of the kind I have suggested in this chapter, look especially for *non-parametric* tests, such as the Mann–Whitney test and the Wilcoxon rank-sum test.

Geertz, C. (1975) *The Interpretation of Cultures*. London: Hutchinson.
Read this for the discussion of 'thick description' (see also Chapter 11 below). Also, try Googling "Geertz deep play notes on the Balinese cockfight" for an example of Geertz actually doing anthropology and thick description.

Goffman, E. (1956) *The Presentation of Self in Everyday Life*. Edinburgh: University of Edinburgh.
The clue's in the title: it's about how we present ourselves ... er ... in everyday life. We do so as actors, performing a series of roles on different stages. It's worth reading even if you don't do a case study.

Hoyle, R.H. (1999) *Statistical Strategies for Small Sample Research*. Thousand Oaks, CA: Sage.
Not on case studies per se, but relevant.

Malinowski, B. (1922) *Argonauts of the Western Pacific*. London: Routledge & Kegan Paul.
Malinowski, B. (1982) 'The diary of an anthropologist', in R.G. Burgess (ed.), *Field Research: A Sourcebook and Field Manual*. London: George Allen & Unwin.
Between 1915 and 1918, Malinowski studied the Trobriand Islanders of the South Pacific. He broke new ground in the way he went about understanding people as fellow human beings rather than as objects of study and, in doing this, he helped to establish the ethnographic tradition. He was a participant observer, keeping a diary of his observations, and his analyses were pioneering in their use of an interpretative approach.

Spradley, J.P. (1980) *Participant Observation*. New York: Holt.
This is a beautifully organised account of the process of ethnography from a master of
the genre.

Thomas, G. (2007) *Education and Theory: Strangers in Paradigms*. Maidenhead: Open
    University Press.
Here, I go into some detail (possibly too much) on the meaning of theory and what it
can offer to researchers.

Whyte, W.F. (1985) *Learning from the Field: A Guide from Experience*. Beverly Hills, CA:
    Sage.
This covers just about everything that an interpretative researcher could wish to know.

YOUR PROCESS: THE SHAPE, STYLE AND MANNER OF YOUR CASE STUDY

How will you go about structuring your case study? What I am talking about here is the style and manner of your study – whether you are doing a case study of one individual or several and, if the latter, whether they are all done at once or one after the other, whether you will separate out nested elements of the single case for special examination or look back at events that have happened in the past or collect data as time proceeds (or both). We will focus in this chapter on the nuts and bolts of the study, as summarised in Figure 9.1.

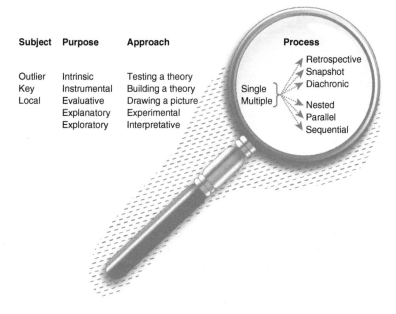

Figure 9.1   The process as part of the design route

The single case

The single case could be called the classic form of the case study. When people think about case studies, they think of one person – a doctor's patient, for example, or a child in a school or, perhaps, a classic legal case. The single thing is studied for the lineaments of its structure, its character, with the emphasis on understanding what is going on, taking one of the approaches I have already described.

The focus, when choosing the single case study, has to be on the characteristics that give it some interest. Let's imagine an example:

Let's imagine that you are a political science student doing a master's degree in security studies. One of your taught courses has been on terrorism and – this having interested you – you wish to follow it up by concentrating on terrorism for your dissertation.

You do some reading and thinking about terrorism to try and shape your ideas, and realise that nearly all terrorism is related to the work of well-organised groups of varying sizes and forms, each with causes that inspire loyalty from a significant proportion of some defined population with a perceived grievance of some kind. The groups that manage to commit terrorist acts successfully do so because they evade detection by the authorities. You decide to make this the key angle of your inquiry – the lever that you will use to force open the issue – and your research question is geared towards it.

You draw your storyboard, which expresses your basic question, 'How do terrorists escape detection?', as shown in Figure 9.2. In it, you sketch out some ideas to follow up.

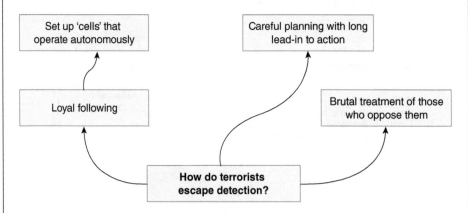

Figure 9.2   Terrorism storyboard

So, you have a question, but there are still a number of options open to you concerning the route that would offer the most illuminating avenues for tackling it. You could, for example, first try to group terrorist acts in some way to see if they shared any characteristics. Then, using information in the public domain, you might pick a couple of these groups to focus on, looking for clues as to how they evaded detection by the security services. While this would be instructive, it would not be likely to offer much data that would provide an enlightening analysis. Really, on the question of evading the authorities, something richer that taps a variety of sources and aims to knit them together is likely to be more helpful. In other words, a case study.

Once you have come to this conclusion, you are at the stage of explaining why a case study would be valuable in the circumstances of your current knowledge and the question that you have sketched out. Your expectation is that a case study of a particular terrorist incident will offer more insight into this question than a range of other approaches. By enabling you to focus in depth, a case study will mean that you can draw out the lines of reasoning, to see the possible strands of causality at play.

You decide to focus on a terrorist incident that will provide a good deal of detail about the people involved in it. The availability of data on the backgrounds of the people involved is the key issue here. Once you have chosen an attack, what might you do to look at how it evaded the gaze of authority? Remembering that the case study is singled out by its emphasis on the richness of the individual account or narrative, you might choose to focus on one of the terrorists in a particular terrorist cell. You could focus on all of them and treat the attack itself as 'the case', but this would necessarily reduce the richness of each terrorist's history and situation. With the depth provided by one account, you can look at a great deal of detail: you can look at the childhood of the terrorist, his education, his early adulthood and his friends – was he a loner or did he have lots of friends? You can look at the reasons for his attraction to fringe religious sects and, ultimately, groups of people who were connected with Al Qaeda.

This initial inquiry might tell you a number of things. It might point, for example, to his childhood in a wealthy family and his upbringing in a British private school, where he developed an especially aggravated feeling of difference and alienation from his host culture. This might give you a clue to his resentment of authority and Western culture and his willingness to engage in acts of this kind. More relevantly for the dimension of escaping capture by the authorities, it might point to a familiarity with isolation and a predilection for 'keeping his head down', avoiding notice by keeping quiet. There is a range of strategies that could be involved in such a way of dealing with life – not getting yourself noticed by being naughty or, indeed, by being particularly good, not volunteering, always fitting in and going along with the majority. In school life, such strategies are easily developed. You could point out how easily such strategies might transfer to life in the adult world.

Then there is the issue of identity – the need for belonging. Having been brought up feeling an outsider, such a need would be particularly exaggerated – he would want to feel what the political scientist Robert Putnam (2000) calls *social capital*. He would want to feel part of a club – not literally a club, like a bridge club or a tennis club, but a group of people who are brought together by a common aim and feeling a sense of togetherness. Not getting this from his host culture – indeed, feeling alienated from

(Continued)

(Continued)

it – he would be vulnerable to all kinds of approaches from those who could offer such an identity.

Always remember to keep your question at the front of your mind when building an interesting pen picture such as this, as it is all too easy to get distracted and go off on a tangent that is not related to your question. Here, your question is about evading detection. How could you use the pen picture you are developing to help you answer this question? Well, the need to feel part of a club might lead a person to particularly strongly bonded groups – groups with a powerful sense of identity. Going back to Robert Putnam for a theoretical framework, he uses the distinction between what he calls 'bridging' and 'bonding' activities to strengthen identity. *Bridging* activity is the more inclusive kind of socialising, looking for new members and looking outwards. With *bonding*, by contrast, members seek to strengthen the group by *excluding* others and making the group exclusive rather than inclusive. Such a group will seek ways to make itself invisible, not draw attention to itself, shun the approaches of outsiders or suspicious newcomers. It will develop rituals of secrecy.

Already, we can see a potentially interesting personality case history developing here, using Putnam's distinction between bonding and bridging as the theoretical 'tool' (which I describe in Chapter 11). We can see a boy who feels different from the crowd and has this feeling exaggerated on going out into the big wide world. We can see the beginnings of an explanation about how he and a group of similar young men might develop a tight-knit, highly 'bonded' group that learned how to avoid being noticed, especially by the authorities. They would be likely to assume low-profile personae wherever they went, assuming these almost automatically, in situations where they were likely to meet with authority figures.

These kinds of personae could be seen as the backdrop, providing the fabric within which their everyday encounters were framed. As an inquirer into a project such as this, you could also seek to understand (within the constraints of your own position, probably as a student inquirer with little power to find out detailed personal information) what the incipient terrorists did specifically to avoid observation. Were they known to have used coded messages? Did they assume disguises? Did they use pseudonyms? These, then, would be evidence of the more deliberate avoidance strategies.

A conclusion to the study might show how these strategies had broken down. Perhaps the group had been infiltrated by the security services? Did those services understand the modus operandi and psychology of groups such as this, looking for psychological profiles and patterns of behaviour, seeking such groups out to penetrate them?

All the time, you as an inquirer would be focusing first and foremost on the individuals involved, building a narrative. Because this is a case study, it is the narrative structure that is important – the story, in other words, building a picture of the personalities involved. Remembering, too, that this is a single case study, the one individual would form the core that would bind together all of the other elements, around whom the tapestry of your story would be woven.

Time as a dimension of the case study

The great historian R.G. Collingwood (1946/1994: 72) pointed to the significance of time and past events when he said that 'truth … is the daughter of time; the best knowledge is a fruit of the ripest and richest experience'. *Time* is a feature in most case study research. You are looking back on a phenomenon, situation or event; or you are studying that phenomenon, situation or event as it happens. For my classification of case studies in this chapter I have divided case studies into *retrospective*, *snapshot* and *diachronic* studies, to indicate the ways in which time is treated and employed differently in each type. I have further divided multiple case studies into parallel and sequential studies.

The retrospective study

The retrospective study is the simplest of these, involving the collection of data relating to the past phenomenon, situation or event. It happened in the past, so you will be looking at documents and archival records such as registers, newspaper stories, diaries, logs and photographs. You may be able to conduct interviews with those who experienced the event or participated in it.

In several of my examples so far in this book I have used a retrospective study – see the Berlin Wall example (page 39) and that of the terrorists (page 162) – so I shall refrain from giving another example here. Do remember, though, that there are several ways of tackling the issue of time in a case study: you don't have to do a simple retrospective. Consider the other frames for your design process that I outline in this chapter before proceeding.

The snapshot

Here, the case is being looked at in one period of time. It could be a month, week, day or even a period as short as an hour. That is the frame – the borders within which the study is undertaken. Remember that a case study is already a bounded study, and the boundaries are defined by *something* – possibly an institution, or the life of the person in question – but here, in the snapshot, it is defined by a period of time.

If this is so, then time should in some way be important. If the snapshot defines the study, then you are not getting contextual information arising from a whole range of ongoing sources of data that you are able to mix and match. Your focus is, if you like, 'a day in the life of' and the skill will lie in being able to draw data into that narrow frame.

In doing this, the snapshot case study is illustrative, demonstrative and analytical, like other forms of case study, but the analysis here is aided by the temporal juxtaposition of events – and that temporal juxtaposition (in other words, things being next to each other in time) will help you and the reader to understand the connectedness of events.

By presenting a narrative from one day, whether it is like a continuous video or more like a scrapbook, you are offering the reader your analysis of the situation. The object emerges out of this analysis. As Walton (1992) puts it, 'Cases come wrapped in theories.' In other words, the view being presented is a three-dimensional picture with all of the colours painted in – the contour lines and the colour provided by your own 'theoretical' stances, which are all of the things that make you who you are and, in turn, your analysis what it is. The case inquirer is the central person providing the theoretical wrappings, and this is done here in the snapshot especially with a view to the picture being presented as a Gestalt over a tight timeframe.

What does this mean in practical terms? I've mentioned that your focus is like 'a day in the life of', and it's useful to think of one of the most famous examples of the genre – Aleksandr Solzhenitsyn's (1963/2000) *One Day in the Life of Ivan Denisovich*. Although it is a work of literature rather than a research report, it is useful as an example since Solzhenitsyn based the book on his own experience and it illuminates his subject and enlightens his readers. Apart from any literary merit, this was an experience worth knowing about since it gave a picture of the author's reflections after his time in a Soviet labour camp – an experience he was forced to suffer because of a derogatory comment he made about Joseph Stalin.

As with all other forms of case study, there should be a purpose for doing it. The case study cannot be *merely* illustrative. If I were to provide a snapshot of my day as *One Day in the Life of Gary Thomas*, it sadly would be nowhere near as revelatory as that of Ivan Denisovich. There would have to be a reason for my writing it and, while Solzhenitsyn's experiences in a Soviet labour camp are an immediate and obvious source of interest, my own in my everyday life are not. Solzhenitsyn's experiences, however, can tell us about a whole range of things. We learn of the desperation brought about by the intense cold and what this does to a human being, the nature of the discourse permitted about Stalin, camaraderie, its nature and its purposes. Then we can put all of this into the context that is known about Stalin's USSR and all that came after it. Not only does telling the story over one day serve the narrative purpose of making it more interesting, real and compelling but also the timeframe connects the bits of the narrative. By describing the cold and its effects on the guards (as well as the prisoners), Solzhenitsyn humanises the guards and helps us to understand their reactions to the prisoners – both sympathetic and unkind. Take this passage from the beginning of the book (Solzhenitsyn, 1963/2000: 7):

> As usual, at five o'clock that morning reveille was sounded by the blows of a hammer on a length of rail hanging up near the staff quarters. The intermittent sound barely penetrated the window-panes on which the

> frost lay two fingers thick, and they ended almost as soon as they'd
> begun. It was cold outside and the camp-guard was reluctant to go on
> beating out the reveille for long.

The camp guard becomes human – he is dispirited by the cold and we empathise
with him. Not only this, by empathising with him we understand better the other
actions he takes. The timeline, whether a week, a day or an hour, focuses the gaze
of the observer and encourages an analysis of the interconnections between parts
of the narrative. It helps an understanding of the ways in which one element of
the story is bound to another. It helps us to understand the fabric of the day, the
ways in which the inmates avoid or gain the guards' attention and their facility
in harnessing from them small treats that could be traded and the ways in which
these became converted to a kind of currency. We learn about this in the context of
the intense and all-pervading cold and the prisoners' single-minded preoccupation
with warmth and survival.

As I said above, *A Day in the Life of Gary Thomas* would not be as compelling
as that of Ivan Denisovich. Ivan Denisovich has the advantage, as a subject, of all
that we have just talked about. Ultimately, it helped to change the world. My being
woken – me and 6 million others – by my radio alarm, the *Today* programme and
John Humphrys competes poorly with the camp guard's reveille. My day *could* be
interesting, however, as could anyone's, if an angle on it could be found. Here are
two possible such angles, which would form the *object* of my study.

- I am a senior member of staff at a university, negotiating a way between
  junior staff members' needs and wishes and the direction of the university's
  management. I could thus focus on the events in a working day that highlighted
  the tensions and dilemmas and how they represent the effects of a culture of
  performativity and audit and what this means for the erosion of trust in the
  context of the traditional working environment of the professional. Choosing
  my day with care, the day's events could exemplify and explicate any or all of
  these issues.

- As a parent of daughters now in their twenties, I could choose a day that in some
  way focused for me the tensions and life changes that are brought about by a
  young person 'leaving the nest'. It might be a special day, such as a graduation
  or moving into the first flat. Moments during the day would provoke reverie,
  reflection, sadness, hope, feelings of rejection (real or unreal) or joy, and these
  could be used as a backdrop to an analysis of changing life circumstances and
  their effects.

As I've noted regarding Ivan Denisovich, this could not simply be a record. I could
not simply say 'this happened, then this happened, then that happened'. That would
simply be a diary, and a not very interesting one. The key in employing a snapshot

is to find those interconnections over the day, week or whatever. It is the finding of these interconnections that would constitute the analytic frame. How did this link to that and what were my reflections on each? This is the stuff of which analysis is made.

Here is another example of a snapshot, this one occurring over three days:

Katrina is on a postgraduate course in educational psychology, for which she has to do a piece of reflective research to be written up into a 20,000-word dissertation. Katrina is on a placement at a young persons' unit of a psychiatric hospital and decides to do her dissertation based on this experience.

Among the patients at the unit is Briony, a 16-year-old young woman admitted because of anorexia nervosa. It is difficult to understand this condition and hugely frustrating for professionals to work with young people who display its symptoms. It's a form of self-destructiveness that seems almost to have its own power source behind it. The difficulty is understanding what this power source is.

Katrina wishes to do a snapshot case study since, she hopes, it will help her to understand Briony's condition by bringing together the interconnectedness of several elements of this young woman's life – the food consumption itself, its antecedents (that is, what went before) and its immediate consequences and how all of these are connected to Briony's social relationships with her family, friends, patients and hospital staff.

Having established clearly the informed consent of Briony and her family, Katrina decides to spend three whole days with Briony, staying at a guest house close to the hospital, so that she can devote the whole of the three days to being with Briony, talking with her, observing what she does and to whom she talks, noting her eating habits, their context, antecedents and consequences.

As part of all of this, Katrina decides to conduct two long interviews with Briony in which she intends to ask this bright, likeable young woman for her own reflections on the condition (see Figure 9.3). She will focus on a recurrent theme in the literature on anorexia – namely that, in dangerously restricting food intake, people with the condition are taking control of their lives in a way that they had hitherto found impossible.

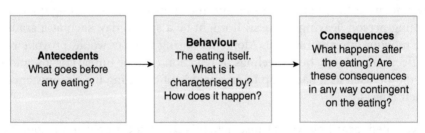

Figure 9.3   An ABC of behaviour, linking events over time

Depending on Briony's responses, Katrina will look to link this theoretical position with the young woman's actual behaviour in situ at the unit. Is there evidence of any kind of implicit or explicit control going on as the day proceeds and as mealtimes approach, are encountered and pass? How does this control take shape? Is it of her physical environment or the people around her or her own moment-to-moment existence? How can any or all of these be understood?

The diachronic study

The diachronic study shows change over time. In this way it contrasts with the snapshot study, which is a here-and-now study. Again, by contrast, it is different from a sequential study in that it is not two or more studies in sequence one after another, but one study that reveals differences as it proceeds. Here is an example:

You may have heard of the Hawthorne effect – a well-known term in organisational psychology. It is about the phenomenon of productivity increasing when an interest is shown in staff (see Figure 9.4). It doesn't matter what the interest is – it seems to have this effect most of the time.

The effect was named after the Hawthorne Works, a factory near Chicago making electrical parts for telephones and radios. In 1924, the US National Research Council sent two engineers to run experiments there in the hope that they would learn how improving lighting on the shop floor influenced workers' productivity.

To cut a long story short, they did discover that improving light levels improved productivity. Not only this, but subsequent analysis showed that any change – the maintenance of tidy workstations, moving benches around, clearing floors and even *reducing* light levels – all had the same effect. The consequence of changes such as this came to be known as the Hawthorne effect, sometimes also called the experimenter effect, and was written up in the literature by Roethlisberger and Dickson (1939).

Why should the Hawthorne effect happen?

Working in a factory that makes car parts, Bev is studying part-time for an MSc in human resource management and decides to study the phenomenon as the topic for her 20,000-word thesis. She decides to use her own place of work to take this question

Figure 9.4 Is everybody happy? The Hawthorne effect

(Continued)

(Continued)

further, clearing with her bosses, and three employees on part of the assembly line, the making of a series of small changes to work routine, during which time their productivity will be assessed. Clearly, this involves gaining the trust of her colleagues, clearance from the staff's trade union and ethical clearance from the university, but, given the good industrial relations at the plant, none of these is too difficult to achieve.

Bev's starting point is that the Hawthorne effect is a *real* phenomenon, even though there has been some evidence (Levitt and List, 2009) to suggest that it might have been a result of the way the data were originally collected in Chicago all those years ago. Bev, however, after having discussed this with her tutor, took the effect to be so well established in subsequent replications that it was worthy of additional study.

She was interested in the *why* and the *how* – why and how does productivity improve when a change is made to working conditions, and why does it not tend to maintain itself over time? A case study, Bev feels, may help to get to the means by which the effect works. It may give clues to its mechanism of action. A time element will clearly be at the core of this study, looking at changes that occur over time as the change is introduced and as it becomes part of the routine. Time, in other words, provides the basis of the analytical frame.

The change that Bev decides to introduce involves raising the height of these three employees' seats by 2 centimetres – not very much, but enough to make a noticeable difference.

Now, remembering that a case study is a bounded case, Bev has the situation she wishes to study bounded by:

- the physical context – the workbench, seat, engine parts zinging down the assembly line

- the social context – the other staff and the group's supervisor

- time – the key one, with changes happening as time proceeds.

Bev has to remember in doing this case study that it is not governed by the same principles as an experiment (unless she were to deliberately set up an experiment as part of the case study, but she is not going to do that). So, she is *not* going to be changing the value of a variable (the height of the seat) while holding the other variables constant in order to assess the effect of the change. Nor is she going to be formally comparing this group with another group of workers further down the assembly line who have not had their seats raised. Rather, she is going to be looking at the case as a whole from a number of directions and interpreting what she finds. Always, in analysing her findings, she will have to have at the front of her mind her purpose for doing the study, which is to understand the Hawthorne effect in her particular circumstance. Her understanding is informed by all of the work on the Hawthorne effect that she has discovered during her literature review. On the basis of the latter and her thinking, she draws up a storyboard about potential explanations, as shown in Figure 9.5.

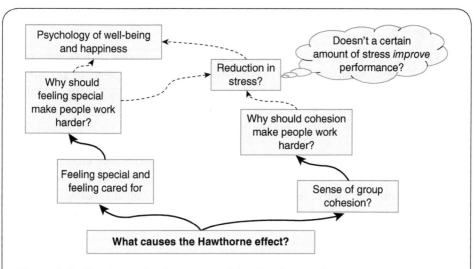

Figure 9.5 Storyboard for the causes of the Hawthorne effect

So, Bev starts the study and raises the seats of the three staff. She assesses their output and finds that it does indeed rise in all three cases. (Suppose it hadn't risen. Would this have been the end of the inquiry? No. Bev could have proceeded with the study, either modifying it in such a way that another change or changes were introduced until an effect was found or else she could simply have continued with the study as an exceptional example, offering reasons for there having been no Hawthorne effect in this case. It could, for example, lend weight to the findings of Levitt and List (2009), who suggested that Hawthorne effects are not real, which would then point to a new direction her inquiry could take.)

On finding a Hawthorne effect – the rise in output of these three members of staff – Bev could proceed to the crux of the study, which is an assessment of the social and psychological processes that might contribute to the improvement in performance.

To guide her data-gathering and its subsequent assessment, she uses the storyboard she drew (Figure 9.5). She has long semi-structured interviews with each of the staff separately and conducts a focus group with them all together. In this she enquires about their feelings of security, 'place', stress and happiness using focus materials – photographs and video clips – that stimulate discussion about safety, confidence and well-being. She asks whether they are getting on better or worse with others participating in the study and with those outside it. She uses the '5 Whys' technique employed by the Toyota Motor Corporation (see Ohno, 2006) for trying to get at the 'root cause'. She also observes what appears to be going on down the assembly line. Is there, for example, any teasing or ignoring or even bullying going on?

Bev focuses especially on the ideas raised in her storyboard and proposes from her findings that the effect is *not* produced as a result of any improved sense of

(Continued)

(Continued)

well-being. Rather, the interviews, focus groups and observation seem to point to a sense of involvement in the work of the company. Rather than being 'us and them', there is more a sense of just 'us', with communication appearing to take place and a sense that the staff involved are being listened to.

An interesting feature of Bev's study is that it involved an alteration in the environment of her staff, in the way that is sometimes thought to be appropriate only for an experimental study. Yet this was not an experiment. It invoked the change in order to provide the basis for an interpretative study – one that is idiographic in nature.

The multiple or collective or comparative case (or cross-case analysis)

> when there is even less interest in one particular case, a number of cases may be studied jointly in order to investigate a phenomenon, population, or general condition. I call this a multiple case study or collective case study.
>
> Stake (2005: 445)

In a multiple case study, because there are several subjects, each individual subject is less important in itself than the comparison each offers with the others. For example, a study of two schools' different responses to a peripatetic education support service might be done to try and throw light on the differences in these schools' biographies and characteristics. The key focus would not be on the shape of relationships per se in one school, but, rather, on the nature of the differences between one and the other. Selection would have to be on the basis of prior knowledge by the researcher of these levels of difference, and the interpretations would also be made in the context of this knowledge. The key to this research would be to drill deeper, to find out more and undertake more searching analysis of the cultures of the two environments. This comparative element is why Schwandt (2001) calls this kind of case study 'cross-case analysis', putting the emphasis on the comparison that is done.

> Another term for multiple case study is 'cross-case analysis', since the emphasis is on the comparison between the cases.

Because you are using multiple studies and making comparisons doesn't mean that you are in some way reinvoking the need for representative samples of each phenomenon. Just as much as in any other case study, a cross-case analysis is about the 'guts' of the case, seen in its wholeness. There is a platform, though, on which sets of wholeness are compared. Remember (once again) that case studies can never form a sample from which you can generalise. In the somewhat pompous language of research methodology, the case you choose to look at will be a non-probability sample. (As I mentioned, though, on page 62, there are good grounds for saying that your case is in no sense at all a 'sample'.) So, if you are comparing cases, you are comparing *these* cases for what they show.

Interestingly, one of the very first case studies ever to have been systematically conducted was a comparative case study. It was undertaken by a French mining engineer, Frédéric Le Play, in nineteenth-century France. Le Play had travelled as part of his work as an engineer, but, perhaps to the chagrin of his employers, became more interested in the people he met than the mines he was visiting. On his travels, he would stay with a family and remain with them long enough to get a full picture of their way of life (Mogey, 1955). Drawing from such intense observations of individual families, he was able systematically to compare the lives of families in rural German mining villages with those of French urban workers. Partly because of the vividness of these first-hand accounts, his comparative case studies achieved literary as well as popular acclaim and led to significant reforms – initiated by employers – in the treatment of workers in urban France.

Returning to the twenty-first century, at several points in his lovely book *The Craftsman*, Richard Sennett (2009: 182–93) uses case comparisons, or cross-case analysis, to set off strands of analytical thought in his readers' minds. I shall draw from one of these here:

The Craftsman is a highly readable work of scholarship about craft knowledge – how it is acquired and how it is passed on to others. Sennett legitimately uses a panoply of different sources to compile his thesis – historical records, case studies, conversations, reminiscences, personal experiences, scientific literature and more.

Sennett uses a comparison to make a point about instructions. His point is 'show, don't tell'. In other words, in helping to share a craft with another person – whether it is woodworking, cooking or whatever – the mentor or craftsperson should give examples rather than try to explain. It doesn't matter how strange the examples are, they are better than instructions based on task analysis. The mind doesn't work like a computer, with watertight sequences of 'do this; don't do that; now do this'. We need real examples from life that we can get inside, like a comfy pair of shoes – we need metaphors from practice.

(Continued)

(Continued)

We learn by empathising, imagining and doing, feeling our way with the guidance of a tutor. Whether this tutor is a real flesh-and-blood person or a book (as in Sennett's examples about recipes) is immaterial. What is needed is the feeling that you are sharing the task, understanding its nooks and crannies, being guided rather than told. For those familiar with the psychology of learning, the congruence with Vygotsky's thinking is clear.

Perhaps I should rephrase the comment I made just now about learning by empathising and doing. It should really be, 'We learn *best* from empathising and doing.' Of course, we could simply learn – no more and no less – from a set of instructions, but our learning would have no depth, no feeling. To bring the craft, the magic, into the learning, to make a wooden box with enjoyment and care – a box with soul rather than just a box – needs skills learned by the side of a craftsperson or those honed over a lifetime's experience.

Anyway, this is the essence of what Sennett is trying to illustrate with his comparison of four chefs and how they cook various chicken recipes. Sennett's case study is:

- *local*, since one of the cases draws from his own experience, and *key* because they all are exemplars

- *instrumental*, since it serves a purpose

- *illustrative*, since it is showing something

- *multiple or comparative*, since the core of the message comes out of the comparison of cases.

So, remembering back to the taxonomy of purposes, approaches and processes, the path that it takes is as set out in Figure 9.6.

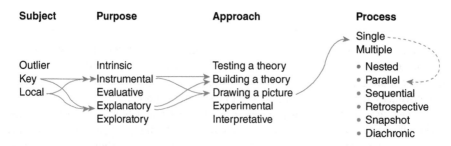

Figure 9.6   Sennett's case study

The first chef Sennett describes is Richard Olney. Sennett picks on his description of how to bone a chicken (see Figure 9.7). The instructions provided by Olney, says Sennett, *tell* instead of show: 'If the reader already knows how to bone, this description might be a useful review; for the neophyte it is no guide. Many unfortunate chickens will be hacked to bits if a beginner follows it.'

Here is a sample of the instructions that Sennett is talking about: 'Sever the attachment of each shoulder blade at the wing joint and, holding it firmly between the thumb and forefinger of the left hand, pull it out of the flesh with the other hand.' He likens this kind of writing to engineering: 'Not only do engineer-writers leave out "dumb things" that "everyone knows": they repress simile, metaphor, and adverbial color. The act of unpacking what's buried in the vault of tacit knowledge can make use of these imaginative tools.'

The second part of the multiple case study consists of a word picture that Sennett draws of chef Julia Child. He gives an account of how Child's recipe is like a story that

Figure 9.7   Preparing a chicken, by four chefs. A comparative case study

gets inside the chef's head, expressing forebodings and sympathy. She uses analogy, focusing on the cook rather than the chicken. She gives clues rather than direct instructions and guides the reader like an expert with an apprentice, anticipating difficulties and suggesting ways around them: 'for a moment Child will imagine holding the knife awkwardly; the cello master will return to playing wrong notes. This return to vulnerability is the sign of the sympathy the instructor gives' (Sennett, 2009: 186).

Part three is a pen portrait of the famous Elizabeth David, who shared her skills with her readers by giving the cultural context of the food. She talks about local cooks in France touching and prodding the bird. She tells stories about when, how and with whom she ate and gives interesting titbits about how tarragon might be used by Bordeaux cooks while, for the same recipe, sage was used by the cooks in Perpignan. So, as a reader you think about the food you are cooking, being encouraged to consider the process as creative, variable and intuitive rather than a rigid set of procedures.

The fourth case study offered by Sennett is perhaps the most interesting. It is of Madame Benshaw and her recipe for poulet à la d'Albufera. Madame Benshaw is different from the others in that she isn't famous – she emerges from Sennett's own personal knowledge – and because she talks almost entirely in riddles, devoid of instructions in the formal sense. Sennett was a student of hers at an evening class and he says that, because her English was poor, she would teach almost entirely by example, 'coupled with slight smiles and emphatic, frowning contradictions of her thick eyebrows'. With Sennett's help, Madame Benshaw wrote down the recipe:

(Continued)

(Continued)

> Your dead child. Prepare him for new life. Fill him with the earth. Be careful! He should not over-eat. Put on his golden coat. You bathe him. Warm him but be careful! A child dies from too much sun. Put on his jewels. This is my recipe. (pp. 190–91)

By the 'dead child', she meant the chicken. The 'preparation for new life' meant boning. 'Filling with the earth' was about stuffing, and 'not overeating' about not overstuffing. The 'golden coat' was about browning before baking. The 'bathing' referred to the preparation of a poaching liquor and the 'jewels' the pouring on of this liquor, basting.

This recipe, then, is told entirely via metaphors, and these allow the novice cook to feel and understand. Calling the chicken a 'child' immediately evokes a sense of intimacy, protection and tenderness, so we understand that we should place the bird only in a cool oven. As Sennett puts it, metaphors 'roll forward and sideways', allowing us to gather different meanings as they do so.

This comparative case study illustrates exactly the point that Sennett wants to, which is that learning a craft is not about simply following instructions but a human process. He builds the theory that in doing this, we do well to follow our noses, to use, if you like, our 'instinct' for learning. This is something that is done by modelling and copying, getting inside another person's head. To build the theory, he draws out the key points and synthesises them, as shown in Table 9.1.

Table 9.1   Chefs cooking chickens – Sennett's multiple case study

Chefs	Style (for comparison)	Analysis
Richard Olney	Straight instructions that give almost clinical directions about what to do	The general point is about learning coming from imagining and doing and using the knowledge you already have to help you learn something new. It does not come through formal instruction
Julia Child	Use of analogy, focus on the cook rather than the chicken and use of the learner's vulnerability	
Elizabeth David	Talking about the culture, taking the reader on a journey, discussing variations – making it, therefore, less rigid, less fixed	
Madame Benshaw	Talking entirely in metaphors that let the reader 'get inside' the mind of the chef and understand what she is saying	

This is where many student researchers go wrong in doing a case study of this kind. There is too much description – and it is *just* description. Too little actually comes from looking at the differences between the cases. It is this that is, in fact, more important than the presentation of the cases. Fascinating though Madame Benshaw's case is, it is far less interesting on its own than it is when compared with the others. The analytical frame is provided by the comparison.

An interesting comparative case in the literature can be found in the work of Jiménez and Gersten (1999). They made comparisons between the teaching styles of two Latina/o teachers and the different ways in which they went about teaching literacy.

Nested case studies

Yin (2009) draws a useful distinction between multiple case studies and what he calls 'embedded' case studies. I prefer to call the latter 'nested' studies, partly because it is one less syllable than 'embedded', but mainly because 'nested' gives more of a sense of a subunit *fitting in* with a larger unit, rather than it being *implanted* there. It is that *fitting in* that is of interest – how does the subunit connect with other subunits and the whole?

With multiple studies, the emphasis is on comparing clearly different examples, and the contrasts found between and among the cases then throw the spotlight on an important theoretical feature. By contrast, with nested studies the breakdown is *within* the principal unit of analysis, such as classrooms within a school. This is summarised in Figure 9.8.

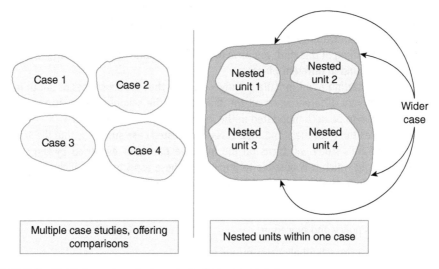

Figure 9.8 Multiple and nested case studies compared

A nested study is distinct from a multiple study in that it gains its integrity, its wholeness, from the wider case.

As with all decisions regarding case studies, there has to be a reason for conducting the study in a particular way and, with the nested study, that reason comes out of contrasting the units *as part of the wider case*. If you were looking at three classrooms within one school, but the school had no significance other than that it physically housed these three classrooms, then the cases would not be seen as nested. They are nested only in the sense that they form an integral part of a broader picture – integral to something that might be happening within the school. Let's flesh out this example a little.

Franklin Drive Primary School has just decided to implement an inclusion policy. Deputy headteacher Lara, who is studying for a master's degree in education, decides to examine the ways in which the policy can be understood and implemented throughout the school. This analysis will be done for the dissertation she has to complete for her degree, but she expects that it will also form the basis for developmental work in the school afterwards.

Lara's starting point is that the kinds of changes expected to result from an inclusion policy of this kind are difficult to implement at a practical level because they depend on the cooperation of individual people, and different people notoriously behave in different ways.

Lara's tutor has referred her to a classic paper, 'The myth of the hero-innovator', by Georgiades and Phillimore (1975). The point that Georgiades and Phillimore make is that implementing change in an organisation is far more difficult than it might at first sight seem. Because of this, the organisational landscape is littered with the carcasses of brave people who have tried to change things but failed. It's almost as if people working within organisations, whoever they are – teachers, doctors, firefighters, zookeepers – conspire to resist change. Allied to this is Lara's knowledge that there are few recipes for success with an innovation such as the implementation of an inclusion policy. If trying to introduce something of this kind, you have to adapt and modify to suit the organisational conditions you find in different places.

This is the starting point for Lara's study – namely, that the six classes of her primary school are all very different since all the teachers in the school have their own styles which will have to be accommodated in the implementation of the policy.

She chooses three teachers and their classes as nested case studies within the school. The core of Lara's study will focus on the inclusive principles espoused by the school and the ways in which it is possible to implement these aspects of the inclusion policy, given the different styles of the teachers working at Franklin Drive. The principles of the inclusion policy include:

- admissions policy and procedure
- the way that the school allocates resources
- assessment procedures
- staff development
- specific inclusion strategies
- the curriculum
- parental involvement.

The first four of these are whole-school issues that will not be affected by the idiosyncrasies of the teachers' styles. Lara is concerned about the last three points, however – namely, specific inclusion strategies, the curriculum and parental involvement. She knows that teaching styles differ greatly in the three classes on which she is focusing. The teachers' attitudes to parental involvement also differ. The teachers are:

- *Jon*, a newly qualified teacher, who does things by the book and enjoys involving parents, but is rather in awe of them

- *Meryl*, who retires next year and is a formal teacher who firmly declines offers of help from parents or volunteers

- *Jane*, mid-career teacher who is spontaneous, dismissive of government directives, popular with parents and works easily with them.

Lara decides to focus in these studies on the ways in which these three teachers can implement the school's new policy, given their different styles. She considers forming a focus group with Jon, Meryl and Jane in which she will present the policy and discuss views on its implementation. On reflection, however, she rejects this idea, realising that it may accentuate any differences in style and make Meryl defensive and alienated from the others. What she needs to do is study each of these classrooms as environments for the development of the policy, each working in its own way. In the sense that the study will help to change practice, this is a case study that is also a piece of action research.

Lara ultimately decides to conduct semi-structured interviews with each of the teachers, in which she will ask about inclusion strategies, the curriculum and parental involvement. These will be analysed using the constant comparative method (see Chapter 11) for both unique and shared ideas about implementation in class. The analytical framework that she will develop will serve as the basis for a summative plenary discussion with the teachers in which their ideas are shared.

As Lara expected, the interviews reveal quite different attitudes to the curriculum, learning and the community, as well as education's place in it. She uses construct maps (Thomas, 2013: 237–9) to show diagrammatically the differences in thinking and try to draw strands of commonality from them. She fails in this last aim, however. While Jon and Jane show some commonality in their thinking, there is no congruence at all with Meryl.

Lara's conclusion is that the units of the school operate as quite discrete elements in the larger structure of the school, and she uses Bronfenbrenner's systems theory (see Chapter 3) to frame her analysis here. She speaks in her write-up of the insularity of the teacher role within the school and of the resilience of this insularity. She also questions if it would, in fact, be a good thing to attempt to break this down, coming back to her starting point about styles – styles that are built on attitude, belief, personality, habit and disposition. These facets of individual teachers' make-up would be difficult if not impossible to break down, and in any case should not be broken down, Lara decides. Lara's conclusion also includes reflections on the role of policy and the extent to which

(Continued)

(Continued)

attempts at the implementation of policy may undermine the teachers' identities and effectiveness. The latter, she suggests, is framed around the characteristics of each teacher and the circumstances of his or her class, and attempting to change this may be counterproductive.

I hope that you can see how the nested study is different from the simple multiple study, comparing particularly the multiple study of chefs with the study of the three classrooms. Comparisons are at the heart of each kind of study, but in the nested study these occur in a wider, connected context.

Parallel and sequential studies

Parallel and sequential studies are both forms of multiple study. In the parallel study, the cases are all happening and being studied at the same time, as in Lara's case above, while in the sequential study the cases happen one after the other and there is an assumption that what has happened in one or in an intervening period will in some way affect the next.

Given that Lara's study suffices as an example of a parallel study, let me give a short example of a sequential case study to complete the picture:

Sarah is studying the accessibility of public spaces – particularly public buildings, roads and parks – for people with disabilities. She works for a large charity that has agreed with a local authority to share funding of the replanning and landscaping of a small city-centre park. This project will be used as a pilot and, on the basis of its findings, the charity will aim to work with other local authorities to make changes elsewhere, informing the conduct and design of these further projects.

Under Sarah's guidance, the park is replanned by a group comprising a landscape architect, disabled people and local authority planners. They work with a computer design expert from the local university to produce virtual reality environments and computer visualisations that enable disabled people to offer their advice on possible changes. The result is that they plan to change paths, signage, access to buildings and the space devoted to various activities.

Sarah's plan is to design two case studies, one before and one after the change, as part of a larger inquiry in which the use of the park by various groups of people is monitored. This therefore involves a before-and-after comparison, so it draws its rationale directly from evaluative research (discussed on page 121). The same considerations that applied there also apply here, and a straightforward piece of research comparing, perhaps, use of the park by disabled people over two periods of time, one before and one after the change, would be a case study, but only in a limited sense. A case study has to entail some element of in-depth examination involving the capture of fine-grained detail about the changes, looking from several angles at perhaps the experience of just a few people. Thus, if the inquiry shows that there has been an increase (or a decline) in the use of the park by disabled people following the changes, the sequential case studies will aim to provide insight into why that increase or decline might have occurred.

Sarah's choice of participants is clearly important given the topic. A selection of people with different kinds of disability will be necessary. So, she chooses to talk in depth to four people before the changes and four people after the changes, making these different people each time, though, on each occasion, two will be wheelchair users and two identified by the local group for people with Asperger's syndrome.

The first part of the study (A1 and A2 in Figure 9.9) does indeed show an increase in use after the changes have been implemented, though, of course, this could have been due to novelty and expectation effects – people being excited to see what is happening and at the same time expecting things to get better.

The second part of the study (B1 and B2) involves the in-depth analysis, with four people on each occasion. Sarah decides to do this – that is, the case study element – by engaging her research participants in unstructured interviews and 'walk-throughs' of the park, with a non-directive invitation to offer ideas and comments about anything that occurs to them about the park's design.

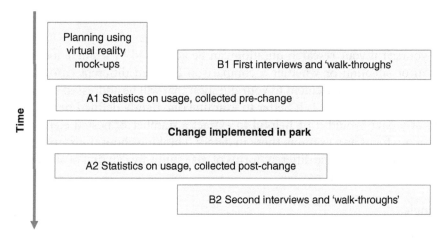

Figure 9.9   Sarah's research, with the sequential case study elements shaded

As noted, the first part of the study (A1 and A2) provided confirmation of an increase in usage and an endorsement of the improvements in access to the park. The case study element (B1 and B2) gave mixed information about the nature of the changes, with

(Continued)

(Continued)

a difference between the wheelchair users and those with Asperger's syndrome in the way they responded in their interviews and walk-throughs. Those using wheelchairs were indeed content with the primarily access-based changes. Those with Asperger's syndrome, however, were unhappy with the assessment that had been made of them as 'disabled', raising ethical issues that Sarah and the charity had to pursue. On the substantive subject of the project – park design – these participants made comments about a sense of security, the need for predictability, reduction in noise and the scale of the buildings and signage used.

By doing her case studies sequentially in this way, Sarah was able to offer useful information to aid the rolling out of the programme to other parks. For example, she had been able to understand how the design that had been produced with the aid of computer visualisation had not met all expectations. She was then able to make suggestions about future projects. Also, although the case studies did not draw from a representative sample of disabled people, they enabled a closer understanding of the needs of these users, pulling in ideas that would not have been garnered from a study with a more one-dimensional focus.

If you take only one thing from this chapter, take this ...

Ask yourself if your research question can be addressed by a single focus on one person or situation or whether a comparison between different cases would be better. Is there a time element to your question that will be addressed by looking at a sequence of events or is it better to examine one tightly defined period in time, such as a day? Would it be helpful to extract a number of nested elements from your main focus and examine these in detail? Thinking about these questions and how we might categorise different forms of case study, we can first of all say that the subject of a case study may be:

- single
- multiple.

Beyond this, *time* can be thought of as a key component in structuring the case study. We have thought about:

- retrospective case studies
- snapshot case studies
- diachronic (or longitudinal) case studies.

Each of these employs time in a different way. And if the study is a multiple one, the multiple subjects may be studied:

- as nested units within a larger whole
- as parallel units, being studied separately
- as sequential elements.

As with all questions about design, thinking carefully about what you need will be repaid in your findings and the analysis you are able to draw. Keep asking yourself, 'What kind of analysis, what kinds of insights am I seeking?', and then structure the case study – thinking about both the subject and the object (pages 15–17) – around these questions.

FURTHER READING 📖

Sennett, R. (2009) *The Craftsman.* London: Penguin.
I offer *The Craftsman* as further reading for this chapter partly because I have drawn on Sennett's examples, but mainly because his thesis is so apposite for the case study. It's about how we *make sense* when we become skilled in a craft, which is as relevant for the case researcher as it is for the goldsmith (one of Sennett's examples), carpenter or chef.

Yin, R.K. (2009) *Case Study Research: Design and Methods* (4th edn). Thousand Oaks, CA: Sage.
Yin draws some interesting distinctions between different kinds of case studies.

PART 3

COLLECTING EVIDENCE, ANALYSING AND WRITING UP

In this third part of the book, I look at:

- ways to collect data for a case study
- ways to analyse those data
- writing up a case study.

10

OUT IN THE FIELD: SOME WAYS TO COLLECT DATA AND EVIDENCE

'In the field' is a term used by researchers to refer to the process of actually collecting data, as distinct from, say, doing a literature review. So, when you are 'in the field', you are doing 'fieldwork'. Fieldwork is a distinct part of a research project. When you are doing fieldwork, you are collecting data and/or evidence.

It is important to remember that there is a distinction between data and evidence. *Data* is another word for 'information' – bits of information of whatever kind, whether they be observation records, numbers (such as test scores), interview transcripts, photographs or documents. *Evidence*, however, is data in support of some proposition. The propositions you come up with in your inquiry will be in the process of developing as your research progresses. As I hope I made clear in Chapter 2, the initial, prima facie questions that you lay out in your introduction are an expression of your first thoughts about a subject, and these are refined as your work progresses – as you read more for your literature review and your ideas become clearer.

> *Data* are bits of information. *Evidence* comes from data that support or refute a proposition.

It is as you go through this process that the propositions become clearer and you, in turn, can be more focused about the evidence you need to support or refute those propositions. If we take the example of the case study on the Hostos-Lincoln Academy (see page 33), Rageh Omaar started with a fairly undefined question, but, as his immersion in the relevant research and literature progressed, he developed ideas, propositions and theories about his questions. The case study that he ultimately conducted was aimed at gathering data that would support or refute the propositions emerging for him.

So, you may be seeking data, pure and simple. Alternatively, you may be seeking evidence in support of a proposition. Which you do depends on the kind of research you are conducting. If you go into your case study *without* a tightly constructed theory or set of propositions to guide your research, you will be seeking data that will gather around ideas which emerge as the study progresses. If, however, you begin with a clear hypothesis or a well-defined theory at the outset, then you have propositions that will be supported (or not) by the data that you collect – you are looking for evidence.

With this distinction in mind, how can you go about collecting information that will help you with your case study? I have mentioned many of the methods that can be used in the examples I have given in Chapters 6–9. Let's do this more systematically now, though, and run through some of the most commonly used ways of collecting evidence as a guide for you when you actually get down to doing your study. This is *only* a guide and an aide-mémoire, though, and I give more details about methods for gathering data in *How to Do Your Research Project* (Thomas, 2013). I summarise these commonly used methods of collecting evidence in Table 10.1. Let's look at each of them in a little more detail.

Table 10.1 Commonly used methods of collecting evidence

• interviews	mainly use words
– structured	
– unstructured	
– semi-structured	
• accounts	
• diaries	
• group interviews	
• focus groups	
• interrogating documents	
• questionnaires	use words, images and/or numbers
• observation	
– structured observation	
– unstructured observation	
– participant observation	
• image-based methods	
• measurements and tests	mainly use numbers
• official statistics	
• other numerical data.	

Interviews

Structured interviews

In a structured interview, you meet with another person and ask a *predetermined list of questions*. The structured interview has a limited range of strengths:

- it can be administered relatively easily and quickly
- interviewees' responses can be easily coded.

But, beyond these, it doesn't have very much in its favour. Because there is no great advantage in giving it in a face-to-face manner, it may as well be given in written form – in other words as a questionnaire (see page 193).

Unstructured interviews

Likely to be used in an interpretative case study (see Chapter 9), an unstructured interview is like a conversation. There is no fixed way to conduct such an interview. You don't present your interviewee with a list of questions. In fact, the idea really is for interviewees to set the agenda. *They* should be the ones who determine the direction of the interview and the topics that emerge. As the researcher, you go in with an open mind and just try to listen and facilitate. This is of course what is wanted in interpretative research: in this kind of research you are looking for your respondents to set the scene and let *them* tell *you* what the issues are.

Beyond this desire to let the interviewee lead the way, there are variations on the theme of just how unstructured the interview should be. If your respondent goes completely off the topic, then you would wish to bring them back to it in some way. However, this would need to be done sensitively, since it may be the case that this is the way that the respondent talks – going 'off message' for a while before they return to the topic. Or they might like to tell a story when they are talking, and the unstructured interview gives them a chance to do this. If it seems the case in this sort of circumstance that something of a delicate or sensitive nature is being disclosed you should clear with your interviewee after the interview that they are happy for the specific information to be used and in what guise. You could reveal it only as a general comment, perhaps, or it may be acceptable to your interviewee to quote from them in an anonymous way on which you can agree. (See also the discussion on ethics and confidentiality in Chapter 5.)

The unstructured interview will be more like a conversation than a formal interview. Sometimes, though, you may wish to move the conversation in a particular direction and prompt the interviewee. How should you prompt without setting the agenda yourself? There are degrees of strength of prompt: you may simply say

'Can you tell me more about that?' or offer something stronger such as 'How did that make you feel?' or 'What happened next?' However, if you really are interested in what the interviewee has to say you would avoid a question such as 'Does that make you feel angry?' This really would be putting words into the interviewee's mouth.

Semi-structured interviews

In a semi-structured interview you provide the structure with a list of *issues* (rather than specific questions) to be covered and you have the freedom to follow up points as necessary. Because of these advantages, it is the most commonly used kind of interview arrangement in small-scale social research.

However, for case study, the fact that it is the most commonly used does not mean that it is necessarily the best. If you really are interested in interpreting your interviewees' comments and if you are a participant observer in the situation that you are researching, an *unstructured* interview may well be a better choice. I make this point because too many students (in my opinion) opt for the semi-structured interview as the most straightforward and seemingly obvious choice, where in fact it can lead them to do a different kind of research from that which they set out to do. If you really do intend to do an ethnographic, interpretative case study, entering your research environment as a participant observer, you are trying to understand how the 'players' in that environment are playing their roles – depending on the meanings that they construct. If this is the case, if this is what you want to do, then the semi-structured interview may be too rigid.

If you decide after reflection that you do need semi-structured interviews, though, you will start with an *interview schedule*, which is a list of issues that you intend to cover. You are not obliged to go through these points in order – or in any way keep to a formal set format for the interview. Rather, it gives you a reminder of what you want to cover. It reminds you not just of the issues but also of potential questions, possible follow-up questions and 'probes', which may encourage the interviewee to say more on these follow-ups. Probes may be verbal – for example 'Go on ...' – or non-verbal, such as a nod, smile or tilt of the head.

Accounts

An account comes from a respondent and is the result of a format that allows him or her to communicate experiences and feelings freely. Accounts are really like the products of unstructured interviews, but without having been collected in an interview. The account could be provided in a long, written piece of prose, like an essay, or recorded in audio form, to be transcribed later. An account is handled in the same way as the data from an unstructured interview.

Diaries

A diary may involve you, or a participant in your case study, making a record of ideas, reflections, thoughts, emotions, actions, reactions, conversations and so on. Alternatively, it may involve making a structured record of activities. Diaries may be divided into three types:

- *interval-contingent*, where participants report on their experiences at regular intervals. This is the most common kind of research diary.

- *signal-contingent* where some signalling device (a phone call or text message, for example) prompts participants to give diary reports at particular intervals (fixed or random).

- *event-contingent*, where participants provide a diary entry each time the event occurs. This enables the capture of rare events that would not necessarily be caught by fixed or random interval assessments.

If you are completing a diary yourself, it is best done immediately after your session in the field, recording an assortment of opinions, views, interpretations, remembered conversations and so on. It can take written form or be an audio or even a video recording.

Some people will be more fulsome in accounts in a private disclosure of the kind given in a diary than they would be in a face-to-face interview. This is often the case with children and young people, as long as they have the writing skills. If they don't have such skills, you could consider the use of an audio diary. You may even wish to keep a video diary, where expressions, gestures, sighs, grimaces, frowns, tears even, may be recorded – features of the situation that would be missed in a written or audio diary.

Group interviews and focus groups

Group interviews

Before you set up a group interview, you need to establish your reason for holding a group rather than individual interviews. If you are interviewing a group, it should be because the group psychology itself has some impact on the situation that is of interest to you. You may, for example, want to find how the group (*as* a group) is behaving, how it might behave in response to an imaginary event, or *compare* a group attitude with individual attitudes within the same group, perhaps to judge the power of one or two group members who may not be at all representative of the general opinion.

People behave differently in groups: particular individuals may become more talkative or less talkative; some people take the lead, while others follow; some will tend to be 'stroppy', others helpful. And there are particular ways a whole group will behave, differently from individuals. So, for example, there is an inclination for a group to display what is called a 'risky shift phenomenon', a tendency well established in social psychology. This is about the likelihood that a group will make a riskier decision than an individual. If you asked a set of groups a question such as 'Would you have a person with a criminal record to stay in your house?' and then asked an equivalent number of people but as individuals, you would probably find a riskier decision (that is, more likelihood of saying 'yes') in the groups. There's safety in numbers, and this maxim applies even if decisions are being made about wholly imaginary happenings.

So there are good, legitimate reasons for using a group interview, beyond the mere fact that it may save you time.

Focus groups

The term *focus group* has come to be used interchangeably with *group interview*, but the two kinds of group are different in important respects. In group interviews the emphasis is on the researcher taking a lead role, asking questions and being in control of the discussion – rather in the way that an interviewer is leading the discussion in a structured or semi-structured interview. So the researcher asks questions and respondents answer. But in focus groups the researcher plays the role of *facilitator* or *moderator*. If you are running a focus group your aim is to facilitate or moderate discussion *among participants*, not between yourself and the participants. The idea is that you take a marginal rather than a pivotal role.

In the focus group, participants, usually eight or so, who have a relevant characteristic or feature of their lives in common will be brought together in an informal setting to discuss the topic in question. As in an unstructured interview with an individual, the idea is to get at the understandings, beliefs and values of the participants. And in the same way that in an individual unstructured interview the aim is to let the *individual* take the lead in setting the direction of the discussion, so in the focus group the aim is to let the *group* take the lead. As facilitator, your role is to stimulate discussion, and you may do this with your comments or you may prepare a range of *focus materials* for the group to discuss. These are materials – for example, objects, artefacts, photographs, drawings, newspaper clippings, short videos, audio recordings – that help the group focus on the topic of interest.

Given that you need your wits about you to facilitate effectively in a group such as this, it is common practice in professionally conducted research to use an observer to record information about context, environment and participants' behaviour. In small-scale research it will not usually be possible to get help in this way, so it may be helpful to make an audio and/or video record of proceedings.

Interrogating documents

Case studies take many and varied forms, and a retrospective case study may depend entirely upon documentary evidence. It may be the case that there are no living survivors of the event, or no one who is accessible to offer their thoughts. Even in the case of an event about which there are potential informants, these people may not be able or willing to be interviewed.

Gathering data from documents represents an entirely different proposition from gathering data from people. Essentially, the knack is to find the right documents, read them and think about them.

There are methods for examining documents with your word-processing program for, for example, readability or the existence of certain kinds of words, but there is no substitute for your own careful reading for meaning and substance in a document. Fortunately, reading documents has been made easier since most are nowadays available in Word, as PDFs or online and can be searched and cut-and-pasted from.

Given the ease with which documents can now be downloaded (particularly government and other policy documents), a key shortcut is in some basic document interrogation using computer software. This is easy if the document is in Word, but a bit trickier if it is in PDF. If the latter, you can, after checking copyright, copy the whole thing and then paste it into Word. (*Tip*: To copy the whole lot in a PDF file, press Ctrl-A, which selects the whole document; then Ctrl-C, which copies it, then switch to a blank Word document and paste it into that with Ctrl-V.) If you are not able to download the relevant document in word-processing or PDF format, the one technical trick that is widely available now is through electronic scanning. Most scanners now are provided with optical character recognition (OCR) software which will do the 'reading' (but sadly not the thinking or understanding) for you. When you scan your text your software should give you the option of enabling the text to be 'read' as text (as distinct from simply taking a picture of the text). It will then save this into a word-processing file, and once this is done there are a number of ways in which your computer can help you to analyse the text; these forms of analysis are covered in Chapter 11.

Questionnaires

A questionnaire is a *written* form of questioning and the questions may be closed ('Do you think parents should be allowed to smack their children? Yes or No') or open ('What are your feelings concerning parents smacking their children?'). You may be collecting facts or, as here, assessing people's attitudes on a topic.

A questionnaire can be tightly structured, but can also allow the chance for a more open responses if required. It may be read out by interviewers (either face-to-face or over the phone) or sent to respondents for them to complete themselves. It may be sent by post or e-mail or presented online. For online questionnaires, there are various Web-based services available (such as SurveyMonkey, available at: www.surveymonkey.com, which lets you construct your own questionnaire free for a survey of up to 100 respondents).

Ways of questioning

The first thing to consider is whether you are going to used *open* or *closed* questions. Open questions leave the response open to the respondent, and I'll come to these in a moment at the end of this section. *Closed questions* limit the response and can be organised in a number of ways.

Dichotomous questions

'Dichotomous' means 'two-way', and the dichotomy is usually 'yes' or 'no'. For example:

Have you ever applied for a managerial position in this company?   Yes   ☐

No   ☐

These can often be screening questions. In other words, you may use the question to separate respondents into groups, who can then be questioned separately. If they haven't applied for a post of responsibility (in this example), why not? Your subsequent questions to this group will pursue this theme. And if they have applied, what happened? A separate route of questioning can be used for this subset.

Multiple-choice questions

These contain two or more answers where respondents can be told either to tick one box or to tick as many boxes as needed.

Rank-order questions

Here, respondents have to rank items (that is, put them in order) on a list according to some criterion – for example, best to worst, most able to least able, or degree of difficulty. Within this ranking, you can either ask for a limited number of choices (for example, first, second and third), or require respondents to rank the whole list.

Rating-scale questions

These require the respondent to rate some experience, attribute, attitude, etc. along a continuum. You may for example wish to ask adults about their experience of testing and assessment when they were at school:

Remembering back to when you were at school, would you say that your experiences of formal assessment and testing were:

Very positive ☐

Positive ☐

Neutral ☐

Negative ☐

Very negative ☐

The respondent will tick only one of these boxes.

Matrix or grid questions

Matrices (grids) provide a series of questions, which all have the same answer scale. For example, if you were interested in canvassing patients on what constitutes a good nurse, you might ask them to suggest how important each of these criteria were, all on the same scale of 1 to 5.

Importance	1	2	3	4	5
Caring	☐	☐	☐	☐	☐
Efficient	☐	☐	☐	☐	☐
Reliable	☐	☐	☐	☐	☐
Kind	☐	☐	☐	☐	☐
Knowledgeable	☐	☐	☐	☐	☐
Understandable	☐	☐	☐	☐	☐
Helpful	☐	☐	☐	☐	☐

Scales

Scales, that is to say, sets of items and responses, appear in some of the question formats above. However, the Likert scale is worth mentioning as an easily used tool for measuring attitudes: respondents indicate their levels of agreement to statements provided by the researcher relating to that attitude, belief or characteristic. The respondent, rather as in rating-scale questions, responds to each item on a five-point or seven-point scale, for example corresponding to strongly agree, agree, neither agree nor disagree, disagree, strongly disagree. To remove the tendency for some people to over-choose the middle option, this middle option is sometimes removed, making a four-point scale. The latter is used in the Rosenberg Self-Esteem Scale, where the first three items are as shown in Table 10.2.

Table 10.2

	Strongly agree	Agree	Disagree	Strongly disagree
1 On the whole I am satisfied with myself.				
2 At times I think that I am no good at all.				
3 I feel that I have a number of good qualities.				

Open questions

You can think of open questions in a questionnaire in the same way that you think about unstructured interviews, diaries and accounts. They are bounded by the same considerations, in that you are aiming to get at the central concerns of an issue as your respondents see them. In a written questionnaire, though, where there is little in the way of stimulus (as there would be in an interview), if you want to use open questions you will have to give more of a prod to jog the mind of your respondent.

Open questions may be simply a question such as 'How would you describe your manager's management style, in two or three sentences?' Or you may structure them differently, for example:

> If I had to sum up the culture at my place of work in a word or phrase, it would be …

> I am/am not enjoying my work because …

Observation

Observation is a key way to collect data, though there are very different ways in which to go about it. The core difference is between:

- the kind of observation in which you systematically look for particular kinds of behaviour
- one in which you watch informally (but methodically), recording important facets of what is happening.

The first kind of observation, where you watch for particular kinds of behaviour, is called *structured observation*. The second kind, where you are in the situation, take part, record and watch from within, is called *unstructured observation*.

If you undertake a structured observation, you make assumptions that the social world is viewable through a prism that enables the breakdown of social activity into quantifiable elements – bits that you can count. You, as the observer, have to define what these bits are. They may be individual pieces of action or language, such as a child physically touching another child or a teacher using a particular kind of question. The next thing that a structured observer has to do is devise some way to count these elements. This can be done in a number of ways.

Structured observation

Duration recording

Here, the observer measures the overall time that a target behaviour (such as 'child out of seat') occurs. You will end up with an overall time, for example 27 minutes in a session of 60 minutes.

Frequency-count recording

The observer records each time a target behaviour occurs. You will end up with an overall number, for example 4 times in a session. (This is also called 'event sampling'.)

Interval recording

You decide on:

- an interval (3 seconds, 10 seconds, 20 seconds, or whatever – depending on the complexity of what you are looking for)
- target individual(s)
- categories of behaviour (for example, on-task, off-task).

You will end up with data that can be processed in a number of ways. The most usual way of processing it is to count up the number of times that the target individual has scored in, say, the behaviour category of interest and then to express this as a percentage of the total number of possible observations.

Unstructured observation

By contrast with structured observation, an unstructured observation is undertaken when you immerse yourself in a social situation, usually as some kind of participant, in order to understand what is going there. This is the more likely scenario in a case study. Often this kind of observation is called *participant observation*, because it is associated with researchers becoming participants in the situations that they are researching. Ethnographers, with whom this kind of observation is usually associated, often discuss social life as if it were a stage, or a set of stages, on which we act out roles (see the discussion of Goffman's work in Chapter 3). Unstructured observation will be geared to understanding how these roles play themselves out on the stage of life.

As Burgess (1982) points out, the term 'participant observation' is a little confusing since it connotes much more than simply observation. It entails talking to people, watching, reading documents, keeping notes and anything else that enables you to understand a situation.

Image-based methods

Here, photographs, videos, films, graffiti, drawings, cartoons and so on are used as data sources. Especially now that digital photographs and videos are more or less free and disposable, image-based methods provide a powerful extension of observation and open up a range of possibilities for case study research. Image-based methods not only slot effortlessly into the illustrative case study but also are a means of recording observations and eliciting responses from your research participants in more or less any kind of case study. There are a number of advantages:

• You can more easily include the person or persons on whom the research focuses. While observation pure and simple is always from researcher to researched, image-based methods offer the reciprocal relationship as well – that is, the researched can set the agenda and the research can be more inclusive. In research with young people in a secondary school, Cremin et al. (2011) explored the students' 'voice' by giving them a camera.

• You can capture a social scene far more quickly than you can with notes. The captured scene will enable you to freeze it in time for your subsequent analysis at leisure.

• The scene can be captured discreetly, with little input from you, ready for your subsequent interpretation. Not only is it more subtle than, say, interviewing, but it can also break the ice and help conversation to start. As Schwartz (1992: 1) put it, the camera was, 'an excuse to start up a conversation, and the longer I made photographs, the more people I met'.

- You can adapt your method to your case study 'process'. For example, in sequential or diachronic studies (see Chapter 9) you may wish to repeat photographs of the same situation over a range of times and dates.

- These methods can be blended extraordinarily easily with other methods. Prosser and Loxley (2008) describe a study about city gentrification that combined photography, ethnographic fieldwork, grounded theory and analysis of detailed field notes over a period of 16 years.

- Images can enable the use of the *photo-elicitation* method – that is, photos (or other images or videos) are shown in interviews to evoke a response. This can be particularly useful with children, with whom it is often difficult to engage if you limit yourself to words. Prosser (1992), for example, showed a photo of 'smokers' corner' (see Figure 10.1) to pupils and staff as a way to compare the priorities of teachers and pupils.

Figure 10.1   Photo-elicitation: smokers' corner.
Reproduced by kind permission of Jon Prosser

- Prosser and Loxley also point to the ambiguity of an image and its unpredictable, almost haphazard capacity to kindle a response that may be quite unexpected. Prosser (1998) gives an excellent overview of this emerging method.

Measurements and tests

Tests are used to check the extent of something, whether this is reading ability or blood pressure. Test results will nearly always be given in the form of numbers. Tests can exist in simple, informal measures devised for a particular and local purpose as well as in complex standardised forms. An informal test assesses something that has been taught or a level of pre-existing knowledge. A teacher may devise, say, a spelling test and give marks out of 20. In the same way, for an evaluative case study, you may devise a test to assess the extent of learning.

Tests can be either norm-referenced or criterion-referenced:

- a *norm-referenced test* compares the person being tested to a sample of similar people
- a *criterion-referenced test* assesses whether or not someone meets some criterion, irrespective of how well other people perform on the test.

Tests of ability and attainment are usually norm-referenced since they seek to tell testers how well those tested compare with other people. The driving test is the usual example given of a criterion-referenced test, since there is no comparison going on with other people doing the test. It doesn't matter how many people can or can't do a three-point turn – if the person being tested can do it, then he or she will get that box ticked.

Official statistics and other numerical data

Official statistics are used surprisingly little in student projects. As I hope I have shown in several of the examples I have used in this book, however, you can do the groundwork that will enable you to undertake a case study really easily using these statistics. For example, in the Hostos-Lincoln case study (page 33) I was able to find out that this school is a fine example of a school that can 'buck the trend', simply by Googling its intake and attainment figures.

There are many websites now from which you can download data of extraordinary detail and richness. In the UK, there is the Department for Education's invaluable document *Education and Training Statistics for the United Kingdom* (available online if you google the title). Another excellent resource – particularly for those undertaking comparative research – is the wide range of statistics gathered by the Organisation for Economic Co-operation and Development (available at: http://stats.oecd.org/source or http://stats.oecd.org/wbos/Index.aspx?usercontext=sourceoecd). The Office for National Statistics Neighbourhood Statistics (available at: http://www.neighbourhood.statistics.gov.uk/dissemination) also gives a mass of information about, for example, census data, which includes accommodation types, numbers of cars, country of birth, distances travelled to work and much more, related to people and regions in the UK. It is especially useful if you wish to relate your data to general statistics for a region or nationally.

For access to all of these sorts of data – UK, US and international – visit Emma Smith's excellent website (available at: www.secondary dataanalysis.com). The US one, for example, leads you to administrative records, archives and gateways, including FedStats and public opinion research, census records, longitudinal and cohort survey data.

There are some other useful sites.

- http://gapminder.org is excellent for comparative data between countries. Not only will it plot, say, countries' national income against their citizens' life expectancy, but it will do this dynamically over 150 years. I used this site for the Kerala case study on page 103. Do try this website.

- www.census.gov/ipc/www/idb/pyramids.html will supply you with animated population pyramids. These show the distribution of people in different age groups in a country.

- http://ess.nsd.uib.no provides general social data from different countries in Europe from the European Social Survey.

If you take only one thing from this chapter, take this ...

Remember that this chapter has only been about tools – data-gathering tools – for enabling you to find stuff out. They do not constitute your case study. Good tools, however, help you to do a good job, so, while they are not a substitute for your analytical skill, they can certainly help by providing you with the right kind of data. Do try to get a grip of the range and variety of data-gathering instruments and understand them as well as you can. In this chapter we have reviewed the use of ...

- interviews
  - structured
  - unstructured
  - semi-structured
- accounts
- diaries
- group interviews
- focus groups
- document interrogation
- questionnaires
- observation

- structured observation

- unstructured observation

- participant observation

- image-based methods

- measurements and tests

- official statistics

Having made use of these tools and techniques to gather together a body of data, you will want to proceed to analysis. To analyse the data you gather you will need to think about analytical techniques, and these are introduced in Chapter 11.

FURTHER READING 📖

Bryman, A. (2001) *Social Research Methods*. Oxford: Oxford University Press.
An excellent compendium on research methods and data-gathering techniques.

McCulloch, G. (2004) *Documentary Research in Education, History and the Social Sciences*. Abingdon: Routledge.
Good for understanding the use of documents – archives, records, newspapers and so on.

Prosser, J. (1998) *Image-Based Research*. Abingdon: Routledge.
The bible of theory and practice regarding using image-based research.

Salkind, N.J. (2004) *Statistics for People Who (Think They) Hate Statistics*. London: Sage.
Good on basic statistics, with some information also on not-so-basic statistics.

Smith, E. (2006) *Using Secondary Data in Educational and Social Research*. Maidenhead: Open University Press.
An excellent discussion of the use of secondary data. See also Emma Smith's website (available at: www.secondarydataanalysis.com), which gives details of a broad range of US, UK and international data websites. The US one leads you to records, archives and national government and public opinion research, census records, longitudinal and cohort survey data.

Thomas, G. (2013) *How to Do Your Research Project* (2nd edn) London: Sage.
Chapter 7 covers data gathering and goes into more detail than I do here about interviews, accounts, diaries, questionnaires and observation.

11

ANALYSIS: A TOOLKIT FOR ANALYSING AND THINKING IN CASE STUDY

I noted in Chapter 1 that there are two parts to a case study: the subject and the analytical frame or 'object'. The way in which you develop the analytical frame takes shape in the context of all of the considerations that I have already touched upon, and these considerations will require that you think long and hard about what you wish your case study to be a study *of*. I gave the example of the choice of World War II as a subject. On its own World War II would not be a case; only with an analytical frame such as 'a case study of a "just war"' would the subject derive meaning as a case study.

So, the analytical frame – the object – is essential. While the development of the analytical frame is crucial – it is, after all, at the core of the study – the way in which you go about actually undertaking the analysis is almost equally important. It's about *how* you do the analysis.

There are myriad ways in which you can analyse data. Since we are concentrating on analysis in a *case study* here, though, I am going to say a little about methods that seek a holistic analysis rather than those encouraging a separate analysis of particular parts. I do hope that you won't feel that these are compulsory or recommended, since case study, as I have been at pains to point out, is not defined by an approach, nor by a method, nor even by a set of methods – even if these conspicuously stress the holistic. Rather, a case study is a container, a wrapper, for a situation or a set of circumstances and it may contain a range of phenomena to be analysed. The analysis of those phenomena may, of course, take multiple shapes or forms depending on the nature of the phenomena, so you may use statistics or sociograms or network analysis (Thomas, 2013) or whatever, and these may all provide perfectly satisfactory means of analysis of these different elements.

You will wish to take a line in your study, however, that explicitly frames your analysis in a holistic context. It's a case study, after all; it is holistic. So, the ways of thinking about analysis that I offer in this chapter stress a view of the whole situation. It is, perhaps, rather an unusual assortment and by no means covers exhaustively the analytical methods that are available, but I have brought these together as means of seeing patterns and developing connections. They are, of course, no substitute for your thinking. In fact, on the contrary, they *require* your thinking, but what they do is help your thinking progress.

Interpretative inquiry: eliciting themes

You may recall that I mentioned in Chapter 8 that interpretative inquiry seems made for case study. It's like love and marriage, because the starting point of the interpretative inquirer, like that of the case inquirer, is the indissolubility of the situation to be studied. The interpretative inquirer starts with the view that situations cannot be fractured into variables. We have to study the meanings that people are constructing of the situations in which they find themselves and proceed from these meanings in order to understand the social world.

So, interpretative inquirers collect data in the form of interview transcripts, informal observations and so on, as noted in Chapter 8. The tricky bit is in drawing something meaningful from all of this qualitative data – interpreting it in such a way that it contributes to a useful analysis. The problem with qualitative data is that it can seem shapeless and without structure. The trick is to find points of congruence and similarity – places of coherence in the seemingly amorphous mass of data. Those mustn't just re-emerge, undigested as ad hoc quotations; analysis requires more than this. Categorisation, sorting, finding coherence, simplifying, synthesising: these are at the heart of analysis and there are various means to help you achieve good analysis.

> Interpretative inquirers believe that you can't fracture the social world into variables like a geologist fractures rock.

Constant comparative method

The *constant comparative* method is the basic method of interpretative inquiry, rather like curry sauce is the basic substrate of Indian cookery. There may be many bells and whistles that are added to the constant comparative method, but, however elaborate, it will always be defined by the simple principle of going through data again and again (this is the *constant* bit), comparing each element – phrase, sentence or paragraph – with all of the other elements (this is the *comparative* bit). That's all there is to it, though it has been pimped up by the addition of many and varied 'improvements', which you can find detailed in textbooks on research methods. You may find some of these useful, but most, in my opinion, make things appear to be more difficult than they really are.

The basic principle governing the process of constant comparison is that you emerge with *themes* that capture or summarise the essence (or essences) of your data. Taylor and Bogdan (1984: 126) sum up the process thus:

> in the constant comparative method the researcher simultaneously codes and analyses data in order to develop concepts; by continually comparing specific incidents in the data, the researcher refines these concepts, identifies their properties, explores their relationships to one another, and integrates them into a coherent explanatory model.

The general process is as follows:

1 Examine all of your data – read the interview transcripts, diaries, notes from unstructured observations and so on, look at videos and listen to audio recordings.

2 Make an electronic copy of all of your raw data and, mark it 'RAW'. You now have two copies: your raw data (which you don't want to lose or corrupt) and your working data files. Keep them separate. In fact, employ belt and braces: keep a copy of your raw data on a memory stick *as well as* on your hard drive.

3 Now, rename your working files, adding the suffix 'WORKING'. Read through them. As you are reading, underline or highlight parts that seem to be important. This underlining or highlighting is sometimes called *coding*. If you have audio or video from which you have transcribed, look at or listen to this as well. So much more comes from that context. As you proceed, you will get an impression of important ideas or subjects that are recurring. These can be called your *temporary constructs*. Make a list of them.

4 Read through the data a second time, using the list of temporary constructs from your first reading to check against. Draw up a grid, with the temporary constructs on the left and page references to where the constructs are evidenced on the right. Make notes and observations on the grid as you do this.

5 Get rid of any temporary constructs that do not seem to have been reinforced in the rest of the data. Don't delete that actual data itself, though – it may form an important counter-example for the general themes that are emerging. Highlight these counter-examples in a different colour in your working data records and keep a separate list of them.

(Continued)

(Continued)

6 From the second reading, come up with *second-order constructs* that seem to be a good 'fit' with your data. These second-order constructs should do a good job of summarising the important themes in your data.

7 Look through once more, refining these second-order constructs now as marker posts for the final organisation of your data. Once you are satisfied that these capture the essence of your data, label these as your final *themes*.

8 Think about the themes. How do they seem to be connecting together? What matches with what? Are there any unanimous areas of agreement? Are there any contradictions or paradoxes?

9 Find ways to *map* your themes (see below).

10 Select good quotations or sections from your work to illustrate the themes.

These *themes*, or *categories*, are the essential building blocks of your analysis. Remember that the aim in using an interpretative approach is to emerge with the meanings that are being constructed by the participants (including you) in the situation.

There are various ways in which you can *map* your themes to show the *interconnections* between them. This mapping is often the weakest part of students' use of interpretative data. While the identification of themes is important, students sometimes go little beyond this and do not manage to explain how ideas are related to one another.

Theme mapping

While the constant comparative method can identify the themes in a case study, on its own it does nothing to show the relationships among those themes. You need to make it clear from your commentary and discussion how the themes interrelate. Theme mapping makes such interrelationships clearer by presenting an interview and its themes in picture form.

Theme mapping begins, as does most qualitative analysis, with the constant comparative method. Once you have established your themes, you go through your working data files and look for good quotations that illustrate those themes. Then, in the order that those quotations appeared in the interview, you can put them into boxes on the page (see Figure 11.1). The page now becomes your 'map'. You may also find other quotations that in some way complement or contrast with these quotations. Put these in boxes on the 'map' too. Now, label the boxes with the names of the themes and draw dotted lines if ideas seem to be connected between themes, and solid lines with arrows where one theme (the theme towards which the arrow points) seems in some way to account for or explain the theme at the other end of the arrow.

The example I have given in Figure 11.1 is a theme map following the analysis of some interviews I conducted with support teachers for children with special educational needs (see Thomas, 1992). Rather than withdrawing children to work with on their own, these teachers had changed their way of work to be in the classroom, working alongside the class teacher. I was interested in their perceptions and feelings about their role in the classroom. Did they feel useful? Were there tensions, and, if so, of what kind? From my interviews and from my own diary, working as a support teacher, I emerged with a number of themes relating to these questions. These were: status and self-esteem, territoriality, threat/suspicion, interpersonal factors, ideology–professional, communication, organisation, school policy and role clarity. You will see that seven of these nine themes are flagged in the interview theme map in Figure 11.1. Aside from anything else, the theme map gives a kind of mini-representation of the interview, because the illustrative quotations are given in the order that they have appeared in the interview.

NVivo

Remember when you are doing all of this that it is the twenty-first century and there are many software tools to help you analyse data in the form of language. You may, for example, find that packages such as NVivo and ATLAS.ti help if you have a large amount of data. Your university will probably have an institutional licence that will give you free access to one or both of these packages.

NVivo enables you to code data – documents, PDFs, audio, video – and sort these data into themes. The process for examining the data is essentially the same as I've noted above for the constant comparative method. In other words, you explore the data, come up with tentative ideas and code interesting bits, search the data for similarities, mark these, group them under 'nodes', and eventually emerge with final themes.

Figure 11.2 gives an example of an NVivo page from a project in which I was involved with my colleagues Liz Ellis and Liz Hodges (Ellis and Hodges, 2014). This was a project funded by the deafblind charity Sense, exploring the life experiences of people with Usher syndrome, which is the most important single cause of deafblindness. Forty-two people with Usher syndrome were interviewed and their interviews were transcribed into a Word document. This document was imported into NVivo, the data were coded and nodes identified. Figure 11.2 shows those nodes.

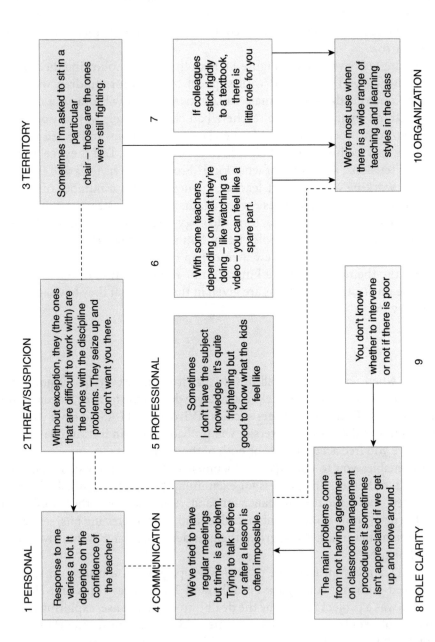

1 PERSONAL

Response to me varies a lot. It depends on the confidence of the teacher

2 THREAT/SUSPICION

Without exception, they (the ones that are difficult to work with) are the ones with the discipline problems. They seize up and don't want you there.

3 TERRITORY

Sometimes I'm asked to sit in a particular chair – those are the ones we're still fighting.

4 COMMUNICATION

We've tried to have regular meetings but time is a problem. Trying to talk before or after a lesson is often impossible.

5 PROFESSIONAL

Sometimes I don't have the subject knowledge. It's quite frightening but good to know what the kids feel like

6

With some teachers, depending on what they're doing – like watching a video – you can feel like a spare part.

7

If colleagues stick rigidly to a textbook, there is little role for you

8 ROLE CLARITY

The main problems come from not having agreement on classroom management procedures it sometimes isn't appreciated if we get up and move around.

9

You don't know whether to intervene or not if there is poor

10 ORGANIZATION

We're most use when there is a wide range of teaching and learning styles in the class

Figure 11.1   Theme map of an interview

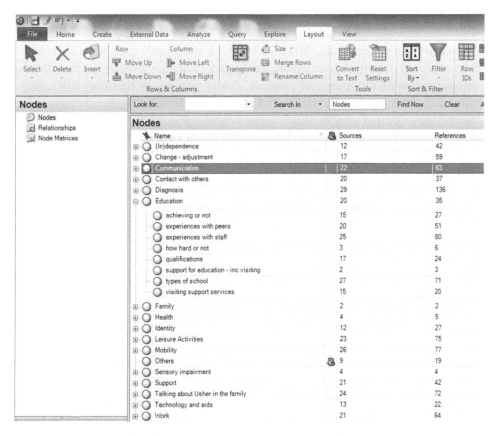

Figure 11.2   Part of a page from NVivo showing nodes and child nodes from the Usher project (Ellis and Hodges, 2014)

You will see that 17 nodes were identified in total; the 'Education' node has been expanded to show its eight 'child nodes'. The 'Sources' column shows how many respondents made reference to each node, and the 'References' column shows how many times the topic (that is, a reference coded by this node) appeared in total. So, for the 'Communication' node highlighted, 22 respondents spoke about something which was coded into this category, while in total there were 63 references made to Communication through all of the interviews.

NVivo has some interesting features that can add to an analysis. You can, for example, make a 'model' to show relationships among nodes, in much the same way as a theme map is drawn.

There is an NVivo 'Getting Started' guide, available as a PDF file, which you can find online. This explains more of the program's features.

Grounded theory

Grounded theory (Glaser and Strauss, 1967) is a commonly used term to describe the process of drawing themes from qualitative data – or, even more broadly, the whole process of interpretative research. Many people say that they are using a grounded theory approach when what they mean, actually, is that they are using the constant comparative method. Some people speak about grounded theory as if it is synonymous with interpretative inquiry – or even as if all of interpretative inquiry depends on it. It's not, and it doesn't.

Perhaps I'm being a bit pedantic, but I find this scooping up of all things interpretative and calling them 'grounded theory' a little irritating. Interpretative inquiry is the Big Daddy; grounded theory is a set of techniques for use in interpretative inquiry. In fact, many of the assumptions behind grounded theory – for example, about grounded theory enabling prediction – seem inappropriate and past their sell-by date now, and I have explored this elsewhere (Thomas and James, 2006). Lincoln and Guba (1985: 339) make a criticism similar to mine, suggesting that constant comparison is the kernel of grounded theory worth preserving.

What *is* helpful about grounded theory is that it offers a neat encapsulation of the essence of interpretative inquiry – in that it puts a heavy emphasis on the way that the ideas (the 'theory') emerge from your immersion in a situation. This is in contrast, of course, to the notion that you can go into a case study with fixed ideas (fixed 'theory') about what may be happening. Again, though, it's important to note that many commentators have queried how far one can clear one's mind of existing ideas and theory and allow these to condense, untainted, out of the data (again, see Thomas and James, 2006). One should, in other words, acknowledge the extent to which already-established ideas and theory may contribute to the illuminations, interpretations and understandings that come through case study inquiry, and this is why it is so important to discuss one's positionality in the methodology chapter of the case study – in order that the reader can have some understanding of the provenance of those interpretations.

Coding in grounded theory

So that you can get your head around some of the different words used to describe similar processes of coding and theme-making in interpretative inquiry, it is worth mentioning that grounded theorists such as Strauss and Corbin (1990) have particular terminology for the coding process as it moves toward the establishment of themes. They talk, in particular, of open, axial and selective coding:

- *Open coding* is the first stage, going through the data, examining it, comparing one part with another and beginning to make categorisations. This is, if you like, the part where you are using your coloured highlighters to mark the text: it's the identifying of the 'temporary constructs' I talked about when discussing constant comparative method.

- *Axial coding* is the second stage, in which you begin to make sense of the open coding. It's where you ask yourself 'What goes with what? What can we call this set of comments? How are these ideas connected to those?' Here you can come up with labels for your codes – labels similar to the 'nodes' used in NVivo, or the 'second-order constructs' I noted in the constant comparative method above.

- *Selective coding* is the final part where the main themes are drawn. As Strauss and Corbin put it (1990: 116), it is 'The process of selecting the core category, systematically relating it to other categories, validating those relationships, and filling in categories that need further refinement and development'. It's the stage where you may be drawing the theme map I discussed above.

Thick description

If you are confident enough, you may wish to forgo the systemisation offered by the constant comparative method and its derivatives and rely on 'thick description'. The term 'thick description' was popularised in interpretivist circles by the great anthropologist Clifford Geertz (1975). It refers to understanding a piece of behaviour – a nod, a word, a pause, for example – in context, and using one's 'human knowing' to interpret it when one describes it.

Geertz (1975: 9) avers that in interpreting meanings you cannot be simply a 'cipher clerk'. You cannot, in other words, just report things 'thinly' without context. The example he uses is the one originally used by philosopher Gilbert Ryle (from whom he borrowed the idea of thick description), of three boys moving their eyes. With one, the movement is a twitch, with another a wink, and with the third a parody of the second one's wink. What turns the twitch into a wink, and what makes the mickey-take a parody? As Geertz puts it, 'a speck of behaviour, a fleck of culture, and – *voilà*! – a gesture'. The trick is, in reporting your observations, to make clear what is going on in a social situation to turn the twitch into the wink, or into the parody of the wink. How do you know which is which? The interpretative researcher has to tell the reader.

When you are offering thick description you are also offering an analysis. You are doing this by intelligently reflecting on the scene, imagining, putting yourself in another person's shoes, and genuinely interpreting what the other person is doing. You are doing this with the knowledge you have not just of people, but also of life and of the contexts that people inhabit – the stages on which they act. If you opt for doing this kind of thick description, it helps, then, to know something of the situation that you observe.

Good examples of this making use of your ready-made knowledge – the knowledge of being human –are found in the great sociologist Erving Goffman's (1956) book *The Presentation of Self in Everyday Life*. Here, Goffman unpacks a storehouse of examples of how people behave in social life as if they were on a stage, always conveying some meaning with their behaviour. In doing this, he is employing thick description.

Word clouds

Think about using something such as a 'word cloud' to represent the verbal data that you collect. I pasted the first few pages of this chapter into a program called Wordle (available at: www.wordle.net, and see Figure 11.3). While the words from this chapter produce a rather dull cloud, I have to admit, the program could produce some very interesting comparisons if you were, say, contrasting the transcripts from long, unstructured interviews in a comparative case study. You can choose the shape of your word cloud – I rather like the idea of the footprint used for this one.

Figure 11.3   Using a word cloud can give a visual impression of an interview

Sociograms

Sociograms are useful for mapping relationships among people. They are often used in case study as they offer interesting insights into the dynamics of a group. Notably, they were used by Paul Willis in *Learning to Labor* (1981). Using a variety of analytical means, Willis untangled how the students at the 'Hammertown' school in which he was observing developed an antagonism towards school. They developed what Willis calls a 'counter school culture'. He intertwined the development of the theoretical narrative about counter-culture with observations and illustrations from the case study itself. As part of this, he used sociometry.

The sociogram given in Figure 11.4 is adapted from research I undertook for the children's charity Barnardo's on the inclusion of children with physical difficulties in mainstream schools. The children in one primary school class were asked to say in confidence who they would like to sit next to or play with.

Sociometry involves asking respondents who they would like to sit next to or who they would like to work with – or the opposite: who they would not like to sit next to, and so on. For each choice an individual makes an arrow is drawn to show the direction of choice. If a choice is returned, the arrow becomes double-headed.

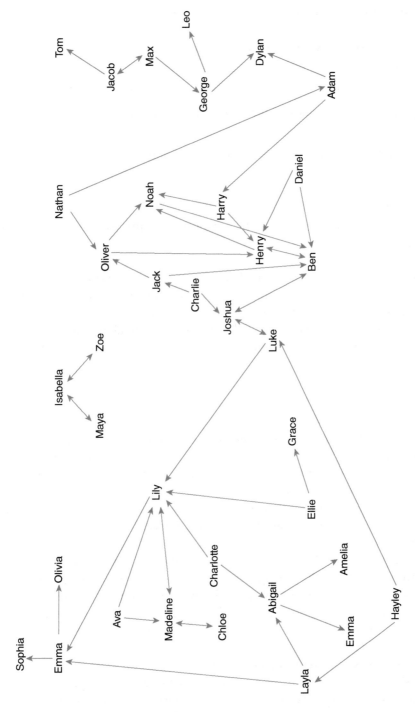

Figure 11.4.   A sociogram of children's seating choices

Various features may emerge from the sociogram:

- one-way choices, where someone chooses another but this choice is not reciprocated
- reciprocated choices, where individuals choose each other
- cliques, tight-knit groups of three or more whose choices are all made within the group
- isolates, those with no choices from other individuals
- clusters, more general groupings
- stars, individuals who have a large number of choices
- power-brokers, individuals who have choices from the stars but not necessarily many others.

Sociometry involves some significant ethical issues. Serious thought needs to be given to the wording of questions and how material is presented to those participating in your project. You must assure your research participants absolute confidentiality and anonymity and take great care not to allow participants to see the papers of others. Pseudonyms are essential, of course, in any write-up.

Systems thinking

I discussed the close ties between systems thinking and the case study in Chapter 3. Because the aim of systems thinking is to try and avoid breaking up a complex web of social activity, it fits naturally with the holistic emphasis of the case study. It's especially useful if there is a problem or puzzle to be solved, which there might be in an action research project, for example. Given that action research is likely to be about your own specific situation, the case study will be particularly appropriate.

I have noted that there have been several models developed for using systems thinking. These have originated in science and technology, but one of the most useful for our purposes has been devised for use in *social* systems, where the problems are often taken to be 'messier' than those in, say, engineering. It is known as the *soft systems methodology* and was conceived by Peter Checkland (1981).

Checkland's soft systems method is particularly useful in what might be called 'purposive' systems – that is, systems with a purpose. You can probably imagine a broad range of purposive systems in your home or university or work life, such as a system for taking out the rubbish on bin day, a university system for ensuring speedy feedback to students on their work, a system for involving parents in their children's school. Almost anything where a purpose is involved and people are expected to do something to achieve the purpose requires a system.

Checkland's soft systems methodology involves seven stages:

1 The problem is outlined, though unstructured, using as many means as possible to achieve this – brainstorming, checklists, Lewin's field analysis (see page 56) and so on. At this stage, however, there is no attempt to make judgements or analyses. It is simply about the facts, in as raw a state as possible.

2 Some attempt is made at organising the problem into its constituent elements. Here a 'rich picture' is drawn – literally a picture. It will be a cartoon of the various elements and how they fit together and include, for example, relationships and attitudes – the 'atmosphere'. Draw stick diagrams of the people, with thought bubbles showing their fears and hopes, agreements and conflicts.

3 This is perhaps the most important stage and involves moving into systems thinking – a bit like going through the back of the wardrobe and into Narnia. Here we have to write 'root definitions', which will say something like 'a system to do A by means of B in order to C in the context of D'. The root definition involves six features of the situation as a system:

   a *customers*, those who benefit from the system

   b *actors*, people who transform inputs into outputs

   c *transformation* from this to that, A to B, inputs to outputs

   d *Weltanschauung*, the broader context and worldviews

   e *owners*, people who 'own' the problem and want it resolved

   f *environment*, the constraints that the environment sets up.

   Checkland gives this set of considerations the acronym CATWOE, created from the first letters of the names of the six features listed above. It can be a bit confusing since, in a simple system, the same person or people can occupy several of the roles (an actor could be the same as the owner, for example). The root definition (see above) enables us to think in systems terms about the roles being occupied by people, the values and objectives that they may hold, who holds power and how it operates in the system.

4 In this stage, you can think about how things might change. You develop what Checkland calls 'conceptual models'. You can be as creative as you like as you do this, imagining how things would work. You should think about what is a 'must-have' in the system and what is simply desirable.

5 You now come back through the wardrobe door and return to the real world. You compare the ideal, coming from the conceptual models, with the real world. You ask why the actual and the imagined are not the same.

6 You look to see what changes may be desirable and feasible, on the basis of the comparison you made in stage 5.

7 Action is proposed to improve the problem situation.

This all perhaps looks a little rigid and mechanical, but I prefer to think of it as a framework for thinking, using the 'let's look at the whole picture' of systems thinking. Dick (2002) provides a useful summary of the approach. He says that Checkland's method has at its heart (see Figure 11.5):

> a comparison between the world as it is, and some models of the world as it might be. Out of this comparison arise a better understanding of the world ('research'), and some ideas for improvement ('action') ... [T]he researchers begin with a real-world problem. They study the systems which contain the problem. Following this, they develop some models of how those systems might work better ... The 'ideal' models are then compared to the actual situation. Differences between the models and reality become the basis for planning changes.

Checkland provides examples and it is useful to look at his book if you wish to go into this method in any further detail. Figure 11.6 gives a summary of the method and Figure 11.7 gives a worked example.

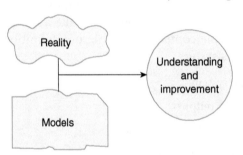

Figure 11.5   Dick's (2002) version of Checkland's soft systems methodology

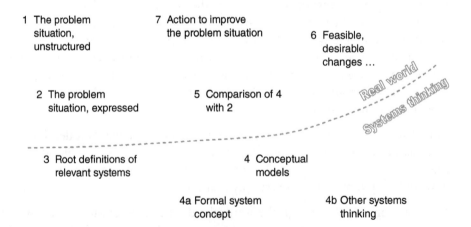

Figure 11.6   Peter Checkland's (1981) soft systems methodology

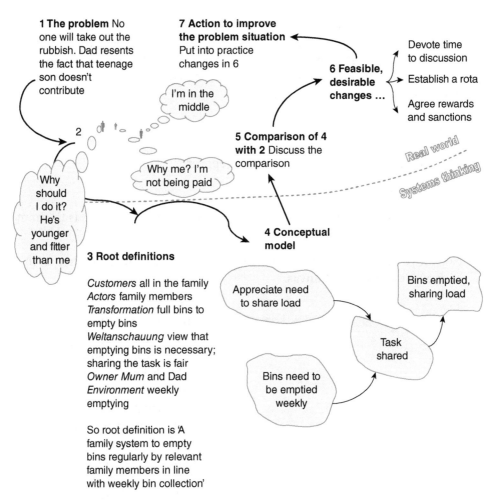

1 The problem No one will take out the rubbish. Dad resents the fact that teenage son doesn't contribute

7 Action to improve the problem situation Put into practice changes in 6

Devote time to discussion

6 Feasible, desirable changes ...

Establish a rota

Agree rewards and sanctions

I'm in the middle

2

5 Comparison of 4 with 2 Discuss the comparison

Real world

Systems thinking

Why me? I'm not being paid

Why should I do it? He's younger and fitter than me

4 Conceptual model

3 Root definitions

Customers all in the family
Actors family members
Transformation full bins to empty bins
Weltanschauung view that emptying bins is necessary; sharing the task is fair
Owner Mum and Dad
Environment weekly emptying

So root definition is 'A family system to empty bins regularly by relevant family members in line with weekly bin collection'

Appreciate need to share load

Bins emptied, sharing load

Task shared

Bins need to be emptied weekly

Figure 11.7   Soft systems with a worked example

Drawing storyboards – the nuts and bolts

On pages 38–44, I discussed how to use a storyboard in the development of your case study, but storyboards are more than merely pictures. Do you remember the scene in *The Terminator* where the cyborg reconstructs itself from all of its broken bits and melted pieces? Well, that's what the storyboard does for you. It's a bit like a silicon chip with the instructions on it for the construction of a case study (rather than a cyborg). It enables you to see all of the disparate elements encased in the case study wrapper and helps you to understand the connections between them so that they can be assembled into a meaningful whole. Not only will you be left with a meaningful whole but also a whole that is more than the sum of its parts.

I've given plenty of examples of storyboards earlier in the book, so I won't give another now. Here are some tips, however, about the nitty-gritty of drawing storyboards in Word. Do remember, though, it is the ideas that are more important than the drawings themselves and they don't need to be done in Word – you could do them just as effectively with sticky notes.

How to draw a storyboard in Word – the basic course

1   Click on **Insert**. Wait for the *full* menu to appear.

2   Then click on **Picture**.

3   Click on **New Drawing** and a 'canvas' will appear on the page. This is the frame for your storyboard.

4   Note: If you are using Word 7, after **Insert**, you will need to go to **Shapes**, then click on **New Drawing Canvas**.

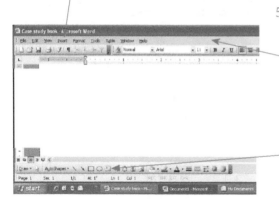

5   Now, into this canvas you can put text boxes to contain your basic ideas. To do this, make sure the drawing toolbar appears by right-clicking on a blank part of the menu bar, tick 'Drawing' and the drawing toolbar will appear at the bottom of your page. On the drawing toolbar click on **Text Box**, then expand your box using the little cross mark and draw and write in your box. (In Word 7, find **Text Box** in the **Insert** menu.)

6   To draw the curved lines between the boxes, click on **AutoShapes** on the drawing toolbar and then on **Connectors**. (In Word 7 click on **Insert**, then **Shapes**, then **Lines**.) Choose the kind of connector you want and 'float' the end of the connector over the text boxes you want to connect. Connect these to the blue dots by unclicking. Now, when you move the box around the canvas later on, the connector stays with the box.

7   Drag boxes around as you wish, change their shapes or whatever. You're in charge.

If you feel life is too short for this, you can draw it by hand and/or use sticky notes, but it is not as hard as it sounds. If you commit to devoting a couple of hours of your life to it, you will find it quite rewarding. If you do proceed, here is the advanced course …

How to draw a storyboard in Word – the advanced course

1 You can alter the 'weight' of lines later on by clicking on one of your arrows or lines and then clicking on the **Line Style** icon on the drawing toolbar. Then choose the line weight that you want.

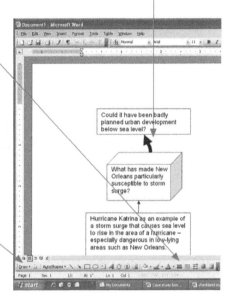

2 You can change the shape of a text box. Click on the outside of the box so that the outside is shaded and there is no cursor in the box, then click on **Draw**. Wait for the full menu to appear, then click on **Change Auto-Shape**. A range of options will appear. For the one I changed here, I chose from the Flowchart range, but you can have whatever you want.

3 To draw a crazy circle, click on **Auto-Shapes**, then **Lines** and choose the 'Curve' line. Practise using it. You'll need to move the cursor round in something approaching a circle (it doesn't matter if it is a bit rough, obviously), left-clicking on and off repeatedly as you move in a circle. You'll find that the ends of the circle join together magically as you get towards closing it. Then, by clicking on the corner points you can enlarge or shrink the shape (as you can with any shape once drawn).

4 To write in the crazy circle, you will need to place a text box over the shape and then write in that. If it disappears or the writing doesn't show, then you'll need to click on **Draw**, then **Order**, then **Bring to front** or **Bring forward**.

That's all there is to it. I can't teach you everything you need to know here, but play with it and you'll find out more and more as you do so.

Developing your theory

I am including developing your theory in the toolkit for analysing and thinking because I think of theory as a tool (Thomas, 2007). It's a tool that can be used in any design frame, not just the case study, but is especially important to it since it acts as the glue that holds the whole thing together.

Glue? Tool? Yes, I'm mixing metaphors a bit. I think of theory as both, really, but let's start with theory as glue.

Theory as glue

I've said that your case study is like a wrapper containing all the bits of your inquiry. The inquiry is defined by a moment in time, a person, place or whatever, and your job in this is usually to drill down to the 'how' and the 'why'. In doing this, you will amass a treasure trove of data that you need to make sense of. For all of the data to provide useful pieces of sensemaking, you need to connect them somehow, which is where theory comes in – it makes the connections between X, Y and Z and holds them together.

It's the 'holding together' bit that is important. Perhaps rather than glue, it's best to think of theory as the sinews and tendons of your study – holding one part to another, yet allowing them to articulate with each other.

Theory as a tool

The great sociologist Pierre Bourdieu was the person who encouraged me to think of theory as a tool. He said of his own work (Bourdieu, in Wacquant, 1989, cited in Jenkins, 1992: 67):

> There is no doubt a theory in my work, or, better, a set of *thinking tools* visible through the results they yield, but it is not built as such … It is a temporary construct which takes shape for and by empirical work.

For Bourdieu, then, theory exists for a purpose. It is *not* the aim of the inquiry, it is *not* an end in itself, it has to do a job, which is to help explain your findings. It comes and goes as you need it, so it may be fleeting, like a shooting star, giving you a flash of inspiration.

This idea of transitoriness is at variance with the idea of theory that is sometimes held in social science. Sometimes, I think, people assume that theory is the end point of an inquiry, but Bourdieu's advice – excellent advice in my opinion – is that it is disposable. It's the explanation the theory provides that is important, not the theory itself. When I shave with a disposable razor, the important part of the process is my silky smooth skin (I wish) at the end, not the razor itself. I don't, on completing my ablutions, carry the razor to work with me to show off to my colleagues, and, when it's blunt, I dispose of it.

Another sociologist, Howard Becker (1998: 3), suggests that theory is a collection of 'generalising tricks' – tricks that help in interpretation and sensemaking. This idea may be a little confusing in the context of a case study, for I have been at pains to point out that you *cannot* generalise from a case study. By adding the word 'tricks', however, I think Becker means something rather different from the usual meaning of generalisation. He is

> Drawing out theory isn't just about making links to 'grand theory' such as that of Marx or Freud. It is about making connections, identifying issues and offering reasoned explanations

talking about our ability to suggest meaningful explanations concerning our findings. How do the parts fit together? What insights emerge? What patterns show up? Here, *generalising* means *finding patterns* or *distilling* or *finding links between*. It's about finding bridges between ideas.

This can be hard to do if you have not had much experience to give you a broad resource of different viewpoints and ideas to make bridges *between*. Using some of the methods that I have outlined in this book, however – such as storyboards, systems thinking, constantly comparing your data – you *can* show that you have weighed up ideas, looked at them critically and tried to form interconnections in the narrative that you are developing; you have tried to develop themes. Always try to extend the process of theorising about what you have done and what you are finding. By doing this you will demonstrate something of not only what you have discovered in your research but also your ability to be creative and insightful.

The process is about not just seeing connections in the data you are collecting yourself but also bringing in and assimilating to your story your reading and knowledge of the world. What use can you make of your own experience, for example on a visit to a different country? Always try to see the relevance of one thing to another and garner and collate thoughts, brainwaves and inspirations as you do so.

In short, theory is about:

- seeing links between ideas
- noticing where patterns exist
- abstracting ideas from your data and offering explanations
- connecting your own findings with those of others
- having insights
- thinking critically about your own ideas and those of others.

Here's an example:

Kayla is following a course in media studies at an American university and on an exchange programme allowing her to study for a year in the UK.

After a while in the UK, Kayla observes what she considers to be a marked difference in the way that the media in the USA and in the UK handle routine national news stories. In the UK, she surmises, there seems to be a reflexively critical, almost routinely deprecatory tone, with shades of adversarialism always thrown into the mix.

Her prima facie questions are: is there a difference in the tone of criticality and disapproval between UK journalism and that in North America, what might be some reasons for this, and what might the consequences be for public discourse?

She begins in her literature review by:

- contrasting intellectual histories of journalism on each side of the Atlantic, looking at the influences of the nations' sizes and political allegiance in such different environments

- examining the influence of UK newspaper magnates such as Beaverbrook and Rothermere on the intensely concentrated market of the UK with its very high density of population

- comparing this with the historically more distributed and local state of affairs in America

- looking at the changes likely to be effected henceforth by the advent of mass communication

- noting the advice given by key figures in the field – people such as Harold Evans (2000), who cautioned against a reflexive jump to the adversarial to attempt to inject spice into a story.

Already, then – in this review of the literature and her reflections on it, informed and bolstered by her own informal observations – Kayla is bringing a theoretical element to her original questions. Already the beginnings of answers are emerging – a little crystal of an idea forming here and there, ready to be followed up and built on. These are embryonic theories, ready for further investigation.

Kayla's prima facie questions did not need much reformulation, but she modified them more precisely to address her interests thus:

- Are there differences between the ways that newspapers report general interest news stories in North America and in the UK?

- If so, how are these manifested in discourse?

- Are differences in discourse likely to impact the nature of journalism and public discourse more generally?

The first of these three questions cannot be answered by a case study since it calls for some kind of representative sample being taken of similar stories in matched newspapers on both sides of the Atlantic. So, such a comparison of stories in matched newspapers using formal discourse analysis is what Kayla did to answer this question in the first part of her inquiry. We'll not delve any deeper into this since it is not relevant to our subject of case studies.

The second and third questions, however, are suitable for exploring using a case inquiry, so Kayla decided to conduct a comparative case study of two newspapers – the *Guardian* and the *New York Times* – over a period of two months, comparing especially their treatment of similar or broadly equivalent news stories.

Kayla was surprised at the degree to which the actuality bore out her expectations. Here is one example of different treatments of stories about something as seemingly innocuous and unadversarial as the weather. The first is from the *New York Times* on 6 February 2010, about a particularly fierce Washington, DC snowstorm:

> The hard edges of Washington were softened as the snow recast the capital of monuments and malls into a postcard town of soft ice cream shapes that had been statues and aerodynamic blobs that had been parked cars: the buried machines of a lost civilization.

Contrast this with a report from the *Guardian* about the unusually snowy and cold winter in the UK exactly one month before the record of Washington's snow:

> A Local Government Association spokesman insisted that councils, which are responsible for gritting many A roads as well as minor and town roads, were prepared: 'As far as we are aware there are sufficient supplies of salt in the country to deal with the current cold snap. How much grit each council holds depends on local circumstances and how much bad weather they tend to get.'

Clearly no general conclusion can be drawn from a simple comparison of the two newspaper stories. Kayla could not suggest that these were representative, but the stories do exemplify the general contrasts that Kayla was noticing in the pieces she was looking at in depth over this two-month period in these two national newspapers. She noticed what she described as a 'defensive, mean and irritable' tone to much of the UK coverage, seeking often to apportion blame, even for natural events such as this. It was not ever-present, and the tone was to be found in the US coverage as well, but her in-depth analysis certainly bore out the findings of the inquiry in response to her first question – namely, that differences existed in the nature of the journalism undertaken in the two countries.

In making this general finding, Kayla was able to contrast excerpts such as those given above. In doing this, she was able to point to the sense of delight shown in the story in the American newspaper and compare this with the inward-looking tone of the UK piece. She was also able to include other news breaking in this period, such as the complaint by the director of the Winter Olympic Games in Vancouver about the treatment of the Games. His complaints centred exclusively on the UK press. Interestingly, one of the allegedly caustic stories to which he pointed came from the *Guardian*, which had claimed that the Games were in danger of being remembered as 'the worst in Olympic history'. The headline in the

(Continued)

(Continued)

Vancouver Sun proclaimed, 'Count on the British media to take the low road', with its first sentence being, 'If there were a gold medal for premature Winter Olympic whining, the British media would be perennial occupants of the middle podium.'

The stories in these two newspapers were a good theme for forming the basis of Kayla's comparison. Using her core case comparison, she was thus able to reflect on her earlier theorisation following her literature review and accept or discard some of her ideas. She could also take some of them further, accepting the idea of adversarialism having emerged from the tight UK market wherein newspaper owners could use everyday news to promote politically loaded messages.

This, then, was the second theoretical element, binding together original and emergent ideas with empirical findings and coming up with new explanatory ideas. These new ideas concerned the oppositional nature of discourse in the two national environments, even where this was not party-based. It affected, Kayla conjectured, all kinds of discourse and extended even into a kind of anti-intellectualism, such as the phrase 'the buried machines of a lost civilization' from the *New York Times*, which, she guessed, would not have been tolerated in the more cynical discursive environment of the UK. Her discussion came to be about the extent to which this affected the intellectual climate more generally (see Figure 11.8) and she sought to discuss this in the context of further reading.

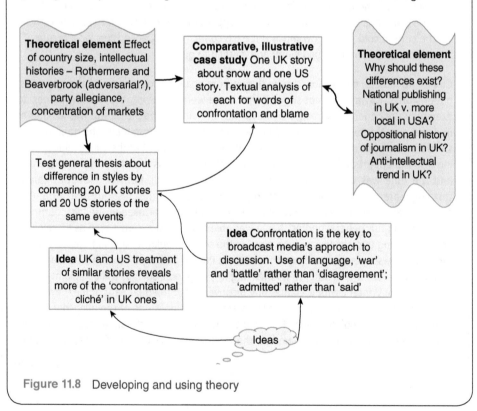

Figure 11.8   Developing and using theory

'Theorisation' and 'theory', then, take a variety of shapes and forms as a study progresses. There are two stages:

1 setting your analysis in the context of everything that has gone before, especially your literature review

2 tying findings together – intertwining ideas, seeing patterns – and then knitting all of this together into a fabric that is called 'theory'.

In doing all of this, the important thing is to use your brain to try and understand what is going on – to *make sense* as you progress.

Elliot Eisner (1991: 238) suggests that theorising is the 'art of the eclectic', wherein we put things together, make multiple interpretations, build bridges and reason by analogy. He makes a plea for 'convincing insight rather than Truth'.

Using narrative

Throughout this book I have stressed the importance of the narrative – the storyline – in a case study.

In the same way that a story has coherence, integrity and progression, so must a case study. In looking at the whole you are eschewing the reductionist, fractionating methods of much social science inquiry – methods that attempt to dissolve the connecting threads and fibres that hold social phenomena together. In a case study you must make sense of the whole by *retaining* the fibres that bind the whole story together. Those fibres concern time, place, meaning, intention and much more, all interrelating.

The interrelationship makes sense in much the way that a story does. We cannot take one page of a novel and make very much sense of it. Nor can we extract and analyse just the sentences that contain a character's name to work out his or her personality – we would probably form a very distorted picture of that character if we did. Rather, each character is understandable only in relation to the whole story. It's the same in a case study.

Not only this, but the structure of a story itself adds a great deal. In stories there are assumptions about, for example, motives, intentions, jealousies and kindnesses. These are things that we all understand from our daily experiences, our understanding of life, and we use this experience and these understandings to deconstruct the narrative of a case study.

The great educator–philosopher Jerome Bruner (1997: 126) goes so far as to say that narrative is at the heart of all meaningmaking, even if it is *scientific* meaningmaking:

> The process of science making is narrative … we play with ideas, try to create anomalies, try to find neat puzzle forms that we can apply to intractable troubles so that they can be turned into soluble problems.

In his famous article in the journal *Critical Inquiry*, he calls this *the narrative construction of reality* (Bruner, 1991: 1). I give below some key ingredients when using narrative in case studies. In doing this I have borrowed heavily from Bruner's (1991: 3) 'ten features of narrative', taking away a few of them and adding a couple of my own. It is an anatomy, if you like, of storymaking. I offer these ideas as ways to extract every possible drop of juice from the story you are telling in your case study.

Questioning and surprise – intelligent noticing and serendipity

You will have 'finds' as you construct your narrative. Be prepared to use these – to use surprise and serendipity. Samuel Johnson (1759/1963) (that's the famous eighteenth-century Dr Johnson) put it well: 'Our brightest blazes of gladness are commonly kindled by unexpected sparks.' We shouldn't ignore these just because they fall outside the bounds of some prescribed method. When inventors and creative thinkers give us an insight into the ways that they think, it is clear that the generalisation, if it is significant, is secondary to metaphor, inspiration and imagination.

Storr (1997: 176) gives many examples of this kind of intuition in which a solution suddenly appears – he quotes from mathematician Gauss, for instance: 'Like a sudden flash of lightning, the riddle happened to be solved. I myself cannot say what was the conducting thread which connected what I previously knew with what made my success possible.' The same happens in social inquiry, and a case study seems to be the ideal vehicle for this kind of insight, as long as it is enabled by a spirit of curiosity and not snuffed out in a relentless search for generality.

Heuristic and incremental chunking

Heuristic comes from the Greek *heuriskein*, meaning 'to discover'. It's from the same root as Archimedes' 'eureka'. Archimedes, of course, jumped out of the bath with the solution to the problem of how to tell if his king's new crown was made of pure gold or had been adulterated with silver. We now use the term 'heuristic' to mean an explanation that is assumed to be the best in the circumstances and 'for the time being'. Heuristics don't have to be the best for evermore.

How do we get to that eureka moment? How, in other words, are the elements woven together? What depends on what? Where are there contradictions or paradoxes? This 'eureka' of intuition, if dissected, is similar to Simon's (1983) tacit processes of incremental chunking. It is the putting together of related information to make a story. Be confident in doing this.

Narrative diachronicity

Narrative diachronicity? Not the most user-friendly term. Thanks, Professor Bruner. 'Diachronic' means changing over time. So, narrative diachronicity means 'a story that changes over time'. (I know: why couldn't he say that in the first place? Someone call the Plain English Campaign.)

Someone doing a case study should be acutely aware of change over time – and not only in a diachronic study (see page 169). He or she notices change as it happens and seeks its antecedents and consequences. We have to find the 'sequence of steps', as Becker (1992: 209) puts it, and understand cause in relation to time, with 'each step understood as preceding in time the one that follows it'. In doing this, we conjecture not only about how one thing is related to another but also how cause and effect change with time as other variables in a situation also change. Becker (1992: 209) gives an example:

> Causes may be seen to operate, but now it is possible to treat a given causal variable as operating in different ways (or indeed not at all) at different steps in the process. In an analysis of heroin addiction, race might be a crucial variable in explaining exposure to the possibility of using drugs, but once a person has started to use drugs, race might play no further part in affecting whether people so exposed in fact use drugs, or, having used them, become addicted to their use.

So, time may switch on or switch off the potency of a variable, and it is important to be aware of this since its significance is one of the ready-made, built-in advantages of the case study. While a reductionist inquiry shows the patchy significance of a variable only with great difficulty, a case study ought – by stressing the importance of the diachronic – to show how a variable such as race (in Becker's example) may ebb and flow in its significance.

Particularity

In her novel *Under the Net*, Iris Murdoch (2002) has one of her characters come out with this line: 'All theorising is flight. We must be ruled by the situation itself and this is unutterably particular.' This is perhaps at variance with the advice I have been giving about the *need* for theorising, and there is an apparent contradiction here. Certainly, if theory is about generalisation, there is a tension to be resolved.

Without going into the ins and outs of this now, what Murdoch is getting at is that there is a uniqueness to a particular situation and we should seek to understand this without what the philosopher Michael Oakeshott (1967: 2) calls the 'irritable search for order'. We should not always judge this situation and its significance by reference to others but by reference to the particular.

This may call for a special effort of will from the student or professional researcher, given the ever-present desire to establish, develop and refer to a certain kind of generalising theory among social scientists.

(Continued)

(Continued)

Intentional state entailment

Bruner notes that we should observe not just what people do, but what they think and feel. It is their beliefs, intentions, hopes, desires and values that are important. There is nothing different here from the thick description of the interpretative inquirer (see page 211). It should be the unselfconscious hallmark of those doing case studies.

Breaching the canon ... and counter-factuality

Using the rather ugly word *canonicity*, Bruner (1991: 11) asks us to consider what is usual, normal, in a line of reasoning or the unfolding of an argument or a story. This is the 'canon' – it's the realm of what we expect. By suddenly throwing a spanner in the works, we can jolt our readers into thinking differently – perhaps differently enough to imagine an alternative explanation or a different state of affairs.

As narratives, case studies have the function of letting us understand and recognise how they differ from what is normal or expected. They let us guess how and why this may be so. Feyerabend (1993) suggested that we may use *counterrules*. These are hypotheses that contradict well-established thinking of one kind or another. Kuhn (1970: 52) suggested something similar in what he called the 'awareness of anomaly'.

Such a breach can be engineered by the deliberate introduction of an *imaginary* change of understanding, which is why I've taken the liberty of adding 'counter-factuality' (Kahneman and Tversky, 1973; Mandel et al., 2005) to the heading above using Bruner's phrase.

Counter-factuality is the imagination of a different state of affairs. This might exist if a particular event (usually, though not necessarily, a key one) had not occurred or if there had been some other outcome from it. Counter-factuality exists, in other words, in 'what if ...?' questions.

This idea has been employed by historians (Ferguson, 1999), though it has not been widely used as part of the method for carrying out a case study in the social sciences. I'd like to see it used more. Ragin (2007: 63) has discussed its use, as has Lebow (2007). Interestingly, Ruth Byrne (2005) discusses how central a role counter-factuality takes in our everyday reasoning, showing how different kinds of reasoning – 'what if ...?', 'if only ...', 'even if ...' – can be refracted through the counter-factuality lens. If only more case study inquiries (or, indeed, inquiries in general) used such aids to the imagination ...

Context sensitivity and negotiability

Perhaps in the same way that Barthes (1974) talks about 'writerly' texts, in which the meaning is (perhaps confusingly) created by the reader (as distinct from 'readerly' texts), so the assumption should be that the interpretation of the case is embedded in the inquirer's (and the reader's) own experiences.

> Interpretation is personal. It is sensitivity to context that enables readers to make sense of the narrative of the case and agree or disagree with the researcher. As Bruner (1991: 17) puts it: 'You tell your story, I tell mine, and we rarely need legal confrontation to settle the difference.'
>
> ### Analogy
>
> We make sense of the unfamiliar by reference to the familiar, drawing likenesses between one situation and another. We use our own knowledge to do this – our 'common sense'. Our understanding is based on myriad personal interpretations we weave together into meaningful stories that help us to make sense of similar events and situations, similar plotlines.
>
> The narrative that a case study lets you draw can be the ideal frame for enabling such analogy and metaphor. Tavor Bannet (1997: 655) discusses analogy and, interestingly, says that it is a 'method of reasoning from the known to the unknown, and from the visible to the speculative' by carrying familiar terms and images across into unfamiliar territory. It is like a form of translation, 'a way of transporting something from place to place, from old to new, from original to copy', and we can therefore move from one context to another. We bring together, juxtapose and see similarities across contexts.

In discussing the importance of narrative in the case study, Abbott (1992) suggests that we should always be seeking what he calls 'causal narrativity', but I personally prefer to suggest that, in social science, we are, as with 'theory', making connections rather than trying to find causes. Becker (1998: 60–61) puts this very nicely: he suggests that the use of the word 'cause' is misleading in social research, given its complexity, so, we should see ourselves as seeking narrative rather than a cause:

> Assume that whatever you want to study has, not causes, but a history, a story, a narrative, a 'first this happened, then that happened, and then the other happened, and it ended up like this.' On this view we understand the occurrence of events by learning the steps in the process by which they came to happen, rather than by learning the conditions that made their existence necessary.

It is the case study that enables such creativity – allows you to suggest these bridges and passages between ideas.

Think drama

In Chapter 3, I looked at the ways in which some sociologists, such as Erving Goffman, have organised their views of the world around *dramaturgy*. This is a view in which life is seen as a set of dramatic performances and has been used by not just Goffman but also a range of interpretivist social scientists. They talk about actors, roles and stages in their discussions of the interactions that take place between people.

If the meat of your case study is about people's interactions and you decide to adopt an interpretivist approach (see page 52), how do you take it forward? I think one of the best ways to make this happen is to extend the theatrical analogy. Think of the substance of the case study as a play, a drama, complete with:

- a script, plot and leitmotif (provided by life and the world)
- a stage and scenery (the wider context)
- a dramatis personae (a list of characters, institutions or agents)
- a director (you)
- an audience (your readers).

The likening of a case study to a play is useful, I think – not just because it stresses the bounded nature of this study (the boundaries in the case of the drama being provided by the script of the play and the walls of the theatre) but also because it emphasises the narrative of the study. In a play, a story is told – of a drama, with a beginning a middle and an end (unless it's *Waiting for Godot*). There are arguments and links intertwined through the story – a plot, with questions, premises, intrigues, subterfuges. Characters come to life as they deal with the obstacles that the plot puts in front of them. The case study is similar on all these counts.

The analogy is not perfect, however, since in a play the work is fictional and in a case study the focus – the person, event, phenomenon or whatever – is there. It is real. If it were *not* real we would not be interested in studying it.

So, there are differences and it is interesting to pursue the dramaturgical metaphor for those differences. In a case study, the *script* is not written by a playwright, but is 'written' by life, by what has occurred. Anyone who has watched a modern-day pro-duction of a Shakespeare play will realise, though, that a script can be interpreted in such a way that a familiar play becomes almost unrecognisable. Directors examine scripts for meanings and impose their own interpretations on them. In the same way, the script provided by a case study is interpretable. Actually, the 'facts' of the case are far more fluid than a play's script since it will be for you (as director) to decide how they are con-stituted and how the various elements intertwine.

> Our social lives can be thought of as a series of stages on which we act out different roles. This metaphor can be useful in the analysis of a case study, thinking of the parts people play in different contexts.

They are, however, the raw materials and it's up to you to knit them together into a convincing narrative. You become the narrator or the playwright, given the storylines and subplots provided by life.

Running through the script will be the *plot*, which will comprise different elements involving the intentions of the characters and their responses to each other and the twists and turns of events.

There will also be a *leitmotif* – the background milieu, the context, the themes that provide the backdrop against which the action occurs.

We can also see the *stage* as the confines or boundaries provided by life. Here we can return to the case study as a container, in the same way that the stage confines the action of the play. There has to be a boundary to a case study and it is up to you to set it.

The *dramatis personae* is perhaps the most important part – that is, the characters, whether they be people, institutions or natural phenomena, such as Hurricane Katrina. What are these characters doing? What are their origins? What, if they are people, gives them meaning and purpose? How far do particular characters react to challenges or make their way around problems?

You are the *director* and, to an extent, the playwright – the latter because you put the people and events together to tell the story as you see it unfolding (the raw materials have been provided by the situation, but you are the one who sees how things fit together). So, you develop and write the plot; you provide the connective tissue.

In doing this, there is an onus on you not simply to be what the great anthropologist Clifford Geertz (1975: 9) called a 'cipher clerk'. In other words, you have to use your imagination for the raw materials available to you.

It is easy to forget the *audience* because its members are not direct participants in the study. They are one of its most important elements, however. Most research – action research excepted – is principally about communicating new information to others. Many students fail to consider the readers, which is a great mistake, given that the main readers of students' theses or dissertations will be markers. Students make the mistake of assuming that if all of the facts are down in more or less the right order, this will suffice.

It won't – and it particularly won't for a case study. Even in a report for an experiment in physics, the structure has to be clear and readers should be able to go through without a double take – without, in other words, thinking, 'Now, what on Earth does this sentence/this paragraph/this chapter mean? How does it fit? What's it doing here?' In my long life, I have read many dissertations and this, sadly, has been an all-too-frequent set of questions in my mind while reading them.

For the readers, reading your report should be like eating a bowl of their favourite ice-cream. It should be smooth, enjoyable, have nice gooey bits that are particularly interesting and, when they have finished, it should leave them thinking 'I enjoyed that, mother. Is there any more?'

Actually, it should be *better* than a bowl of their favourite ice-cream because it should get them *thinking* – and there's nothing better in life than thinking.

There are various techniques that can be adopted when writing up your case study that will make it more interesting and more polished – I shall discuss a few of these in Chapter 12.

Being intuitive and imaginative

[We need] ways of expanding the reach of our thinking, of seeing what else we could be thinking and asking, of increasing the ability of our ideas to deal with the diversity of what goes on in the world.

(Becker, 1998: 7)

In Chapter 1, I noted that Einstein had said of the process of science, 'There is no logical path, but only intuition' and this sentiment – with the obsession of social science to be methodologically exact, rigorous and innovative – has sometimes been forgotten. The philosopher Karl Popper (1968: 32) made a comment similar to Einstein's: 'there is no such thing as a logical method of having new ideas, or a logical reconstruction of this process. My view may be expressed by saying that every discovery contains "an irrational element", or "a creative intuition".' He proceeds to liken this to Einstein's comment (in an address on Max Planck's sixtieth birthday) that scientific advance depends on 'intuition, based upon something like an intellectual love (*Einfühlung*) of the objects of experience'.

So, it's intuition and *intellectual love* that we have to nurture. A tough call, perhaps, since intuition and intellectual love are qualities that don't grow on trees, nor do they lend themselves to bullet-point breakdowns. Given the elusive nature of intellectual love, imagination and intuition, how should we consider them and how should we foster them?

Where to start? Sadly, thinking about how we should foster an intuitive mindset has not been a central consideration in the social sciences. The social sciences have instead become obsessed with correctness, reliability and design exactitude, at the expense of imagination and intuition.

With the paradigm wars that I spoke about on page 48 it is almost as though a false opposition has been set up wherein one cluster of ideas – positivist, normative, experimental, objective – has been set against another – interpretative, subjective, intuitive. This leads to a regrettable hunkering down and a defensiveness in each of the positions. It leads ultimately to an inward turn, wherein there is more concern for process than there is for questions, arguments and conclusions. The consequence is that curiosity in inquiry is diminished and research becomes less interesting.

As astute critic of social science, Stanislav Andreski (1972: 108), says that how we achieve creativity is just as much a mystery [today] as it was in the days of Socrates: all that is known is that, in order to conceive fruitful original ideas, one must have talent, must immerse oneself in the available knowledge, and think very hard.

Is Andreski right about this? Can we really not offer useful advice on creativity and intuition?

In large part I think he *is* right. I quoted the first line from Wittgenstein's *Tractatus* right at the beginning of this book, and he said such beautifully gnomic things that I cannot resist quoting from him again. This time, I shall quote the last line, in the context of Andreski's advice (Kenny, 1993: 31): 'Whereof one cannot speak, thereof one must be silent.'

How true, though I think Wittgenstein was saying a little more than just 'Keep your mouth shut if you have nothing to say' (this is something I have often wanted to stand up and shout out at conferences, but I have never had the courage). Indeed, Frank Ramsey – philosopher, genius, admirer and translator of Wittgenstein – after translating the *Tractatus* (at the age of 19!) suggested in a subsequent commentary that what Wittgenstein was getting at here was 'What we can't say we can't say, and we can't whistle it either'. Ramsey died at the age of 26. How tragic that someone so gifted *and* so funny should die so young.

I can't do better than Ramsey's explanation about whistling, save to offer a very ungnomic deciphering of what these superbrains were going on about. It is this: some things are beyond our words; they exist in what the philosopher Michael Polanyi (1958) has called 'tacit knowledge'. Included in tacit knowledge are your knowledge of how to ride a bicycle (if you can) and your intuition about how to solve difficult puzzles. What the case study offers here, then, is the capacity – or, better, a predilection – to see wholes rather than fractured parts and, with this predilection, we can perhaps have some expectation of a greater emphasis on intuition than is offered otherwise.

Assuming that you are still with me and you don't think I've bicycled off into an academic's cloud-cuckoo-land wearing odd socks, where does all this leave us? It leaves us with a view of certain things being very difficult to teach – intuition being one of them. If I weren't writing a textbook, I would leave it at that, but, since I am, I will proceed with one or two ideas that I have gleaned from Richard Sennett.

Sennett (2009: 211) talks about intuition coming in three main stages:

1 from *imagination*, depending on looking back on sensations already experienced – depending, in other words, on memory

2 from establishing *adjacency*, similar to analogy, where two unlike ideas are brought together

3 from *surprise*, which comes from 'dredging up tacit knowledge into consciousness to do the comparing'.

All of this is similar to the 'imagery' that Becker (1998: 12) speaks about. He suggests that, in studying society, we start with images and end with them. Our aim 'is the production and refinement of an image of the thing we are studying'. The rest of Becker's book, *Tricks of the Trade*, is excellent further reading on this.

Well, I haven't done very well in advising you how to be intuitive, have I? No. Perhaps, then, I should sum it up by saying that we all have intuition – it's part of the human condition – and when you are doing a case study, treasure it and don't let it become suffocated by concern over what you consider to be correct procedure.

If you take only one thing from this chapter, take this ...

The analysis is the most important and enjoyable part of your case study project. Here, you will be tying everything together, intertwining elements so that arguments make sense and have integrity. You will be looking back to the original questions that you posed, seeing how they changed in the context of your reading of the literature and your preliminary inquiries and assessing how well your project – using whatever methods of analysis – has answered those questions.

The richness of your analysis will be determined in large part by how much time and thought you are prepared to devote to it, but I have offered in this chapter some ways in which you can give integrity and coherence to your analysis. To review some of these ways of making an analysis:

- the constant comparative method offers a means of drawing themes from interpretative data

- theme mapping allows you to present in diagram form the ways in which themes may interconnect

- packages such as NVivo enable the easier management of coding and theme-making where large amounts of qualitative data are involved

- 'grounded theory' offers a specialised operationalisation of an interpretative approach

- 'thick description' captures the essence of interpretative analysis in its synthesis of reporting, reflecting and meaningmaking

- systems thinking lets you understand how separate bits of behaviour may be interconnected

- the storyboard offers a way of navigating along different potential routes to develop your argument

- you have always in your analysis to be thinking of developing theory – it's about seeing links, noticing patterns, abstracting ideas from your data and offering explanations

- thinking about narrative – or how the events in your study can be seen dramaturgically – can help to give structure to the events that unfold. In doing the analysis, it is important to understand how you may be both using and developing your theory and how you can be intuitive and imaginative in making sense of your findings.

FURTHER READING 📖

Becker, H.S. (1998) *Tricks of the Trade*. Chicago: University of Chicago Press.
Becker's take on research is refreshingly independent of formulae and bullet points. He encourages readers to use their own resources of imagination and intuition to make shape and sense out of their data.

Bruner, J. (1991) 'The narrative construction of reality', *Critical Inquiry*, 18 (1): 1–21.
The essence of a scientific approach, says Bruner, is in meaningmaking, while narrative, with its 'grammar', its rules and its structure, provides a vehicle for meaningmaking.

Eisner, E. (1991) The *Enlightened Eye: Qualitative Inquiry and the Enhancement of Educational Practice*. New York: Macmillan.
Eisner has some interesting ideas on what constitutes theory in qualitative inquiry.

George, A.L and Bennett, A. (2005) *Case Studies and Theory Development in the Social Sciences*. Cambridge, MA: MIT Press.
Taking quite a traditional view on theory, the authors give a perspective on the case study that is located principally in political science. It thus draws on a different disciplinary base from most commentary on the case study and offers some interesting discussion on comparative case studies.

Loader, D. (1997) *The Inner Principal*. London: Falmer.
Loader tells stories from his own experiences. He compares the outer and inner influences on change.

Taylor, S.J. and Bogdan, R. (1984) *Introduction to Qualitative Research Methods: The Search for Meanings*. New York: Wiley.
A key text, and excellent on constant comparative method.

Wright, T. (2010) 'Learning to laugh: a portrait of risk and resilience in early childhood', *Harvard Educational Review*, 80 (4): 444–63.
An excellent and moving study, told in a narrative form.

12

WRITING YOUR STUDY

Ultimately, your case study is written up as a research project, dissertation or thesis. So, it needs to conform to what is expected of one of these. How, then, should it be structured, and is it different from the balance and shape of the write-up of a project that follows a different research design?

Structure

The following gives a breakdown of a typical dissertation or thesis. Be aware, however, that there are few 'typical' dissertations; all are different, and yours may be rather different from this. For example, a literature review may comprise not one, but two or more chapters. The findings and discussion may be conflated into one chapter or expanded to form several, depending on the nature of your work.

A case study will often be unusual in its structure because of its typically narrative form, but you should remember that there are essential elements to any project that must be incorporated in the write-up. Here is a summary.

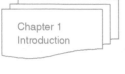

Chapter 1
Introduction

You need an introduction that explains how you came to be interested in the topic of the study. Here, you will lay out your prima facie questions (see page 29).

Chapter 2
Literature review

You need a literature review that looks at what other inquiries have been done on this or related topics and helps you to understand their contribution to your own question. As I explained in Chapter 2, this enables you to refine and reformulate your prima facie research question(s). It may comprise more than one chapter if there are different elements of the literature that you feel warrant their own treatment.

Chapter 3
Method

You then need a methodology chapter to explain why you have chosen to conduct your research in the way you have. That is to say, why have you done a case study? You also explain here why you have picked your chosen design pathway (see Chapters 2 and 6–9) and why you have used the data-gathering techniques and analytical methods that you have (see Chapters 10 and 11). Here, you can also set out details of the research setting in which you have chosen to work: who, where, what, when, how many and so on? Alternatively, given that the setting in which you are studying is likely to be especially important in a case study, you can make this into a separate, subsequent chapter all on its own, rather than being incorporated in the method chapter.

Chapter 4
Findings

In this chapter you set out your findings – what you actually did and found. This and the next chapter really are the 'guts' of your research and the write-up, and in a case study they may be conflated. In other words, findings, analysis and discussion may all occur together in one combined chapter. If this is the case, you may wish to break up this 'mega-chapter' in some other way – perhaps by subject or theme.

Chapter 5
Analysis and
discussion

In the analysis and discussion chapter (which may be divided into two chapters) you offer an analysis of your findings using the tools for analysing and thinking outlined in Chapter 11. You discuss this analysis in the light of your research questions and any issues highlighted in the literature review.

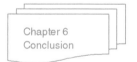
Chapter 6
Conclusion

Your final chapter, the conclusion, draws together the threads and assesses how well the question has been answered by your inquiry.

Figure 12.1 shows the rough proportions (in terms of numbers of words) given to each of these sections, though I should warn you that this is only indicative – some case study write-ups will have a very different balance. As I have noted, your fieldwork, findings, analysis and discussion may, in an interpretative case study, all be merged together because you will be reporting observations almost simultaneously with discussing them.

Is the structure of a case study different from that of other research?

In a case study write-up, it is especially difficult to decide on the balance of the elements I have just outlined. Because of the holistic nature of the worldview taken when doing a case study, it is sometimes less than easy to divide a write-up into sections.

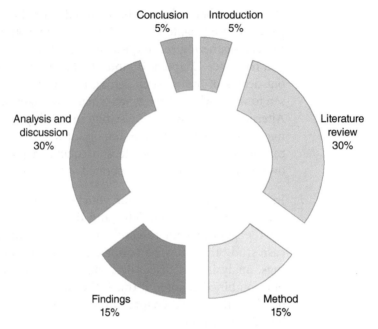

Figure 12.1   Elements of the write-up of a formal, traditional study and their *rough* proportions

In a formal study, you can sometimes take a straightforwardly linear approach, wherein *findings* precede the *analysis*, which precedes the *discussion*. For a case study, however, you may not want to separate out sections in this way since all the time you will be testing out your emerging findings against your thoughts. If this is the case, it is inappropriate to impose a strict line between analysis and discussion since one infiltrates and merges into the other. The differences between the different kinds of study are shown in Figure 12.2.

Formal linear study	Findings ──────▶	Analysis ──────▶	Discussion
Case study	Findings, analysis and discussion		

Figure 12.2   Different kinds of analysis and discussion

Writing up your case study

Why is research done at all? It is done in the spirit of inquiry – to find things out.

An essential part of this is the communication of the findings of that inquiry to others – telling other people. There isn't much research that is of benefit to only the person undertaking it. Perhaps simply keeping the findings to yourself is all right with certain kinds of action research, but nearly always the communication of findings to others is an essential part of the inquiry process.

Certainly this communication is a necessary part of any university-based research, when the people you will be communicating your findings to will be principally your tutor and other markers. The audience may be wider than this, though. It may include fellow researchers, other students, colleagues and other interested professionals – even the general public or local politicians.

Because it is about communication, your write-up has to be interesting. Indeed, interest is the key and you will not establish it simply by dredging up as many facts as possible and flinging them down in front of your readers in more or less the right order. This is true for any kind of research reporting, but with a case study it is especially true.

> Avoid the 'mushy heap syndrome' when writing up your case study – that is to say, avoid an undifferentiated list of quotations and reportage with little commentary or analysis to glue it together. Remember, you need narrative, explanation and theory. Make it all hang together.

A case study is not about finding facts but gathering evidence. This evidence, though, is gathered for the purpose of developing an argument, and there are two important aspects to this. One is the way in which your argument is constructed and the other is about the critical reasoning that you demonstrate. I shall come on to these in a second, but let us pause for a moment to consider the structure of a case study, for, alongside its undoubted strengths, there are some significant risks associated with adopting it as a frame for your work.

The risks come from your 'freedom to roam' when doing a case study. All research has fences around it – barbed wires that define the territory and its integrity, but also have the effect of holding you in place. With some research there are so many fences, enclosures, and enclosures within enclosures, there is hardly any room for the researcher to roam at all. The fences structure the research so that it meets the standards expected of it so that its conclusions can be said to be valid. For example, your choices in terms of how to conduct an experiment are constrained by the limited number of established designs; the conduct of surveys is circumscribed by expectations about samples and the nature of questioning. So, these kinds of research have formidably sturdy fences around them.

The methods that may be used inside the case study wrapper may be constrained by the same kinds of fences, but the case study itself is defined more by your own imagination than methodological boundaries. You thus have freedom to roam, without fences. Marvellous. With this freedom, though, the onus is on you, the researcher, to provide the structure and meaning for the work. With a case study, at its worst, this can lead to the mushy heap syndrome to which I referred earlier (see page 29). Sometimes, what goes under the name 'case study' can amount to not much more than an undifferentiated collection of thoughts and quotations from interviews with very little in the way of glue to hold the whole thing together. This is what you must avoid.

The point I am trying to make is that the quality of a case study cannot be guaranteed by simply following a procedure correctly. Instead, it is determined by your imagination, the way in which you construct your narrative and theory, your critical reasoning and the way in which you develop your argument using evidence. The whole of this book, really, has been about your imagination, so I won't dwell on this now and I have discussed narrative and theory in Chapter 11, but it is important to say a little more about critical reasoning and argument.

Employ critical reasoning

Your findings, the original knowledge that you produce – the guts of your research – are, of course, important. Almost as important, though – particularly when doing a case study as a student – is your *attitude* to knowledge.

In any kind of inquiry, not just a case study, it is not so much about the *amount* of knowledge that you can show you possess, but, rather, whether or not you can show how you have acquired evidence and analysed it and argued from it with a critical frame of mind. Your approach to knowledge should always be as a sceptic – you should show appropriate suspicion and doubt. You will be expected to be aware that there are always different ways to interpret an observation, different ways to argue a case, different interests at play in any argument. In short, you'll be expected to recognise – and demonstrate that you recognise – that truth is hard to come by.

You will need to be tentative about conclusions that you feel you are able to make. Try to avoid phrases such as 'this proves' and, instead, say things such as 'this indicates' or 'the evidence suggests' or 'points towards'. Try to use phrases that moderate the strength of an assertion, such as 'tends to' or 'one might conclude that'. Academic writing is an area where it pays to be tentative: no one will give you high marks for making unwarranted claims about your own research or for innocently swallowing the reports of others.

Doubt *everyone's* findings, even your own. Many great minds have attested to the importance of this. René Descartes (1647/1996) said that 'Doubt is the origin of wisdom', summing this up in the aphorism 'De omnibus dubitandum' (meaning 'Doubt everything'), which Karl Marx took as his own motto for life. Similarly, the great biologist J.B. Haldane concluded his famous essay *Possible Worlds* (1928: 224) with the words 'science has owed its wonderful progress very largely to the habit of doubting all theories'. Jeremy Paxman summed up the sentiment a little more demotically in his personal rallying cry, 'Why is this lying bastard lying to me?' Actually, Paxman claims that what he meant was that he always approaches people with 'a degree of scepticism, asking "why are they saying this?" and "is it likely to be true?" ... Scepticism is a necessary and vital part of the journalist's toolkit' (Wells, 2005). Scepticism is a necessary and vital part of the researcher's toolkit, too.

The great philosopher of education John Dewey (1920/2004) also championed scepticism. He said that we should be suspicious of certain kinds of thinking, particularly those arising from tradition and authority. We should be cautious in trusting the reasoning of others; we should think for ourselves. We should also be especially wary of any line of reasoning (in others or in ourselves) that comes from a strongly held opinion. He promoted *reflective thought*, which is being sceptical about our thoughts and always looking for evidence for a line of reasoning. This brings me on to the way in which your argument is developed.

> Be critical. Remember:
> 'De omnibus dubitandum'
> or 'Why is this lying bastard
> lying to me?'

Develop your argument

Much of this book has been about developing the argument of a case study, stressing the importance of coherence, integrity and the need to weave a storyline – often with a storyboard – from the information that you have collected. While I don't want to go into that again, I do want to stress something that I have not touched on so far, which is the way in which your argument is actually built – the chassis, if you like, of your argument.

There are two main elements to this chassis that, in my experience, are often weak in research project write-ups:

1 establishing the problem to be solved
2 establishing the argument itself.

Let us look at these in turn and see what each should contain.

The problem

The problem must be the sandwich filling between two elements: the context and the response:

The opening context sets out some common ground on which everyone can agree. The problem or 'angle' has two parts:

- some missing evidence or contradictory reasoning

- the consequences of not having an answer.

The response concerns your promise of a solution.

    An example of how this works, presented in Table 12.1, is an 18-month case study that I undertook for the children's charity Barnardo's (Thomas et al., 1998). The case studied was of a school closing and moving all of its staff and students to the local secondary and primary schools. This forms the foundation stone of the entire thesis and it is important that it is stated clearly. I have borrowed the broad structure from Booth et al.'s (2003) excellent book *The Craft of Research*.

Table 12.1   Locating an angle and promising a solution

Context ... *Common ground* ↓	Inclusion of children with special needs in mainstream education is happening increasingly. The move towards inclusion, backed by anti-discrimination legislation, is occurring principally in response to concerns over the loss of social and educational opportunities for those who are segregated in special schools ... and so on.
Problem or angle stated ... *What are the consequences of not knowing? Who cares? So what?* ↓	Little is known about the experiences of students who transfer to mainstream schools. Concerns have been expressed about: • the ability of mainstream teachers adequately to meet the needs of young people with serious difficulties • the readiness of mainstream students to help accommodate special school students • ... and so on. Much comparative research has been undertaken *[brief outline of what it is prior to a full explanation in the literature review]*, but little work has been undertaken to examine the quality and 'texture' of students' experiences in the new environment and how this changes over time – improving or deteriorating – as the process of inclusion becomes 'bedded in' ... and so on. Without information on these issues, the policy to include children with special needs risks failure ... and so on.
Response ... *Promise a solution*	A diachronic case study focusing intensively on the experiences of the students of a recently closed special school promises to add to the knowledge about students' social and educational adaptation over time and will offer insight into the means by which such closures are effected.

    Beyond this, your literature review will help you to refine and revise the issue that you wish to research. After doing this, you will begin your research using your case study and the methods that you have chosen to conduct it. Your case study wrapper encases all of the methods and instruments you choose to address the issue.

So, in the example of the special school that was closing, my fellow researchers and I had started with some notions about the ways in which inclusion operated, and these notions were further informed by our reading of the literature. We then had ideas – a theory, if you like – about the challenges and opportunities that the project might face as it proceeded. We made observations, held interviews with staff and students, kept diaries, conducted documentary analysis and drew sociograms, and these helped to 'thicken' or, alternatively, tone down or soften the various strands of theory that we had developed.

The argument

The evidence that emerges as you proceed contributes all the time to the question that you originally posed. Does the question still seem valid in the light of the new information? Do you want to change course?

Remember that evidence is nothing on its own: it is data in support of a proposition or a claim, so you will be modifying and adapting the claims that you are making as you continue with your empirical work.

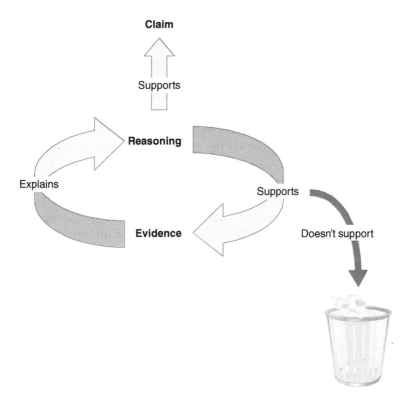

Figure 12.3 The relationship between evidence and reason supporting a claim (adapted from Booth et al., 2003)

So, the process of argument involves recursion (retracing your footsteps), summary, synthesis, putting ideas (yours and those of others) next to each other to see how they shape up together.

This is the way that your argument develops. It involves a revisiting and reassessment of your original ideas and arguments to see which seem more or less valid. Some ideas may be rejected or put into abeyance. Tell readers about this – tell them about your process of acceptance, rejection and reformulation and the conclusions you have come to. Booth et al. (2003) suggest that the process is like that set out in Figure 12.3. I have added the bin to their diagram – I hope they don't mind.

Two examples of good analysis, argument and writing

In the previous chapter as well as this one, I have noted that analysis and argument are difficult subjects on which to offer advice. It may help to provide a couple of examples of first-rate analysis, and there are many examples of such quality. I give several examples of such quality elsewhere (see Thomas and Myers, 2015). As you explore the methodological literature about the case study, you will repeatedly find the same iconic studies used as examples. Again and again, you will find case studies done as part of the sociological tradition, such as Howard Becker et al.'s (1961/1980) *Boys in White* and William Foote Whyte's (1955/1993) *Street Corner Society*. You will probably also find reference to *The Polish Peasant in Europe and America* by Thomas and Znaniecki (1927/1958).

I think it's a pity, though, to treat the case study as the sole prerogative of the interpretative sociologist, so, in seeking examples of good analysis I have tried to take a broader disciplinary approach to it. In the points that I make in this section, I should like – for the sake of freshness – to use different examples of the genre. They are interesting not only in terms of what they have to offer as case studies but also because their authors do not flag the fact that they have undertaken case studies. Perhaps they don't even care that they are doing case study research. As I said earlier, those who research in disciplines outside the social sciences seem delightfully unselfconscious about the methods they use.

I will concentrate on two sets of case studies – those done by a neurologist and a biologist – for the insights that they have to offer.

Oliver Sacks (1996) is a neurologist by professional training, but he discards some of his neurological education to assume the clothes of a storyteller and researcher in his book *An Anthropologist on Mars*. His book relates how he talked with and observed people who exhibited unusual kinds of behaviours – for example, in the syndromes that lead people to display the characteristics of autism and Tourette's.

In doing his case studies, Sacks offers a set of sparkling insights into and understandings of the worlds of a number of people who behave differently. Such insights have been largely curtained off from us by the understandings offered by the traditional kinds of analysis found in medicine and psychology.

Sacks gives reasons for eschewing many of the procedural and methodological habits of his own discipline, neurology, in making his analysis. Neurologists focus on helping people who are, for whatever reason, uncomfortable, unhappy, disaffected, unable or unwilling to 'fit in'. Sacks's insight is that the methods which have been used to examine this discomfort or disaffection, while they can be successful up to a point, fail to address the real issues at stake – human issues. He says (Sacks, 1996: xvii–xviii):

> The exploration of deeply altered selves and worlds is not one that can be fully made in a consulting room or office. The French neurologist François Lhemitte is especially sensitive to this, and instead of just observing his patients in the clinic, he makes a point of visiting them at home, taking them to restaurants or theatres, or for rides in his car, sharing their lives as much as possible. (It is similar, or was similar, with physicians in general practice. Thus, when my father was reluctantly considering retirement at ninety, we said, 'At least drop the house calls.' But he answered, 'No, I'll keep the house calls – I'll drop everything else instead.')

A case study is like keeping the house calls. Sacks spent days and weeks with people with different kinds of behavioural issues – ones that caused them or those around them concerns of one kind or another. He made every effort, however, to put those behaviours in context, not seeing them as disembodied, decontextualised medical or psychiatric conditions but, rather, as valid ways to deal with the world, sometimes very successfully. For example, an autistic woman who found great difficulty relating with other people but who felt great tenderness for animals, combined the latter with her skill in drawing and planning. She used this to help in the design of more humane slaughterhouses that minimised, as far as possible, any potential distress to the animals. Rather than defining a condition or trying to exemplify or generalise from a condition with a supposedly typical example, Sacks used the intimate knowledge he was gathering to illustrate the idiosyncrasy, the particular story, of her case. He showed the individual at work and at home. He showed her autonomy, strength, individuality and the integrity of her life. This is not something that could be said of most medical or psychological writing about autism.

Sacks makes no attempt to generalise from this or from any of his vignettes, and his method is almost invisible since he lays out no mental map at the beginning of his work. Rather, readers are left to make up their own minds; they are left to piece together conclusions for themselves.

(Continued)

(Continued)

The conclusions – conclusions, note, rather than generalisations – are about the ways in which difference can be respected rather than pigeonholed. The pigeonholing comes from the obvious categories of clinical and administrative convenience and the emotions associated with those stereotypical categories leading too easily into hackneyed emotions of pity or admiration so familiar to those with the conditions concerned. By using the case study, Sacks expects to move away from the rut of categories and offers us instead rich analyses of people's lives.

The second set of case studies is from the work of well-known biologist Jared Diamond (2005). While Sacks leaves us to make what we will of his case studies, with each one being a little jewel in and for itself, Diamond develops from the case studies a complex argument and thesis.

He looks at a range of communities and societies that have collapsed or are currently in the process of collapsing. Each one – the Montana of today, the Easter Island of the seventeenth century, Pitcairn, the Mayans, the Vikings, modern Haiti – is very different from the others, but they are connected by decline and collapse.

Diamond's thesis is that the decline of a society happens because of a number of potential factors, ranging from hostile neighbours to environmental change and the society's response to that change. His first point, then, was to establish a connection between these communities. The second was to look for threads that might form the basis of the connection.

Let's look briefly at one of Diamond's case studies. Easter Island has always been a mysterious phenomenon to explorers because of its huge, ghostly statues gazing out to sea. Yet, today, aside from these striking megaliths, there is virtually nothing there. These sculptures were clearly the product of a centuries-old, highly sophisticated civilisation, but why did it evaporate, leaving nothing behind other than these remarkable statues?

It's fanciful to suggest that Diamond had a 'method' for answering these questions since his inquiries consisted of not much more than reading widely about the island, using existing research – botanical, cultural, historical (he wasn't fussy) – visiting it for an extended period and *thinking*. He looked at Easter Island's history and geography. He looked at what the people ate, drawing from research using pollen and charcoal remains that gave clues about now-extinct crops. Using archaeological evidence and oral history, he looked at the likely structure of the society, people's attitudes to death and the afterlife, how the statues might have been sculpted, transported and erected.

The case study is about using many and varied sources of evidence. It's about imagining and using your intuition in arguing a case.

Most importantly, he looked at how all of this might be connected, in the way that the islanders sought and used resources – from the intensification of their agriculture using windbreaks and pits for better growing to the division of the island into 11, eventually competing, territories. All of this he pieced together using intelligent questioning and intelligent answering – often called the *Socratic method*. This method was formalised by Plato and involved the posing of questions by Socrates to a pupil or other person. Diamond does this, but he does it with himself and an imaginary interlocutor. Here's an example (Diamond, 2005: 99):

> How did all those Easter Islanders, lacking cranes, succeed in carving, transporting, and erecting those statues? Of course we don't know for sure, because no European ever saw it being done to write about it. But we can make informed guesses from oral traditions of the islanders themselves ... from statues in the quarries at successive stages of completion, and from recent experimental tests of different transport methods.

For me, two things are interesting about this passage. One is the self-questioning that I have just mentioned. The other is the humility and deference with which Diamond approaches knowledge. 'Of course we don't know for sure' should be the motto of anyone doing a case study. I'll go further: it should be the motto of *any* inquirer. We don't know anything for sure – we don't even know for sure if the sun is going to rise tomorrow morning.

The second thing is that Diamond goes on to point out that we make *informed guesses*, which is a point I have made throughout about the case study. Guessing – using our imagination on the basis of the available evidence – is one of the main tools of the researcher, not just someone working on a case study.

Diamond's method of informed questioning, reasoning and case construction works powerfully – and intelligent guessing is at the centre of all this. It happens not just as a result of combining inert hard facts (which are, of course, never as hard as we might like them to be) but also a chemistry, a bubbling cauldron in our brains. Thus, while he is making his case, Diamond is imagining, linking here, there and everywhere, from prehistory to Hollywood. He tells a story and develops an argument.

We're not all as imaginative or knowledgeable or energetic as Diamond, but we can replicate his process to an extent. We can weave a narrative, using the information that we garner not just as part of our formal inquiries but also from our everyday lives – as professionals and ordinary people.

Some rules for writers

Writing is one of those crafts that just has to be learned on the job, but most of us – even if we don't think that we're writers – are writing all the time in some shape or form, so the good news is that we are always learning how to write.

Writing up a case study, however, requires a particular set of awarenesses and skills and I think these can be split into two broad types:

- those concerning writing as an imaginative construction
- those to do with simply getting the thing completed.

Thus, it's about the creative and the pragmatic. The *Guardian* (2010) asked 20 leading novelists and writers to offer their own 'rules for writers' and these, interestingly, split into the creative and the pragmatic. In fact, it was so interesting that I have extracted some of the ones most pertinent to our own focus here and taken the liberty of offering my own comments in Table 12.2.

A last thought about writing up a research report. You do have to consider *register*. 'Register' means the accepted form and style of writing for a particular audience or forum – to write your dissertation using text-speak, for

Table 12.2   Rules for writers, taken from the *Guardian* (2010)

Author	My comment
Diana Athill	
• Read it aloud to yourself	Then you will hear as the reader will hear. Does it sound right? Does it make sense? Will the reader understand?
• cut (perhaps that should be CUT): only by having *no* inessential words can every essential word be made to count	Do cut out words that you think sound impressive. Avoid – like the plague – pretentious words such as 'hegemony' and 'inscribe'
Roddy Doyle	
• Chances are the words that come into your head will do fine, e.g. 'horse', 'ran', 'said'	As above. Ordinary words are usually best, though you will sometimes need technical ones in a piece of academic work. Think about the possible words you could use and judge which will be right
Helen Dunmore	
• Reread, rewrite, reread, rewrite	Excellent advice. You might add … and read it out loud to someone else
Anne Enright	
• Keep putting words on the page	One of the ways to make sure you get the thing finished is just to keep writing. Every day. Set yourself a target number of words per day. Even if you write rubbish, you are keeping the momentum going and you can cut out anything that doesn't work later
Jonathan Franzen	
• The reader is a friend, not an adversary, not a spectator	Do think of your readers. Your readers are not some inert, bodyless phenomena. They are human beings who breathe, burp, yawn and make sense of your work (or don't), depending on how you write it. Imagine your readers.

Author	My comment
Michael Morpurgo	
• Record moments, fleeting impressions, overheard dialogue, your own sadnesses and bewilderments and joys	Particularly in a case study, you make sense of others' intentions, feelings, words and emotions. Keeping a record of your own may help you to interpret the emotions and ideas of others
Andrew Motion	
• Honour the miraculousness of the ordinary	Look for what is special in ordinary moments ... the gaze that is a second too long, the turn of the head, the uncomfortable moment of silence ... What can you glean from anyone doing a case study?
• Think big and stay particular	Could be the motto of anyone doing a case study. While seeing the big picture – the model you are developing – always root it in the concrete, the particular
Will Self	
• Always carry a notebook. And I mean *always*. The short-term memory only retains information for three minutes; unless it is committed to paper you can lose an idea for ever	Self-explanatory and very true
Jeanette Winterson	
• Turn up for work. Discipline allows creative freedom. No discipline equals no freedom	She means 'get down to work – and regularly'. Nothing gets written if you don't write
• Never stop when you are stuck	As above – it's the momentum thing again.

example, would obviously be unacceptable. A student of mine told me that she had tried to write like I do in another of my books. Flattering as this was, I had to remind her that in the book I was writing for a particular audience – namely, students who wanted to learn something and who are sometimes intimidated by academic style and jargon – so my register was as light as I could make it without it actually blowing away. The register you need for a report is, sadly, more formal.

If you take only one thing from this chapter, take this ...

Think carefully about the shape of your written-up study. It needs to conform to certain expectations. Those expectations concern structure (it needs a beginning, middle and end), quality of argument and style. It also has to be good to read. Do think about your readers – put yourself in their shoes. Remember:

- A certain structure is expected in any research report, of whatever kind. Before embarking on the findings and analysis of the case study itself, you have to make it clear why you thought this was a good topic to study, and why you considered case study to be an appropriate design frame for your research. You also need to show that you have contextualised your own work in that of others and show that you have read around the area.

- In a case study, findings, analysis and discussion will usually be conflated.

- The heart of the case study is in the reasoning to support the argument being made; readers should be able to see not only rigour in your collection of evidence, but also imagination and originality in the conclusions you draw. For inspiration, look at some iconic case studies, such as those discussed briefly in this chapter, and in the further reading below.

- There are some basic rules of writing: continually proof-read and edit your work; think about the reader; be disciplined. Perhaps most important for case study: 'think big and stay particular'.

... and this – a final thought

This is the end of the book and I'll finish with a story since I have been stressing the importance of narrative and meaning since the beginning.

I once saw a television programme in which a theoretical physicist was describing how difficult it was for him and his colleagues to build accurate models and theories of the universe, given the fragmentary data to which they had access. He described it as trying to work out the rules of chess by watching a game with your view restricted to the four squares at the bottom left-hand side of the board, seeing pieces emerge and disappear at different angles and at different times, seemingly without rhyme or reason. I guess he would have given his eye teeth for more information about the physical universe – for a view of all 64 squares.

The irony is that, in social research, while we will never, ever work out all the rules of social life, we *can* gain access to much more than the bottom left-hand corner of the chess board. No one is restricting our view and, while we cannot see everything we want to see, we can see a great deal.

More importantly, there's no need deliberately to restrict our own view. Sometimes, of course, it might be sensible to structure the ways in which we organise our scrutiny of the worlds in which we are interested. We should not imagine, however, that there is any requirement to split the world into manageable-sized chunks since, by that splitting, we may force ourselves to sidestep scrutiny of some key aspect of the whole.

I've cautioned in this book against the 'mushy heap syndrome' in case studies – a syndrome in which a case is loosely focused without care for the elements of design and conduct that I have stressed. At its worst, a case study can be a bit like an unmade bed, with an untidy collection of quotes and observations without object, direction, argument or conclusion. At its best, though, it can provide sparkling insight and analysis that is unrivalled by any other kind of research. I hope that in this book you will have found advice that helps you to conduct such research. Enjoy your case study research, and good luck.

FURTHER READING 📖

Becker, H.S. (2007) *Writing for Social Scientists* (2nd edn). Chicago: University of Chicago Press.
Good advice on writing, but it has to be read, like most of Becker's work, a bit like a novel. Very good on the idea that there is no *single* way of writing something well. You can say things in a variety of ways. Lots of good examples. No bullet points.

Becker, H.S. (2014) *What About Mozart? What About Murder? Reasoning from Cases*. Chicago: University of Chicago Press.
More wisdom from Becker, this specifically on case study.

Booth, W.C., Colomb, G.C. and Williams, J.M. (2003) *The Craft of Research* (2nd edn). Chicago: University of Chicago Press.
I've mentioned this book in relation to its advice about establishing a rationale (Chapter 6). It is equally good on the question of writing – not just how to construct good sentences but also how to build good argument.

Diamond, J. (2005) *Collapse: How Societies Choose to Fail or Survive*. London: Penguin.
This book is a collection of case studies that can be read separately or all together. About the collapse of societies due to environmental degradation, together the studies offer an integrated thesis that Diamond unrolls as he proceeds through this multiple case study.

Myers, K. (2011) 'Contesting certification: mental deficiency, families and the state', *Paedagogica Historica: International Journal of History of Education*, 47 (6): 749–66.
Two examples are given in this chapter of good analysis and writing. This is another one. The study is of a working-class family in the 1930s which successfully resisted the pressure of the local authority to send the youngest child of the family to a residential special school. It raises a range of issues, among them eugenics, the employment of psychometrics, the use of authority and professional power, and the changing role of parents. It brings these together to provide a rich analysis of the ways in which forces interplay to develop, enact or resist policy.

Sacks, O. (1996) *An Anthropologist on Mars*. London: Picador.
In this fine collection of case studies, Sacks is focusing on difference and differences – the differences that exist between people, which are sometimes magnified by a disability or condition of some kind. Each is a vignette in itself, but, as a whole, the book offers a multiple case study par excellence, since the whole is more than the sum of its parts. Each study is, in a way, refracted through the others.

Thomas, G. (2012) 'Changing our landscape of inquiry for a new science of education', *Harvard Educational Review*, 82 (1): 26–51.
Here I talk about the power of case study as a form of social inquiry vis-à-vis other forms of inquiry. The article was written in the context that the use of case study research has waned as policymakers have sought 'evidence-based' policy informed by randomised controlled trials. They seem unable to understand the frailties of such trials in social research and the potential contribution of case study evidence.

Thomas, G. (ed.) (2013) *Case Study in Education. Volumes I–IV*. London: Sage.
This collection gives many examples of iconic case studies and less well-known but equally good ones. Some of these provide excellent examples of good writing.

Thomas, G. and Myers, K. (2015) *The Anatomy of the Case Study*. London: Sage.
In this book, Kevin Myers and I try to work out what is going on 'inside' the case study. In Chapter 6 we offer ten examples of what we consider to be good analysis.

Wolcott, H. (1992) 'Posturing in qualitative inquiry', in M.D. LeCompte, W.L. Milroy and J. Preissie (eds), *The Handbook of Qualitative Research in Education*. New York: Academic Press, pp. 3–52.
Wolcott, H. (2009) *Writing Up Qualitative Research* (3rd edn). London: Sage.
Wolcott is good not just on writing but also positioning yourself as a researcher.

Other reading

Bendix, R. (1963) 'Concepts and generalization in comparative sociological studies', *American Sociological Review*, 28: 532–9.
Bradshaw, Y. and Wallace, M. (1991) 'Informing generality and explaining uniqueness: the place of case studies in comparative research', *International Journal of Comparative Sociology*, 32: 154–71.
Feagan, J., Orum, A.M. and Sjoberg, G. (eds) (1991) *A Case for the Case Study*. Chapel Hill, NC: University of North Carolina Press.
Kurtz, M.J. (2000) 'Understanding peasant revolution: from concept to theory and case', *Theory and Society*, 29 (1): 93–124.
Rosenblatt, P.C. (1981) 'Ethnographic case study', in M.B. Brewer and B. Collins (eds), *Scientific Inquiry and the Social Sciences: A Volume in Honor of Donald T. Campbell*. San Francisco: Jossey-Bass, pp. 194–225.
Snyder, R. (2001) 'Scaling down: the subnational comparative method', *Studies in Comparative International Development*, 36 (1): 93–110.
Stoeker, R. (1991) 'Evaluating and rethinking the case study', *Sociological Review*, 39: 88–112.
Thomas, G. (2010) 'Doing case study: abduction not induction; phronesis not theory', *Qualitative Inquiry*, 16 (7): 575–82.
Thomas, G. (2011) 'The case: generalisation, theory and phronesis in case study', *Oxford Review of Education*, 37 (1): 21–35.
Tobin, J. (2005) 'Scaling up as catachresis', *International Journal of Research & Method in Education*, 28 (1): 23–32.

REFERENCES

Abbott, A. (1992) 'What do cases do? Some notes on activity in sociological analysis', in C.C. Ragin and H.S. Becker (eds), *What Is a Case? Exploring the Foundations of Social Inquiry*. Cambridge: Cambridge University Press.

Alderson, P. (2004) *Ethics, Social Research and Consulting with Children and Young People* (2nd edn). London: Barnardo's.

Althusser, L. (1979) *For Marx*. London: Verso.

Andreski, S. (1972) *Social Sciences as Sorcery*. London: André Deutsch.

Back, S. (2002) 'The Aristotelian challenge to teacher education', *History of Intellectual Culture*, 2 (1) (available online at: www.ucalgary.ca/hic/files/hic/back_forum.pdf).

Ball, S. (1981) *Beachside Comprehensive: A Case-Study of Secondary Schooling*. Cambridge: Cambridge University Press.

Barker, R.G. (1968) *Ecological Psychology*. Palo Alto, CA: Stanford University Press.

Barrow, J.D. (1997) 'The values of science'. Amnesty International Science Lecture, Oxford University.

Barthes, R. (1974) *S/Z* (R. Miller, trans.). New York: Hill & Wang.

Bassey, M. (1999) *Case Study Research in Educational Settings*. Maidenhead: Open University Press.

Bateson, G. (1972/1999) *Steps to an Ecology of Mind*. Chicago: University of Chicago Press.

Becker, H.S. (1992) 'Cases, causes, conjunctures, stories, imagery', in C.C. Ragin and H.S. Becker (eds), *What Is a Case? Exploring the Foundations of Social Inquiry*. Cambridge: Cambridge University Press.

Becker, H.S. (1998) *Tricks of the Trade*. Chicago: University of Chicago Press.

Becker, H.S. (2014) *What About Mozart? What About Murder? Reasoning from Cases*. Chicago: University of Chicago Press.

Becker, H.S., Geer, B., Hughes, E.C. and Strauss, A.L. (1961/1980) *Boys in White*. Edison, NJ: Transaction Publishers.

Belmont Report (1979) *Ethical Principles and Guidelines for the Protection of Human Subjects of Research: The National Commission for the Protection of Human Subjects of Biomedical and Behavioral Research*. Washington, DC: U.S. Department of Health & Human Services (available online at: http://www.hhs.gov/ohrp/humansubjects/guidance/belmont.html).

Biletzki, A. (2009) 'Ludwig Wittgenstein', in E.N. Zalta (ed.), *Stanford Encyclopedia of Philosophy* (summer 2009 edition). Stanford, CA: Metaphysics Research Lab, Center for the Study of Language and Information, Stanford University (available online at: http://plato.stanford.edu/archives/sum2009/entries/wittgenstein/).

Blumer, H. (1992) *Symbolic Interactionism: Perspective and Method*. Berkeley, CA: University of California Press.

Booth, W.C., Colomb, G.C. and Williams, J.M. (2003) *The Craft of Research* (2nd edn). Chicago: University of Chicago Press.

Bronfenbrenner, U. (1979) *The Ecology of Human Development*. Cambridge, MA: Harvard University Press.

Bronfenbrenner, U. and Morris, P.A. (1998) 'The ecology of developmental processes', in R.M. Lerner (ed.), *Handbook of Child Psychology, Vol. 1: Theoretical Models of Human Development*. New York: Wiley, pp. 993–1028.

Bruner, J. (1991) 'The narrative construction of reality', *Critical Inquiry*, 18 (1): 1–21.

Bruner, J. (1997) *The Culture of Education*. Cambridge, MA: Harvard University Press.

Bryant, G. and Monk, P. (2001) 'Summary of the final report of the investigation into the North Leicestershire cluster of variant Creutzfeldt-Jakob disease'. Leicestershire Health Authority (available online at: www.cbsnews.com/htdocs/pdf/vcjd.pdf).

Burgess, R.G. (1982) *Field Research: A Sourcebook and Field Manual*. London: Routledge.

Byrne, R.M.J. (2005) *The Rational Imagination: How People Create Alternatives to Reality*. Cambridge, MA: MIT Press.

Caldwell, J.C. (1986) 'Routes to low mortality in poor countries', *Population and Development Review*, 12 (2): 171–220.

Checkland, P. (1981) *Systems Thinking, Systems Practice*. Chichester: John Wiley.

Collingwood, R.G. (1946/1994) *The Idea of History*. Oxford: Oxford University Press.

Cremin, H., Thomas, G. and Vincent, K. (2005) 'Working with teaching assistants: three models evaluated', *Research Papers in Education*, 20 (4): 413–32.

Cremin, H., Mason, C. and Busher, H. (2011) 'Problematising pupil voice using visual methods: findings from a study of engaged and disaffected pupils in an urban secondary school', *British Educational Research Journal*, 37 (4): 585–603.

de Vaus, D.A. (2001) *Research Design in Social Research*. Thousand Oaks, CA: Sage.

Descartes, R. (1647/1996) *Meditations on First Philosophy*. Cambridge: Cambridge University Press.

Dewey, J. (1920/2004) *How We Think*. Whitefish, MT: Kessinger Publishing.

Diamond, J. (2005) *Collapse: How Societies Choose to Fail or Survive*. London: Penguin.

Dick, B. (2002) *Soft Systems Methodology*, Session 13 of Areol – action research and evaluation on line. Southern Cross University and Southern Cross Institute of Action Research (available online at: www.aral.com.au/areol/areol-session13.html).

Dickens, W.T. and Flynn, J.R. (2001) 'Heritability estimates versus large environmental effects: the IQ paradox resolved', *Psychological Review*, 108: 346–69.

Eckstein, H. (1975) 'Case study and theory in political science', in F. Greenstein and N. Polsby (eds), *The Handbook of Political Science: Strategies of Inquiry*, Vol. 7, London: Addison-Wesley, pp. 79–137.

Eisenhart, M. (2009) 'Generalization from qualitative inquiry', in K. Ercikan and W.M. Roth (eds), *Generalizing from Educational Research*. Abingdon: Routledge.

Eisner, E. (1991) *The Enlightened Eye: Qualitative Inquiry and the Enhancement of Educational Practice*. New York: Macmillan.

Ellis, L. and Hodges, L. (2014) 'Life and change with Usher: the experiences of diagnosis for people with Usher syndrome'. Birmingham: University of Birmingham (available online at: http://www.birmingham.ac.uk/Documents/college-social-sciences/education/projects/final-report-on-life-and-change-with-usher.pdf).

Evans, H. (2000) *Essential English for Journalists, Editors and Writers*. London: Pimlico.

Ferguson, N. (1999) *Virtual History: Alternatives and Counterfactuals*. New York: Basic Books.

Feyerabend, P. (1993) *Against Method* (3rd edn). London: Verso/New Left Books.

Field, A. (2013) *Discovering Statistics using SPSS* (4th edn). London: Sage.

Fish, S. (1989) *Doing What Comes Naturally*. Oxford: Clarendon Press.

Flynn, J.R. (1987) 'Massive IQ gains in 14 nations: what IQ tests really measure', *Psychological Bulletin*, 101: 171–91.

Flynn, J.R. (1998) 'IQ gains over time: toward finding the causes', in U. Neisser (ed.), *The Rising Curve: Long-Term Gains in IQ and Related Measures*. Washington, DC: American Psychological Association.

Flynn, J.R. (1999) 'Searching for justice: the discovery of IQ gains over time', *American Psychologist*, 54 (1): 5–20.

Flynn, J.R. (2003) 'Movies about intelligence: the limitations of g', *Current Directions in Psychological Science*, 12 (3): 95–9.

Flyvbjerg, B. (2001) *Making Social Science Matter: Why Social Inquiry Fails and How It Can Succeed Again*. Cambridge: Cambridge University Press.

Flyvbjerg, B. (2006) 'Five misunderstandings about case-study research', *Qualitative Inquiry*, 12 (2): 219–45.

Foucault, M. (1981) 'Questions of method: an interview with Michel Foucault', *Ideology and Consciousness*, 8 (Spring): 3–14.

Freud, S. (1957/2009) *Five Lectures on Psychoanalysis*. London: Hogarth for the Institute of Psychoanalysis.

Geertz, C. (1975) *The Interpretation of Cultures*. London: Hutchinson.

Geoghegan, T. (2007) 'History lessons: for Americans, Herodotus has better ones to offer than Thucydides', *The American Prospect*, 12 March (available online only at: https://prospect.org/article/history-lessons-1).

Georgiades, N.J. and Phillimore, L. (1975) 'The myth of the hero-innovator and alternative strategies for organizational change', in C.C. Kiernan and F.P. Woodford (eds), *Behaviour Modification with the Severely Retarded*. Amsterdam: Associated Scientific Publishers.

Glaser, B.G. and Strauss, A.L. (1967) *The Discovery of Grounded Theory: Strategies for Qualitative Research*. New York: Aldine.

Goffman, E. (1956) *The Presentation of Self in Everyday Life*. Edinburgh: University of Edinburgh.

Grinyer, A. (2002) 'The anonymity of research participants: Assumptions, ethics and practicalities', *Social Research Update*, 36: 1–6.

Guardian (2010) '10 rules for writers', *Guardian*, Guardian Review, 20 February: 2–5.

Haig, B.D. (1995) 'Grounded theory as scientific method', in A. Neiman (ed.), *Philosophy of Education Yearbook, 1995: Current Issues*. Champaign: Philosophy of Education Society, University of Illinois Press at Urbana-Champaign, pp. 281–90.

Haldane, J.B.S. (1928) *Possible Worlds and Other Essays*. London: Chatto & Windus.

Hammersley, M. (2005) 'Assessing quality in qualitative research', paper presented to ESRC TLRP seminar series: Quality in Educational Research, University of Birmingham, 7 July (available online at: www.education.bham.ac.uk/research/seminars1/esrc_4/index.shtml).

Hammersley, M. (2007) 'The issue of quality in qualitative research', *International Journal of Research and Method in Education*, 30 (3): 287–306.

Hammersley, M. and Gomm, R. (2000) 'Introduction', in R. Gomm, M. Hammersley and P. Foster (eds), *Case Study Method*. London: Sage.

Hearnshaw, L.S. (1979) *Cyril Burt: Psychologist*. London: Hodder & Stoughton.

Holton, G. (1995) 'The controversy over the end of science', *Scientific American*, 273 (4): 168.

Houser, N., Kloesel, C. and the Peirce Edition Project (eds) (1992) *The Essential Peirce*, 2 vols. Bloomington, IN: Indiana University Press.

James, W. (1890/1981) *The Principles of Psychology*. Cambridge, MA: Harvard University Press.

Jenkins, R. (1992) *Pierre Bourdieu*. London: Routledge.

Jiménez, R.T. and Gersten, R. (1999) 'Lessons and dilemmas derived from the literacy instruction of two Latina/o teachers', *American Educational Research Journal*, 36 (2): 265–302.

Johnson, S. (1759/1963) 'The Idler, no. 58, Universal Chronicle', in W.J. Bate, J.M. Bullitt and L.F. Powell (eds), *Works of Samuel Johnson, Vol. 2*. New Haven, CT: Yale University Press.

Junghans, C., Feder, G., Hemingway, H., Timmis, A. and Jones, M. (2005) 'Recruiting patients to medical research: double blind randomised trial of "opt-in" versus "opt-out" strategies', *British Medical Journal*, 331: 940 (available at: www.bmj.com/cgi/reprint/331/7522/940.pdf).

Kahneman, D. and Tversky, A. (1973) 'On the psychology of prediction', *Psychological Review*, 80 (4): 237–51.

Kamprad, I. with Toreleull, B. (2000) *Leading by Design: The IKEA Story*. London: HarperCollins.

Kellett, M. (2005) *How to Develop Children as Researchers*. London: Paul Chapman Publishing.

Kelly, D.H. (1993) 'Case: grammar and terminology', *The Classical World*, 87 (1): 35–9.

Kenny, A. (ed.) (1993) *The Wittgenstein Reader*. Oxford: Blackwell.

Kounin, J. (1970) *Discipline and Group Management in Classrooms*. New York: Holt, Rinehart & Winston.

Kuhn, T.S. (1970) *The Structure of Scientific Revolutions*. Chicago: University of Chicago Press.

Lebow, R.N. (2007) 'Counterfactual thought experiments: a necessary teaching tool', *The History Teacher*, 40 (2) (available online at: www.historycooperative.org/ journals/ht/40.2/lebow.html).

Levitt, S.D. and List, J.A. (2009) 'Was there really a Hawthorne effect at the Hawthorne plant? An analysis of the original illumination experiments', NBER Working Paper No. 15016. Cambridge, MA: National Bureau of Economic Research.

Levy, P. (1981) 'On the relation between method and substance in psychology', *Bulletin of the British Psychological Society*, 34: 265–70.

Lewin, K. (1951) *Field Theory in Social Science: Selected Theoretical Papers*. New York: Harper.

Lewin, K. (1997) *Resolving Social Conflicts: Field Theory in Social Science*. Washington, DC: American Psychological Association.

Lewis, A. and Lindsay, G. (2000) *Researching Children's Perspectives*. Buckingham: Open University Press.

Lewis, A. and Porter, J. (2004) 'Interviewing children and young people with learning disabilities: guidelines for researchers and multi-professional practice', *British Journal of Learning Disabilities*, 32 (4): 191–7.

Lincoln, Y.S. and Guba, E.G. (1985). *Naturalistic Inquiry*. Beverly Hills, CA: Sage.

MacIntyre, A. (1985) *After Virtue: A Study in Moral Theory*. London: Duckworth.

Mandel, D.R., Hilton, D.J. and Catellani, P. (2005) *The Psychology of Counterfactual Thinking*. Abingdon: Routledge.

Merriam, S.B. (1988) *Case Study Research in Education: A Qualitative Approach*. San Francisco: Jossey-Bass.

Milgram, S. (1963) 'Behavioral study of obedience', *Journal of Abnormal and Social Psychology*, 67 (4): 371–8.

Milgram, S. (1981) 'Behavioral study of obedience', *Social and Behavioral Science*, 9: 18 (available online at: www.garfield.library.upenn.edu/classics1981/A1981LC33300001.pdf).

Miller, S. and Fredericks, M. (1999) 'How does grounded theory explain?', *Qualitative Inquiry*, 9: 538–51.

Mitchell, J.C. (2006) 'Case and situation analysis', in T.M.S. Evens and D. Handelman (eds), *The Manchester School: Practice and Ethnographic Praxis in Anthropology*. Oxford: Berghahn Books.

Mogey, J.M. (1955) 'The contribution of Frédéric Le Play to family research', *Marriage and Family Living*, 17 (4): 310–15.

Mouzelis, N. (1995) *Sociological Theory: What Went Wrong?* London: Routledge.

Murdoch, I. (2002) *Under the Net*. London: Vintage.

Norton, J.D. (2004) 'Einstein's investigations of Galilean covariant electrodynamics prior to 1905', *Archive for History of Exact Sciences*, 59: 45–105 (available online at: www.pitt.edu/~jdnorton/papers/Einstein1905.pdf).

Oakeshott, M. (1967) *Rationalism in Politics and Other Essays*. London: Methuen.

Oakley, A. (1999) 'Paradigm wars: some thoughts on a personal and public trajectory', *International Journal of Social Research Methodology*, 2 (3): 247–54.

Ohno, T. (2006) 'Ask "why" five times about every matter', Toyota Motor Corporation (available online at: http://www.toyota-global.com/company/toyota_traditions/quality/mar_apr_2006.html).

Omaar, R. (2009) *Race and Intelligence: Science's Last Taboo*. London: Channel 4 Television.

Parlett, M. and Hamilton, D. (1987) 'Evaluation as illumination', in R. Murphy and H. Torrance (eds), *Evaluating Education: Issues and Methods*. Milton Keynes: Open University Press.

Patrick, J. (1973) *A Glasgow Gang Observed*. London: Methuen.

Polanyi, M. (1958) *Personal Knowledge: Towards a Post-critical Philosophy*. London: Routledge & Kegan Paul.

Popper, K.R. (1968) *The Logic of Scientific Discovery*. London: Hutchinson.

Popper, K.R. (1977) 'On hypotheses', in P.N. Johnson-Laird and P.C. Wason (eds), *Thinking: Readings in Cognitive Science*. Cambridge: Cambridge University Press.

Prosser, J. (1992) 'Personal reflections on the use of photography in an ethnographic case study', *British Educational Research Journal*, 18 (4): 397–411.

Prosser, J. (1998) *Image-Based Research*. London: Routledge.

Prosser, J. and Loxley, A. (2008) 'Introducing visual methods', ESRC National Centre for Research Methods Review Paper NCRM/010'. Southampton: ESRC NCRM (available online at: http://eprints.ncrm.ac.uk/420/1/Methods ReviewPaperNCRM-010.pdf).

Putnam, R. (2000) *Bowling Alone: The Collapse and Revival of American Community*. New York: Simon & Schuster.

Ragin, C.C. (1992) 'Introduction: cases of "What is a case?"', in C.C. Ragin and H.S. Becker (eds), *What Is a Case? Exploring the Foundations of Social Inquiry*. Cambridge: Cambridge University Press.

Ragin, C.C. (2007) 'Comparative methods', in W. Outhwaite and S.P. Turner (eds), *The Sage Handbook of Social Science Methodology*. Los Angeles: Sage, pp. 67–81.

Roethlisberger, F. and Dickson, W. (1939) *Management and the Worker*. Cambridge, MA: Harvard University Press.

Rutter, M. and the English and Romanian Adoptees (ERA) Study Team (1998) 'Developmental catch-up, and deficit, following adoption after severe global early privation', *Journal of Child Psychology and Psychiatry*, 39: 465–76.

Sacks, O. (1996) *An Anthropologist on Mars*. London: Picador.

Schatzman, L. (1991) 'Dimensional analysis: notes on an alternative approach to the grounding of theory in qualitative research', in D.R. Maines (ed.), *Social Organization and Social Process: Essays in Honor of Anselm Strauss*. New York: Aldine, pp. 303–14.

Schwandt, T.A. (1996) 'Farewell to criteriology', *Qualitative Inquiry*, 2: 58–72.

Schwandt, T.A. (2001) *Dictionary of Qualitative Inquiry* (2nd edn). Thousand Oaks, CA: Sage.

Schwartz, D. (1992) *Waucoma Twilight: Generations of the Farm*. Washington, DC: Smithsonian Institution Press.

Sen, A. (1999) *Development as Freedom*. New York: Alfred A. Knopf.

Sennett, R. (2009) *The Craftsman*. London: Penguin.

Silverman, D. (2010) *Doing Qualitative Research* (3rd edn). London: Sage.

Simon, H. (1983) *Reason in Human Affairs*. Oxford: Basil Blackwell.

Simons, H. (1989) 'Ethics of case study in educational research and evaluation', in R. Burgess (ed.), *The Ethics of Educational Research*. Lewes: Falmer, pp. 114–40.

Simons, H. (2009) *Case Study Research in Practice*. London: Sage.

Smail, D. (1993) *The Origins of Unhappiness*. London: HarperCollins.

Smith, J.K. and Deemer, D.K. (2000) 'The problem of criteria in the age of relativism', in N.K. Denzin and Y.S. Lincoln (eds), *Handbook of Qualitative Research* (2nd edn). Thousand Oaks, CA: Sage.

Solzhenitsyn, A. (1963/2000) *One Day in the Life of Ivan Denisovich*. London: Penguin.

Stake, R.E. (1995) *The Art of Case Study Research*. Thousand Oaks, CA: Sage.

Stake, R.E. (2005) 'Qualitative case studies', in N.K. Denzin and Y.S. Lincoln (eds), *The Sage Handbook of Qualitative Research* (3rd edn). Thousand Oaks, CA: Sage.

Storr, A. (1997) *Feet of Clay: A Study of Gurus*. London: HarperCollins.

Strauss, A. and Corbin, J. (1990) *Basics of Qualitative Research: Grounded Theory Procedures and Techniques*. Newbury Park, CA: Sage.

Tavor Bannet, E. (1997) 'Analogy as translation: Wittgenstein, Derrida, and the law of language', *New Literary History*, 28 (4): 655–72.

Taylor, S. J. and Bogdan, R. (1984) *Introduction to Qualitative Research Methods: The Search for Meanings*. New York: Wiley.

Thomas, G. (1992) *Effective Classroom Teamwork: Support or Intrusion*. London: Routledge.

Thomas, G. (2007) *Education and Theory: Strangers in Paradigms*. Maidenhead: Open University Press.

Thomas, G. (2009) '"What works" as a sublinguistic grunt, with lessons from catachresis, asymptote, football and pharma', *Research Intelligence*, 106: 20–2.

Thomas, G. (2010) 'Doing case study: abduction not induction; phronesis not theory', *Qualitative Inquiry*, 16 (7): 572–82.

Thomas, G. (2011a) 'A typology for the case study in social science following a review of definition, discourse and structure', *Qualitative Inquiry*, 17 (6): 511–521.

Thomas, G. (2011b) 'The case: generalisation and theory in case study', *Oxford Review of Education*, 37 (1): 21–35.

Thomas, G. (2013) *How to Do Your Research Project* (2nd edn). London: Sage.

Thomas, G. and James, D. (2006) 'Reinventing grounded theory: some questions about theory, ground and discovery', *British Educational Research Journal*, 32 (6): 767–95.

Thomas, G. and Loxley, A. (2007) *Deconstructing Special Education and Constructing Inclusion* (2nd edn). Maidenhead: Open University Press.

Thomas, G. and Myers, K. (2015) *The Anatomy of the Case Study*. London: Sage.

Thomas, G., Walker, D. and Webb, J. (1998) *The Making of the Inclusive School*. London: Routledge.

Thomas, W.I. and Znaniecki, F. (1927/1958) *The Polish Peasant in Europe and America* (2nd edn). New York: Dover.

Vaughan, D. (1992) 'Theory elaboration: the heuristics of case analysis', in C.C. Ragin and H.S. Becker (eds), *What Is a Case? Exploring the Foundations of Social Inquiry*. Cambridge: Cambridge University Press.

Vincett, K., Cremin, H. and Thomas, G. (2005) *Teachers and Assistants Working Together*. Maidenhead: Open University Press.

von Bertalanffy, L. (1950) 'The theory of open systems in physics and biology', *Science*, 111: 23–9.

Wacquant, L.D. (1989) 'Towards a reflexive sociology: a workshop with Pierre Bourdieu', *Sociological Theory*, 7: 26–63.

Walton, J. (1992) 'Making the theoretical case', in C.C. Ragin and H.S. Becker (eds), *What Is a Case? Exploring the Foundations of Social Inquiry*. Cambridge: Cambridge University Press.

Wells, M. (2005) 'Paxman answers the questions', *Guardian*, 31 January (available online at: http://guardian.co.uk/media/2005/jan/31/mondaymediasection.poli ticsandthemedia).

White, H.C. (1992) 'Cases are for identity, for explanation, or for control', in C.C. Ragin and H.S. Becker (eds), *What Is a Case? Exploring the Foundations of Social Inquiry*. Cambridge: Cambridge University Press.

Whittemore, R., Chase, S.K. and Mandle, C.L. (2001) 'Validity in qualitative research', *Qualitative Health Research*, 11: 522–37.

Whyte, W.F. (1955/1993) *Street Corner Society: Social Structure of an Italian Slum*. Chicago: University of Chicago Press.

Whyte, W.F. (1985) *Learning from the Field: A Guide from Experience*. Beverly Hills, CA: Sage.

Wieviorka, M. (1992) 'Case studies: history or sociology?' in C.C. Ragin and H.S. Becker (eds), *What is a Case? Exploring the Foundations of Social Inquiry*. Cambridge: Cambridge University Press.

Wiles, R., Crow, G., Heath, S. and Charles, V. (2008) 'The management of confidentiality and anonymity in social research', *International Journal of Social Research Methodology*, 11 (5), 417–28.

Willis, P.E. (1981) *Learning to Labor: How Working Class Kids Get Working Class Jobs*. New York: Columbia University Press.

Yin, R.K. (2009) *Case Study Research: Design and Methods* (4th edn). Thousand Oaks, CA: Sage.

INDEX

Abbott, A., 73, 229
ABC of behaviour, 168
abduction, 69–73, 77, 121, 252
accounts, 188–191, 195, 201, 202
action research, 36–7, 50, 56, 118, 179,
    214, 231, 239
adopted Romanian children, 99, 108–9
Alderson, P., 87, 93
Althusser, L., 70
analogy, 51, 141, 175–6, 225, 229, 230, 233
analysing data, 203–35
analysis and discussion (in write-up), 237,
    238, 250
analytical category, 16, 18, 20, 136
analytical frame, 15–24, 99, 100, 102, 103,
    110–12
    See also, object of the case study
Andreski, S., 232–3
anecdotal evidence, 4
Anna O, 18, 19, 20
anomalies, 69, 225
anonymisation, 82, 88
anonymity, 80–3, 93, 94, 214
anorexia nervosa, 86, 168
Anthropologist on Mars, 244, 251
anthropology, 148, 159
appendix, use of, 90
approaches to case study research,
    134–59
archival records, 164
    See also, document interrogation and
        documents
Aristotle, 48–9, 72, 73
artefacts, 192
Athens, 48
ATLAS.ti, 207
attitudes to knowledge. *See* critical
    reasoning

audiences, 66
audio, 88, 190, 191, 192, 205, 207
audit society, 65

Bacon, F., 48
Bailey, M., 24
Ball, S., 38, 45
Barker, R., 29, 55, 57, 61
Barthes, R., 228
Bassey, M., 113, 118
Bateson, G., 55, 61
Beachside Comprehensive, 38, 45
Becker, H., 4, 9, 21, 24, 34, 45, 61, 132,
    221, 227, 229, 232, 234–5, 244, 251
Bell Burnell, J., 5–6
Belmont Report, 79, 81
Bendix, R., 252
BERA, 91, 93
Berlin Wall, 39, 40–3, 115–6, 164
biography, 68
biologists, and case study, 25
Blumer, H., 52
Booth, W., 133, 242, 244, 251
Bourdieu, P., 70, 149, 220
Bradshaw, Y., 252
brainstorming, 40, 43, 100, 126, 215
British Educational Research Association
    (BERA), 91, 93
Bronfenbrenner, U., 56–9, 179
Bronx, 33
Bruner, J., 122, 225, 226, 228–9, 235
Bryman, A., 202
BSE. *See* mad cow disease
Burgess, R., 61, 159, 197
Burt, C., 65–7

Caldwell, J.C., 103–6
Campbell, D., 24, 252

capability, Sen's notion of, 106
cartoons, 198
case
    as argument, 14
    as container, 12–13
    Latin derivation of, 12
    as situation, 13
    of something, 14–17
    what is a case?, 11–17
        See also, analytical category; analytical
            frame; object of the case study;
            subject of the case study; types of
            case study
causal narrativity, 229
causation, 9, 11, 21, 37
cause, and Becker's 'sequence of steps', 227
census data, 200
Checkland, P., 57, 61, 214–6
chefs' recipes, 174–9
classrooms, 34, 118, 125, 177–9
closed questions, 194
code of conduct, 91
coding, 210–11
    See also, constant comparative method
Coffey, A., 94
Cohen, M.F., 24
collecting data, 157, 187–202
collective case study, 172
    See also, comparative research; multiple
        study
Collingwood, R., 73, 164
comparative research, 36, 37, 200, 242, 252
    See also, multiple study
concealment, ethics of, 81, 87
conceptual model, in soft systems, 215
confidentiality, 80–8, 94, 189, 214
consent, and ethics, 79–89, 91, 93, 108
constant comparative method, 179, 204–6,
    207, 210, 211, 234, 235
contextual antecedents, 127
control group, 156
conversations, 81
correlation, 103
Costa Rica, as outlier, 103, 104
craft knowledge, 48, 72, 173

creativity in designing research, 229, 232, 233
Cremin, H., 156–7, 198
Creutzfeld-Jakob Disease, 38, 127, 131
criteriology, 65, 75, 77
criterion- *v* norm-referenced, 200
critical awareness, 67, 221
critical inquiry, 105
critical reasoning, 239, 240
cross-case analysis, 172, 173
    See also, multiple study
Cuba Missile Crisis, 3, 86
cultural expectations, 101
curiosity, 69, 108, 120, 226, 232

data
    analysis, 203–35
    collection, 187–202
    security and stewardship, 82, 93
debriefing for participants, 81, 89
deception, ethics of, 81, 87
deduction and deducing, 71
    See also, interpretative inquiry
Denzin, N., 24
Department of Health, 91
dependent variable, 157
Descartes, R., 240
description, 15, 75, 100, 115, 159,
    174, 176, 211
    See also, thick description
design of research, 25–45, 90, 91
Dewey, J., 7, 241
diachronic case study, 242
Diamond, J., 246–7
diaries, 38, 164, 188, 195, 201–22, 205, 243
disability, 79, 181, 251
discourse analysis, 223
discussion, as part of write-up, 236–8
dissertations, 231, 236
document interrogation, 193, 201
documents, 83, 101, 164, 187, 188, 193,
    197, 202, 207
dramaturgical perspective, 51–2, 61, 230

Easter Island, 246–7
Eastern Europe, 39, 40, 42

ecological model, 55
ecological psychology, 29, 53–60
Education and Training Statistics, 200
Einstein, A., 6, 8, 9, 34, 51, 65, 66, 232
Eisenhardt, K., 159
Eisner, E., 225, 235
empathy, 182
empirical findings, 224
engineering, as source of systems thinking,
    56–8, 214
epidemiological inquiry, 105
epistemology, 132
ethical clearance, 81, 87, 90–93, 170
ethics, 78–93, 94, 122, 189
ethnicity, 68
ethnography, 24, 94, 148, 160
    See also, interpretivism; interpretative
        inquiry
Eureka moment, 226
European Social Survey, 201
evaluation, 36, 37, 75, 94, 122
evaluative case study, 199
Evans, H., 7, 222
evidence
    abduction and, 69–73, 77, 121, 252
    accumulation of, 187–202
    corroborative, 4
    reasoning from, 203–35
    triangulation of, 67–8
    See also, data
examples of case studies
    adopted Romanian children (as local
        knowledge case study), 108–9
    adults' employment in schools (as
        explanatory case study), 123–6
    anorexia nervosa (as snapshot case
        study), 168–9
    Berlin Wall (designing a case study),
        39–44, 116
    chefs' recipes (as multiple or
        comparative case study), 173–6
    a day in the life of ... (as snapshot case
        study), 166–8
    dentists in training (as illustrative–
        demonstrative case study), 143–6

examples of case studies *cont.*
    dynamic hip screw (as illustrative–
        demonstrative case study), 146–7
    Easter Island (as multiple or comparative
        case study), 246–7
    fear of SAT tests (as exploratory case
        study), 126–7
    Freud's Anna O (generalising from a
        case study), 18–20
    Hawthorne Effect (as diachronic case
        study), 169–72
    hospital infection with MRSA (as
        theory-testing case study), 139–40
    Hostos-Lincoln Academy (from idea to
        question), 33–5
    hung parliament (as analytical frame,
        or object), 16
    Hurricane Katrina (as key case study),
        100–102
    IKEA as a business (defining boundary
        of case), 3, 21–3
    IQ and ethnicity (from idea to question),
        31–4
    Kerala, longevity in (as outlier case
        study), 103–8
    Korean War (and analytical frames), 14–5
    'mad cow' disease (as exploratory case
        study), 127–31
    media styles, contrasting US and UK
        (drawing theory from), 222–24
    office productivity (as evaluative
        case study), 122
    park design (as sequential case study),
        180–2
    pulsars (as case study in science), 5–6
    reading difficulty (as local knowledge
        case study), 109–10
    school governor (as interpretative case
        study), 150–3
    school inclusion policy (as nested case
        study), 178–80
    teaching assistants (as experimental case
        study), 123–6
    terrorism (as theory-building case
        study), 136–8, 162–4

exemplary knowledge, 69, 73
experimental study, 153–8
explanatory study, 123–6
exploratory study, 126–32
eyeballing of statistics, 157

fabrication, 65, 66
facilitator in interviews, 192
Feagan, J., 252
FedStats, 200
feedback to participants, 57, 80, 89, 146, 214
Ferguson,N, 228
Feyerabend, P., 228
field theory (Lewin), 56
fieldwork, 32, 33, 90, 131, 148, 187–202, 237
films, 198
    See also, image-based methods
findings, analysis of, 203–35
first person, using the word 'I', 68
Fish, S., 71, 72
Flynn effect, 32
Flynn, J., 32, 33
Flyvbjerg, B., 6, 7, 48, 61, 143
focus groups, 172, 188, 191, 192, 201
focus materials, 171, 192
Foucault, M., 4, 5, 67, 105
Freud, S., 18, 19

gangs, 7
Gapminder, 106
Geertz, C., 151, 159, 211, 231
gender, 50, 68
generalisation and generalisability, 4, 7, 9,
    11, 17, 19, 23, 48–51, 61, 68–73, 76–7,
    118, 121, 221, 226–7, 252
George, A., 52, 159, 235
Georgiades, N., 178
Gestalt, 50, 56, 166
gestures, 191
Glaser, B., 71, 210
Glasgow Gang Observed, A, 6, 24
Goffman, E., 52, 61, 111, 142–3, 159, 197,
    211, 229–30
Gomm, R., 10, 11, 24
Googling, 159, 200

graffiti, 40–3, 198
grand theory, 150, 221
grounded theory, 199, 210, 234
group, 90
group interview, 188, 191, 192, 201
guesses, informed, 105, 247

Haig, B., 70
Haldane J.B.S., 240
Hammersley, M., 10, 11, 24, 70, 74–5
harm to participants, 82, 83, 85, 89, 90
    See also, ethics
Harvard referencing system, 235, 252
Hawthorne effect, 169–71
health service managers, 140
Herodotus, 73
heuristics, 70
Hightown Grammar, 45
holism, 47, 49, 56, 60
Holton, G., 8
Hostos-Lincoln Academy, 33–4, 99, 112,
    187, 200
How to do Your Research Project, 30, 64,
    67, 77, 99, 155, 188, 202
hung parliament, 16
Hurricane Katrina, 99, 100, 101, 102, 111, 231
Husserl, E., 53
hypothesis, 34, 101, 104, 130, 131, 153, 188

idiographic research, 5, 7, 49, 60, 113, 172
idiographs, 51
IKEA, 3, 21, 22
illustrative case study, 141, 146–7, 198
image-based methods, 188, 198, 202
imagery, 234
imagination, 48, 108, 226, 228, 231, 232–5,
    239, 240, 247, 250
implied consent, 84, 85, 88, 89
    See also, consent
incremental chunking, 226
in-depth analysis, 33, 109, 223
induction, 17, 69, 70, 71, 73, 77, 252
inductive reasoning, 70
informed consent, 80, 93, 144, 168
    See also, consent

insight, 21–2, 43, 121–2, 146, 152, 163, 181, 225–6, 242, 245, 251
institutional review, 90
instrumental case study, 121
intellectual love, Einstein's notion of, 232
intelligent noticing, 226
interaction, 52, 55
interdisciplinarity, 57
international comparison, 106, 108
   See also, comparative study
interpretative case study, 134–53
interpretative inquiry, 204–35
interpretivism, 52, 149
interviewing, 189–91
intrinsic case study, 120
introduction, 68, 90
intuition, 8, 9, 226, 232, 233, 234, 235, 246
IQ, 31, 32
IRB (Institutional Review Board), 90, 92

James, W., 6, 32, 71, 154, 210
Jimenez, R., 176
journalism, 7, 222–3

Kahneman, D., 228
Kamprad, I., and IKEA, 22
Kellett M., 87
Kerala, 4, 99, 103–5, 116, 201
key case, 99, 100, 112, 116
kinds of case study, 29, 97–118
   See also, examples of case studies
kinds of question, 35–7, 153
Köhler, W., 50
Korean War, 14, 15
Kounin J., 155
Kuhn, T., 228
Kurtz, M., 252

Lacey, C., 45
language, difficulty of translating, 68, 84, 89
Le Play, F., 173
leitmotif, of case study as drama, 41, 230, 231
Lewin, K., 50, 56

Lewis, A., 79, 87
library, 73
Likert Scale, 195
linear study, 238
literacy, 177
literature review, 26, 30–3, 39–40, 44, 170, 187, 222–37, 242
Loader, D., 235
local knowledge case, 98–9
logs, 164
Loxley, A., 31, 199

MacIntyre, A., 49, 61, 69, 70, 71, 72
macrosystem. *See* ecological systems theory, 58
mad cow disease, 127
making sense, 51, 235
Malinowski, B., 148, 159
Marx, K., 240
McCulloch, G., 202
Mead, G.H., 52
media, 41, 43, 84, 86, 116, 139, 140, 222, 224
medical education, 18
Merriam, S., 113
mesosystem. *See* ecological systems theory, 58
metaphors, use of, 4, 58, 143, 173, 176, 220
methodology, 25–6, 30, 46, 64–5, 68, 72, 90, 173, 210, 214–6, 236
methods. *See* approach taken in the case study; data collection; data analysis; purpose of the case study; types of case study
microsystem. *See* ecological systems theory
Milgram experiments, 78
Milgram S., 78, 81
Miller, S., 70
Mitchell, J.C., 13, 113
Mouzelis, N., 71
MRSA infection, 139
multiple case study, 116, 172, 175–7, 251, 180
mushy heap syndrome, 29, 239, 250

narrative, 73, 90, 101, 111, 122, 140, 163–7, 221, 225–31, 235–6, 240, 247, 250

narrative diachronicity, Bruner's concept
of, 226
natural sciences, 7, 47–9, 65, 69, 153–4
nested case studies, 34, 177–8
network analysis, 203
newspaper stories, 164, 223
Newton, I., 51
Nietzsche, F., 6
normal distribution curve, 32
NVivo, 207–9, 211, 234

Oakley, A., 48
object of the case study, 15–7, 20–1, 23,
86, 111–2, 115, 119–132, 135, 149,
166–7, 183
See also, analytical frame; subject of the
case study
observation, 38, 67, 85, 86, 154, 157, 164,
172, 187, 188, 196–8, 202, 240
Office for National Statistics, 200
official statistics, using, 188, 202
Omaar, R., 31–4, 187
One Day in the Life of Ivan Denisovich.
See Solzhenitsyn, A.
online, 92, 101, 193, 200, 209
optical character recognition (OCR)
software, 193
Organization for Economic Co-operation
and Development (OECD), 200
outlier case, 102–8, 112, 114–7

paradigms, 160
paradigm shift, 58
paradigm wars, 48, 232
parallel and sequential studies, 164
Parlett, D. and Hamilton, D., 8, 9
participant observation, 188, 197, 202
particularity, versus generalisation, 10, 13, 120
Patrick, J., 6, 7, 24
pattern-finding, 50
Paxman, J., 240
Peirce, C., 69–71
personal experience, 15, 72, 99, 173
PGCE qualification, 109
photo-elicitation, 199
photographs, 137, 164, 171, 187, 192, 198–9

phronesis, 72–3, 77, 121, 142, 252
pilot, 35, 63, 92, 101, 180
Plato, 48, 73, 247
plausibility, 65–7
Polanyi, M., 72, 233
polyhedron of intelligibility, 4, 5, 67, 105
Popper, K., 50, 232
population, sample drawn from, 4, 11,
62–3, 85,
positionality, 62, 65, 68, 210
postgraduate, 40, 83, 92, 109, 143, 168
potential explanations, 21, 103, 123–4,
128, 131, 170
practical theory, 72
practitioners, 143, 147
prediction, 49, 210
prima facie question, 29, 30, 31, 33–4, 39,
187, 222, 236
process of the case study, 161–83
Prosser, J., 199, 202
protocols, ethical, 92
pseudonyms, 82, 164
psychiatry, 18
psychology, 8, 50–61, 108, 109, 110
psychometrics, 64, 251
public health, 127, 128, 131
public opinion research, 201, 202
purpose of the case study, 17, 119–132, 144
purposes of research, 17
purposive systems, 214
Putnam, R., 163, 164

qualitative, 76, 204, 206, 210
See also, interpretative inquiry
quantitative, 76, 132
Queniborough vCJD cluster, 38, 127,
128, 131
questionnaires, 38, 188, 193–6, 201, 202
questions, kinds of, 78, 79, 80, 88, 92,
207, 214
See also, research questions
quotations, 204, 206, 207, 240

Ragin, C.C., 11, 21, 24, 228
Ramsey, F., 233
recipes, as comparative case, 174, 178

reductionism, 47–9
reflective thought, 241
register of writing, 147, 248
registers, as documents, 164
reliability, 62, 64, 67, 71, 74, 76, 77, 232
repeated measures design, 156
replicability, 24
representative or typical case, 114
representativeness of data, 10
research
   approach, 36
   design, 25–45, 97, 103, 153, 236
   questions, 27, 32, 35–7, 237
retrospective study, 113–6, 165, 193
risky shift, 192
Roethlisberger, F., 169
Roman, L., 49
room management, 156–7
root definition, in soft systems, 215
Rosenberg Self Esteem Scale, 195
Rosenblatt, P., 252
Rutter, M., 108, 109
Ryle, G., 211

Sacks, O., 244, 245, 246, 251
Salkind, N., 202
samples and sampling, 4, 10–11, 13, 62–5,
   173, 182, 200, 222, 239
SATs, 126, 127
scales, 32
scattergram, 108
scepticism, 241
Schatzman, L., 70
school governor (as interpretative case
   study), 150–3
school inclusion policy (as nested case
   study), 178–80
Schwandt, T., 65, 75, 77, 172
scientific method, 69
secondary data, 200, 202
   See also, official statistics
second-order constructs, 206
   See also, coding; themes
selecting a case, 95–118
Sen, A., 105, 106
Sennett, R., 143, 152, 173–6, 183, 233

sequential case study, 180–2
serendipity, 11, 226
simile in multis, 48
Simons, H., 10, 24, 87, 94
single case study, 115, 162, 164
Smail, D., 59
Smith, E., 200, 202
snapshot case study, 165, 168
Snyder, R., 252
social capital, 163
social sciences, 4, 5, 8–9, 25–7, 32, 49,
   66–73, 79, 90, 154, 159, 228, 232, 244
sociograms, 203, 212, 243
sociology, 52, 53, 56
sociometry, 203, 212, 243
Socrates, 48, 233, 247
soft systems, 57–8, 61, 214–7
Solzhenitsyn, A., 166
special needs, 242
special schools, 242
Spradley, J., 160
SPSS, 159
Sri Lanka, 103, 104
Stake, R., 9, 10, 14, 24, 113, 120,
   121, 172
Stanford Law School, 147
statistics, 38, 40, 131, 155, 159, 200–3
Stoeker, R., 252
Storr, A., 226
storyboard, 38–44, 100, 102, 106,
   111, 124, 137–8, 140, 145, 156, 1
   62, 170–1, 217–9, 234, 241
Street Corner Society. See Whyte, W., 149, 244
structured reflection, 71
subject of the case study, 15–17, 23, 86,
   119, 132
   selecting a subject, 97–118
   See also, object of the case study; types of
      case study
subjectivity, 68
survey, 10, 193, 201, 202
SurveyMonkey, 193
symbolic interactionism, 52, 54, 59
systems theory, 56–8, 179
systems thinking, 56, 57, 58, 60, 214,
   215, 216, 234

tacit knowledge, 72, 175, 233
taking notes, 25, 110
teacher aides. *See* teaching assistants
teachers, 34, 80, 88, 126, 143, 152, 177–9,
    199, 207, 242
teaching assistants, 88, 123, 126, 156
temporary constructs, 205, 210
    See also, coding; second-order
        constructs; themes
terrorism, as theory-building case study,
    136–7, 162
tests, 123, 159, 188, 199, 200, 202
textbooks, 63, 204–5
The Craftsman 152, 173, 183
theme mapping, 206, 234
themes, 128, 138, 204–7, 210–1, 221, 231, 234
theorisation, 115, 149, 150, 152, 224
theorising, 21, 71, 152, 221, 225, 227
theory, 70–2, 115–7, 134–59, 188, 219–25,
    239–40
  building, 33, 111, 113–7, 134–59
  developing, 219–25
  as glue, 220
  generating. *See* theory building
  grand, 150, 221
  grounded, 199, 210, 234
  versus phronesis, 72–3
  practical, 72
  testing, 111, 113–7, 134–59
theory *cont.*
  theory-seeking study. *See* theory
      building
  as a tool, 220–5
theory-building case study, 135, 136, 137
theory-testing case study, 139
thick description, 6, 159, 211, 228, 234
thinking critically. *See* critical awareness
Thomas, G., 9, 24, 31, 65, 67, 71, 73, 77,
    99, 155, 160, 166, 167, 179, 188, 202,
    203, 207, 210, 219, 242, 244, 252
thought experiments, 6, 34, 65, 66
Thucydides, 73
timeline, 167
title, of thesis, 87
Tobin, J., 77, 252

Toyota Motor Corporation, the ' Whys', 171
Tractatus, 12, 233
transcripts, 76, 187, 204, 205, 212
triangulation, 67, 105
Trobriand Islanders, 148, 159
types of case study, 97
  diachronic case study, 169–72
  evaluative case study, 122
  experimental case study, 123–6
  explanatory case study, 123–6
  exploratory case study, 126–31
  illustrative–demonstrative case study,
      143–6
  interpretative case study, 150–3
  key case study, 100–102
  local knowledge case study, 108–9
  multiple or comparative case study,
      173–6, 246–7
  nested case study, 178–80
  outlier case study, 103–8
  sequential case study, 180–2
  snapshot case study, 166–8
  theory-building case study, 136–8, 162–4
  theory-testing case study, 139–40
    See also, examples of case studies

undergraduate, 40, 83, 92, 108, 143
uniqueness, 3, 10, 18, 20, 40, 44, 111, 227, 252
USSR, 166

validity, 7, 62–9, 72–7, 154
variables, 8–11, 29, 47, 50, 54, 60, 65, 149,
    154–7, 170, 204, 227
verbal and non-verbal cues, 190
verisimilitude, Bruner's concept of, 122
verstehen, 53
video, 124, 138, 157, 166, 171, 190–2,
    198–9, 205, 207
    See also, image-based methods
von Bertalanffy, L., 57
vulnerable groups, 79
Vygotsky, L., 174

walk-throughs, 182
websites, as sources of data, 200, 202

Wertheimer, M., 50
'What happens when?' questions,
    36, 37
wheelchair users, 181
White, H., ix, 21, 24, 34, 45,
    111, 244
Whyte, W., 149, 160, 244
Wieviorka, M., 15, 16, 20, 136
Windelband, W., 49, 50
Wittgenstein, L., 12, 13, 233

Wolcott, H., 252
word clouds, 212
World War II, 11, 15, 203
'writerly' and 'readerly' texts, 228
write-up of the study, 79, 88, 90,
    179, 214,
  structure of, 236–51
writing, quality of, 238–50

Yin, R., 113, 114, 177, 183